EXCEL IN CIVICS

LESSONS IN CITIZENSHIP

About the Authors

Stephen Jenkins is director of the Resource Center for Law-Related Education of the Bar Association of Metropolitan St. Louis. A high school social studies teacher with ten years of classroom experience, he also served as law-related education specialist with the Law and Education Unit of the St. Louis Public Schools.

Susan Spiegel is an attorney in private practice, a former coordinator of the Resource Center for Law-Related Education of the Bar Association of Metropolitan St. Louis and a former Assistant Professor, St. Louis University School of Law. She has developed law-related curriculum materials, conducted teacher training workshops and organized high school mock trials.

Editors:

Edward T. McMahon, attorney, Deputy Director, National Institute for Citizen Education in the Law and author of numerous articles and books on law-related education including *Street Law: A Course in Practical Law.*

Linda Riekes, Director, Law and Education Unit, St. Louis Public Schools, co-author *Law in Action Series, Sports and Law* and other law-related education publications.

EXCEL IN CIVICS

LESSONS IN CITIZENSHIP

AUTHORS

STEPHEN JENKINS
SUSAN SPIEGEL

EDITORS

EDWARD T. McMAHON
LINDA RIEKES

A cooperative effort of Law in Action and the National Institute for Citizen Education in the Law

Copy Editor: Mary Hough
Compositor: Metro Graphic Arts, Inc.

Library of Congress Cataloging in Publication Data
Jenkins, Steve.
  Excel in Civics.

1. United States — Politics and government. 2. Civics.
I. Speigel, Susan. II. Title.
JK274.J39 1985   320.473   84-28422
ISBN 0-314-83797-3

Table of Contents

Note to Students

Do you think the law affects your daily life? In what ways? Of course you are aware of the state laws that affect your attendance at school. Local, state, and national laws that control use of cars may come to mind immediately. But do you know the how and why of lawmaking? Have you ever thought about the effect of presidential and judicial decisions on your life? Do you know how you can influence governmental decisions?

Excel in Civics will provide you with a working knowledge of our legal system and the opportunity to develop your citizenship skills. This knowledge and these skills should enable you to take an effective role in shaping new laws and determining the direction of public policy. *Excel in Civics* has these features:

> YOUR TURN Activities — several action activities in each chapter to be done in class. YOUR TURN gives you the opportunity to use your critical thinking and problem-solving skills to simulate lawmaking, to decide cases as a judge, and to examine contemporary issues.

ON YOUR OWN Activities — enrichment opportunities, often to be done out of class. ON YOUR OWN takes you beyond the classroom to other resources in your community to examine issues, help interpret complex concepts, analyze the consequences of conduct, and evaluate policy alternatives. You will be encouraged to use law libraries, to interview fellow students and other citizens, and, as a concerned citizen, to take a more active role in community affairs.

UNITED STATES CONSTITUTION — complete text of the Constitution. You will be using information from the Constitution in many of the activities.

CASE CITATIONS — complete legal citations for each example case cited in the text provide reference for further study.

GLOSSARY — definitions of important words in the text in **bold face** type.

More than one hundred fifty years ago Thomas Jefferson wrote:

> I know of no safe depository of the ultimate powers of the society but the people themselves; and if we think them not enlightened enough to exercise their control with a wholesome discretion, the remedy is not to take it from them but to inform their discretion by education.

Excel in Civics represents our commitment to Jeffersonian democracy. The knowledge you gain while studying this textbook may help create a better world in which to live.

Steve Jenkins
Susan Spiegel

EXCEL IN CIVICS

LESSONS IN CITIZENSHIP

1

THE LAW IS ...

Purpose of Laws

"Sale of Alcoholic Beverages to Persons under 21 Is Prohibited"
"No Food or Beverages Permitted on The Bus"
"Speed Limit 55"

Signs like these appear everywhere. Why is buying alcoholic beverages limited to persons twenty-one or older? Why is the speed limit at 55 MPH and not 65 MPH? Why are food and beverages prohibited in certain public places? Because it is the law. But who makes the law? How is the law made? Why do we need such laws?

The answers to these questions help to explain our system of government. The United States is a nation governed by law, not by the whims of kings or queens. The United States Constitution is the foundation of American law. It establishes the powers and describes the limits of government to enact, interpret, and enforce laws. Laws are sets of rules that tell individuals what they must do and what behavior they must avoid. The rules also tell government what it can and cannot do. Imagine a day without any laws, without any limits

1

The Public School

State Law Legal Responsibility for Accidents on School Property	**State Law** Building Standards	**Local Law** Building Codes

State Law Child Abuse Reporting	**Federal Law** Privacy of School Records	**State Law** Establishment of School Districts	**State Law** Required Subjects

Federal Law School Lunch

Federal Law Due Process

State Law Free Public Education	**Federal Law** Education of Disabled Students	**State Law** Vaccinations	**State Law** Teacher Qualifications

State Law Required Tests	**State Law** School Board Duties	**Local Law** 15 MPH School Zone	**Local Law** School Crossings

State Law Compulsory Education	**Local Law** School Taxes	**Federal Law** Freedom of Speech

2

on what people can do and what government can do. What would be the problems?

Our nation and our Constitution have a strong commitment to a republican form of government — a representative democracy where citizens have the power to govern themselves wisely. The concept of a government of, by, and for the people was expressed in a famous court case approximately a hundred years ago:

> Sovereign power in our government belongs to the people, and the government of the United States and the Government of the several states are but the machinery for expounding or expressing the will of sovereign power.
> *Cherokee Nation v. Southern Kansas Railway Company,* 33 F. 900 (D.D.C. 1888).

The sovereign power, the people, has established the government of the United States and the government of the states and local communities. The sovereign power is expressed in daily rules of conduct, like the 55 mile-per-hour speed limit.

This chapter examines the sources and purposes of laws and the ways laws change as times and values change. The examination begins by a look at the laws governing public schools. Look at the drawing on the previous page. Select at least three laws and explain why you think these laws were written — in other words, what is the *purpose* of each law?

Laws exist in every society. But why are laws necessary? Some of the purposes of law are the following:

Purposes of Law   ## Examples of Law

☆ To Establish Order.

> Laws that require all workers to have a social security number.

> Laws that establish standards of measurement (like pounds, feet, meters, and grams).

☆ To Provide for the Continuation of the Society.

> Laws that require students to study civics.

> Laws that protect freedom of speech.

3

☆ To Enforce Values by Setting Standards of Behavior.

- Laws that prohibit public nudity.
- Laws that require parents to support their children.

☆ To Create Institutions to Serve the Public.

- Laws that create police departments.
- Laws that create school systems.

☆ To Provide an Orderly Way to Change the Society's Rules.

- Laws that require voter approval of changes in state constitutions.
- Laws that establish a legislature.

☆ To Provide an Orderly Way to Settle Disputes.

- Laws that establish consumer protection agencies.
- Laws that create courts to help people resolve disputes.

☆ To Protect the Powerless from the Powerful.

- Laws that permit workers to organize into unions.
- Laws that prohibit discrimination against members of minority groups.

☆ To Establish Ownership of Property.

- Laws that protect the creative work of individuals, like authors, painters, musicians and inventors.
- Laws that provide that people can give away their property in a will.

☆ To Prevent Harm to Life,
Health, and Property.

> Laws that protect endangered species.

> Laws that establish 55 mile-per-hour speed limits.

☆ To Punish Persons who
Violate the Rights of
Others.

> Laws that make armed robbery a crime for which the robber may be sent to prison.

> Laws that make people who falsely injure someone's reputation **liable** to pay **damages.**

YOUR TURN: Examining the Purposes of Specific Laws

Review the purposes of law stated on pages 3-5. Then read the laws below. List the purposes of law which apply to each law, and state what would happen if the law did not exist. You may list more than one purpose for each law.

Law	What purposes of law does this law serve?	What might happen if this law did not exist?
Example: Murder is a crime punishable by death or imprisonment.	To protect lives. To punish persons who violate the rights of others.	Possibly more murders. People might take the law into their own hands to revenge murders.
1. All medicine sold in this country must be tested and approved before it may be sold.		

5

Law	What purposes of law does this law serve?	What might happen if this law did not exist?
2. A landlord cannot evict a tenant without going to court. 3. The city is responsible for operating a building inspection department. 4. A person who sells a car must sign the title over to the buyer.		

★ ★ ★ ★ ★ ★ ★ ★ ★ ★ ★

People often do not think about the purposes of law as described on pages 3-5. Instead, they consider the purpose to be taking care of a specific problem. For example, Congress passed laws to regulate the employment of children. The purpose was seen as preventing employers from taking advantage of children by making them work long hours and in dangerous conditions. More generally, such laws are designed to prevent harm to life and health and to protect the powerless from the powerful.

The Necessity of Law

The overall purpose of law is to permit society to function smoothly. The law prevents problems by setting standards of conduct. It can also solve problems when they arise. Sometimes the law may even get involved in what seems to be private activity because the activity affects others in society.

For example, most cities have housing codes. These laws require owners to keep houses and apartments in good repair. Such laws generally make it illegal to have big holes in the floor, outdoor plumbing, or exposed electrical wiring. Even though it is the owner's private property, other people in society may be affected. Visitors may fall through the hole and injure themselves. The owner may fall and require medical treatment for which others have to pay. The law is involved in many activities like these that seem to be private. People cannot always do just what they want, because others may be harmed in some way.

Some activities, though, are so private that they have little effect on others. Then the law does not need to get involved. For example, family members may argue about what color the living room should be painted. The color of the living room has little effect on others in society, so a law is not needed. What is considered private activity varies from one country to another. Many activities that we consider private — that is, up to individuals to decide — are controlled by law in totalitarian countries. For example, in some countries there are laws to discourage married couples from having more than one child.

The law also does not need to get involved when people are able to take care of a problem themselves. An example is the motion picture industry. The motion picture industry opposes censorship. Therefore, it sets its own standards for movie viewing. The industry uses its own code — X, R, PG-13, PG, G — to tell young persons which movies they may watch.

Taking care of problems without law, however, requires cooperation. If the person or company causing the problem does not cooperate, a law may be needed. A law has the power to force a particular solution. For example, for many years people did not understand exactly how much banks and loan companies were charging their customers to borrow money or make purchases on credit. Many banks and loan companies did not give explanations, and borrowers were unable to force them to give explanations. Congress then passed the Truth-in-Lending Law which requires banks and loan companies to explain their charges. The banks and loan companies could have avoided having the law tell them what to do if they had been more cooperative in making explanations on their own. Laws are necessary, therefore, when there are no other effective ways to take care of situations.

YOUR TURN: Not the Law's Business?

Read the following situations. For each situation, decide whether this problem is one in which the law should be involved. Be prepared

to explain your answer in terms of both the pros and cons of the law being involved. Discuss what problems there might be in enforcing this law. Use the purposes of law on pages 3-5 to help explain your answer.

Should the law decide . . .

1. The number of children a family may have?

2. Which books a person may read?

3. Whether a person may gamble?

4. Whether a terminally ill patient is allowed to choose to die?

5. Which products may be advertised on television?

6. What newspapers may print?

7. When a person may marry?

8. The time of night a teenager must go home?

What is the Law?

No one person knows all the law. In order to answer questions about the law, a person must do research on the law. In the United States, laws are found in court decisions, **constitutions, statutes,** and **regulations.** For some legal questions there are only court decisions — no statutes, regulations, or constitutional provisions. Other questions involve only statutes and court interpretations of statutes. Still others involve only the Constitution and court interpretations of the Constitution. Some may involve all of these.

In our country, many laws developed from **common law.** Common law consists only of court decisions. Judges use earlier decisions of courts on the same legal question to guide decision making on new cases. If a court has ruled on the same question in another case, the judge must follow it. If not, the judge looks at decisions on similar questions and decisions in other states. Based on these, the judge then makes a new decision.

Common law came from England with the original colonists. But as the new nation developed, many leaders wanted to define clearly certain rights and responsibilities. They met and wrote the U.S. Constitution in 1787. A constitution is a written legal document that provides a framework of law within which orderly processes of government may operate. It can provide protection of basic personal, political, and property rights.

The U.S. Constitution is the supreme law of the land. Any law — federal, state, or local — that conflicts with it is invalid. For example, state laws requiring segregated schools conflicted with the constitutional right to equal protection of the law. These laws were therefore ruled invalid.

Within a state, the state constitution is the highest law other than the U.S. Constitution. All state and local laws are subject to the state constitution. State and local laws must follow both the U.S. Constitution and the state constitution.

Another source of law is a statute or **ordinance.** Statutes and ordinances start as bills proposing new laws or changes in existing laws. Generally, a bill becomes a statute or ordinance when a majority of the lawmaking body approves the bill. Statutes are laws enacted by Congress or state legislatures. Ordinances are laws enacted by local lawmaking bodies. These laws can define **crimes,** set up government agencies, authorize government spending, provide for collection of taxes, and define some **torts** and other **civil** wrongs.

Statutes can take a particular subject from the area of common law to the area of statutory law. One example of this is the law on **contracts.** Originally, the law on contracts was developed through common law, by judges on a case-by-case basis. In recent years, many questions of contract law have been covered by statutes. These questions are now questions of statute, not common law.

Understanding most statutes, ordinances, and constitutional provisions usually requires looking at court decisions that interpret them. The U.S. Supreme Court is the final decision maker on interpretations of the U.S. Constitution. As Chief Justice Charles E. Hughes, who served from 1930-1941, said, "We are under the Constitution, but the Constitution is what the judges say it is."

A regulation is a **rule,** issued by a government agency, that interprets statutes and ordinances. It also establishes specific standards for enforcing the statutes and ordinances. Regulations must follow the statute that gives an agency power to make the regulations. Regulations that go beyond what a statute authorizes are invalid.

YOUR TURN: Putting the Law Plainly

Following are illustrations of the different sources of laws. As the illustrations show, the law is often difficult to read and to understand because of the language used. Your class has the task of restating the examples in plain language. Read each illustration of constitutional law, statutory law, and regulatory law. Then rewrite each law in language that plainly shows the meaning of the law.

Example:

Common Law: "It was **(defendant's)** intent to force **(plaintiff)** to leave the place where the game was in progress. The push, or the force intentionally exerted by him to that end, was the . . . cause of plaintiff's fall and the resulting injuries. For these injuries and their consequences, the (six-year-old) defendant is liable although the proof fails to show an intent on his part to inflict bodily harm or that the fall and the resulting injuries were or should have been foreseen."
Baldinger v. Banks, 201 N.Y.S. 2d 629 (Sup. Ct. N.Y. 1960).

Plain Language Version: A defendant, even though six years old, is legally responsible for the injuries he caused by intentionally pushing another child and causing the other child to fall. This is true even if the defendant did not intend to hurt the other child and did not expect the child to be hurt from the push.

1. Constitutional Provision: "Congress shall make no law respecting establishment of religion or prohibiting the free exercise thereof; or abridging the freedom of speech, or of the press; or the right of the people

to peaceably assemble, and to petition the government for redress of grievances." First Amendment, U.S. Constitution.

2. Constitutional Provision: "The legislature shall provide for the maintenance and support of a system of free common schools, wherein all the children of this state may be educated." Article IX, Section 1, New York State Constitution.

3. Statute: "There is hereby created a voluntary registry for the matching of adopted persons and biological parents. The purpose of this registry shall be to help voluntary contact between the adopted person and the biological parents." Louisiana State Voluntary Registry Act.

4. Ordinance: "Every dwelling unit shall contain a proper space for the storage, preparation and cooking of food, which shall include space for a stove or other cooking facilities and space for dry food storage and space for refrigerated food storage; and shall include a kitchen sink installed. The sink shall be in good working condition and properly connected to hot and cold running water system under pressure and sewer system, which sink and systems shall be installed and maintained in a manner prescribed by ordinances, rules and regulations of the city." Housing Code, New Haven, Connecticut, Section 300.

5. Regulation: "Every educational agency or institution shall permit the parent of a student or an eligible student . . . to inspect and review the education records of the student. The agency or institution shall comply with a request within a reasonable period of time, but in no case more than 45 days after the request has been made." Regulation §99.11, U.S. Department of Education.

The Source of Law for Specific Cases

The following cases illustrate how a lawyer may consult different sources of law to solve a legal problem.

CASE #1:

Joseph Evans, a supermarket cashier, was accused of stealing from the cash register. Many customers and other workers saw his arrest. In reality, no money was missing from the cash register and the boss should have known it before calling the police. There was extra money in another cash register. Because of the embarrassment of being arrested, Mr. Evans wants to sue his boss for false arrest. Does Mr. Evans have a claim against his boss?

To find out, a lawyer must research the law of false arrest. In most jurisdictions, false arrest is a common law tort. That means that the courts have recognized that causing someone to be arrested based on false information is a wrong for which someone can sue. No section of the Constitution nor any statute or ordinance or regulation gives a right to bring a lawsuit for being arrested falsely. The only guidelines for whether Mr. Evans has a claim are cases previously decided by the courts.

CASE #2

Leila Sharpe worked for the State Highway Department. She and all the other women working in her section have been fired. Ms. Sharpe thinks this is sex discrimination. Is the Highway Department's treatment of women, including Ms. Sharpe, illegal discrimination?

To decide this, a lawyer will look at the U.S. Constitution, at state and federal statutes, and at interpretations of each of these by courts and agencies. The Equal Protection Clause of the U.S. Constitution prohibits states from discriminating. Cases interpreting that part of the Constitution explain what kind of conduct by the state is considered unconstitutional discrimination. In addition, a federal statute, the Civil Rights Act of 1964, prohibits sex discrimination by employers. A state law also prohibits discrimination in employment. A lawyer must look at cases interpreting those statutes. By looking at all of these laws, the lawyer can decide whether the Highway Department discriminated illegally by firing the women and what the women can do about it.

★ ON YOUR OWN: A Lawyer's Analysis of a Case ★

Arrange to interview an attorney, or ask your teacher to invite an attorney to class to discuss several cases he/she has handled and how he/she determined which law applied to the specific legal problem. Inform the attorney that you are studying both sources of law and how attorneys may consult various sources of law to solve a problem. Ask the attorney to describe a case he or she may have had that required researching these sources of law. Prepare a report and include the following:

— statement or description of the legal problem in the case;
— identify the sources of law consulted;
— briefly explain how the legal problem was resolved.

Be prepared to share your report with your class.

★ ★ ★ ★ ★ ★ ★ ★ ★ ★

The Law Changes Over Time

Law changes as society changes. Changes in technology often trigger changes in the law. For example, years ago, the roads were filled with horses-and-buggies. Then, laws required the cleaning of roads after the horses. Now cars have replaced horses. Therefore, laws now set speed limits and require driver's licenses.

Changes in values also cause changes in law. What was important in the past may not be considered important today. In the past, for instance, teachers in some communities were not allowed to marry. Teachers were expected to devote all of their attention to teaching. Today, people no longer think that teachers have to live differently than others. A new awareness of old problems may also result in changes in the law. For example, until the 1970s, persons in wheelchairs could not visit many public buildings because they could not get up the steps. The disabled had few rights. Today people recognize that disabled persons have a right to participate fully in our society. Laws now require public buildings to be accessible to wheelchairs.

A Look at Changes in the Law on Voting

Voting rights law has also changed dramatically since our nation's beginning. Voting is the essence of democracy. Yet, the U.S. Constitution, when adopted, contained no broad guarantee of the right to vote. State law provided little more guarantee.

In 1789, when the Constitution was ratified, the only people allowed to vote in most states were free (not slave), white, male, Protestant landowners over twenty-one years of age. Soon after the adoption of the Constitution most states abolished the requirement that voters be Protestant. This meant Catholics, Jews, Moslems, and other non-Protestants could now vote. But white men who did not own property still could not vote. And blacks and women had no right to vote.

Over the years, the democratic trend continued. By 1821 most states had eliminated the qualifications of owning property or paying taxes. Voters then included all free, white, male citizens over twenty-one.

The next group given the right to vote in some states was aliens, that is, persons who were not born in the United States. States newly admitted to the Union gave the right to vote to aliens in order to attract settlers. By 1875, twenty-two states allowed aliens to vote. But, by the end of the 1800's, more and more states began to include citizenship as a qualification for voting.

After the Civil War, Congress passed the Reconstruction Act of 1867. This law took the right away from all men who had fought for the South during the Civil War. But these Southern veterans of the Civil War had their right to vote restored in 1890.

Two other voting qualifications were changed as a result of the Civil War. The Fifteenth Amendment to the U.S. Constitution, adopted in 1870, prohibited states from refusing the right to vote to persons because of their race or because they had been slaves. Voters now included all males over twenty-one years of age.

By 1890, however, Southern leaders had begun a campaign to take the vote away from blacks. Instead of openly taking away the vote, Southern states passed laws that created new voting qualifications. Although the laws applied to both blacks and whites, the laws were enforced to keep blacks from voting. Some of the new laws required voters to (1) own land, (2) pay a poll tax, and (3) pass an educational or literacy test. In some places, the literacy test required the person to read a section of the Constitution. Then the person had to give a "reasonable interpretation" of the section. White election officials could decide whether a person's interpretation was reasonable. As a result, few blacks passed the tests. In Southern states, the vote again belonged only to white males over twenty-one.

The next voter qualification to change was sex. The organized struggle for voting rights for women began in the 1800s. The first state to give women the right to vote was Wyoming in 1869. By 1912, six states had granted women this right. During World War I, women worked in factories, businesses, and farms more than ever before. They demanded the right to vote. In 1920 their active demonstrations and petitions paid off. The Nineteenth Amendment to the U.S. Constitution gave women the right to vote.

The next group to receive voting rights was the native American. Indians had lived in North America for thousands of years. But they were not made citizens until 1924 when Congress passed the Indian Citizenship Act. Then they were eligible to vote. Some states, like Arizona, still tried to deny native Americans the right to vote by classifying Indians on reservations as "disabled." In 1948, however, the Arizona Supreme Court struck down this law, and native Americans were granted the right to vote.

Legal discrimination against blacks and other minority voters finally ended in the 1960s and 1970s. This occurred in response to the civil rights movement. The Twenty-Fourth Amendment, adopted in 1964, prohibited states from requiring voters to pay a poll tax. The next year, Congress passed the Voting Rights Act, which made it possible for Spanish-speaking persons to vote. Congress passed a second Voting Rights Act in 1970. That law prohibited using literacy tests to qualify voters. It also eliminated the last legal voting barriers for native Americans.

The most recent change in the law occurred in 1971 when the Twenty-Sixth Amendment was adopted. This Amendment changed the voting age for national elections from twenty-one to eighteen. Most states have passed laws allowing citizens over eighteen to vote in all elections. Today, after all these changes, the qualifications for voting simply read: citizens over eighteen.

YOUR TURN: Analyzing Change in the Laws on Voting

List the changes in the law on who can vote. For each group that was given the right to vote, answer the following questions:

1. Identify the groups of persons denied the right to vote and later granted the right to vote.

2. Explain why each group was denied the right to vote.

3. For each group, what changes in society caused changes in the law granting the group the right to vote?

Today groups who usually do not have the right to vote include the following:

— Persons under eighteen years of age
— Non-citizens
— Persons convicted of a **felony.**

Do you think the law should change to give these groups the right to vote? Why? Why not? What purposes of law are served by not letting them vote? By letting them vote?

ON YOUR OWN: Survey on Changes in Law

Survey three adults in the community. Ask them the following questions:

1. Name one law that has changed during your lifetime.

2. Explain why you think the law was changed.

3. Explain how the change in the law affected your life.

Be prepared to report your survey findings.

Law and Change in Technology

Technology is changing our society at an ever-increasing pace. This often requires changes in the law. For example, improvements in the testing of blood types have led to changes in the law on the use of blood tests to prove that a man is the father of a particular child. Other changes may be new laws on new subjects. Today laws control the use of video games, computers, and electronic transfers of money. Several years ago, neither the laws nor the activities regulated by the laws existed. What will the law be like in the future?

YOUR TURN: Law in the Future

Imagine what life will be like in the 21st century as technology changes. List the laws that are likely to change. Follow these steps:

1. Describe the existing law. Then describe the change in the law that is likely to occur. What is the new technology that is likely to cause the change in the law?

2. Describe a new law on a new subject. Also identify the new technology that will require the new law. Why will a new law be required?

2

FEDERAL LAWMAKING

The Need for Federal Lawmakers

A traveler on an interstate highway thought, "What state am I in now? These interstates all look so much alike." Such observations, and such travel, have not always been possible. Less than two hundred years ago, travelers to other states found a wide variety of road conditions. Travelers faced rock roads, dirt roads, log roads, and toll roads. Roads were governed by state and local governments. The differences among these governments caused some very rugged roads for travelers. The conditions of the roads and quality of travel reflected a number of problems facing people living during the early years of the Republic.

At that time the United States was governed under the **Articles of Confederation**. The power and authority of state governments was as great, if not greater, than those of the federal goverment. Most state governments had their own militias, money standards, and laws on trade and commerce. Conflicts often occurred among the states or between a state and the federal government.

The following illustrations show the kinds of conflicts that the states and the federal government faced.

YOUR TURN: There Ought to be a Law: That's a Good Idea

Examine the following illustrations showing conflicts among the states, and then do as follows:

1. Briefly describe the problem(s) shown in each illustration;
2. Recommend at least one idea for a law to solve the problem(s).

Be prepared to share your ideas with the class.

ILLUSTRATION 1
CURRENCY CONFUSION

100 lbs. gold =
$1,000,000.00

400 lbs. gold =
$1,000,000.00

ILLUSTRATION 2
TALE OF TWO MAJOR ROADS

THE STATE X ROAD
RESTRICTED ROAD

THE STATE Y ROAD
TOLL ROAD

The road on the left was built by the government of State X to be used only by citizens of State X. All other citizens were subject to prosecution and imprisonment. The road on the right was built and maintained by the government of State Y as a toll road. A fee was charged to anyone traveling the road who was not a citizen of State Y.

The U.S. Constitution: Guidelines for Federal Lawmaking

How could the above conflicts be resolved if each state could only make and enforce laws regulating that particular state? These problems needed national attention. In 1787 representatives from the original thirteen states met and developed the framework for a federal government. This framework became the Constitution of the United States. The need for action was so great that even before all states had ratified the new Constitution, the first national elections were held. In January 1789 the first federal lawmakers were chosen.

HOUSE OF
REPRESENTATIVES   SENATE

U.S. CONGRESS

THE HOUSE TODAY:
435 representatives.
Apportioned to states by
population and elected by
the people of each state.

THE SENATE TODAY:
100 senators.
Two senators elected by the
people to represent each of
the fifty states.

FIRST HOUSE (1789):
59 representatives from
eleven states.*

FIRST SENATE (1789):
22 senators from eleven
states.*

*Two of the original thirteen states, North Carolina and Rhode Island,
did not ratify the Constitution until after the first national election
and, therefore, were not officially represented in the first Congress.

The new Constitution granted Congress the power to make laws for the entire country. (See Article I, Section 1 of the Constitution in the Appendix.) Some of the lawmaking powers of Congress are specifically named in Article I, Section 8 of the Constitution. These are called expressed powers. Other powers are not identified in the Constitution but are implied from the expressed powers. For example, Article I, Section 8 grants Congress the power "to establish post offices and post roads." This provision gives Congress the expressed power to create post offices. A power implied from this provision is the power to punish persons who steal mail from the post office. Another implied power is the power to regulate the price of postage stamps.

YOUR TURN: Expressed Powers in Action

Read Article I, Section 8 of the U.S. Constitution on page 222, and do the following activity.

Listed in the left-hand column are laws passed by Congress. Read each law. Then identify the constitutional source of power enabling Congress to pass the listed law.

Laws Passed by Congress	Expressed Constitutional Powers
Example: In 1913 Congress passed the Federal Reserve Act establishing the Federal Reserve System, which controls the amount of money in circulation.	Article I, Section 8: To coin money, regulate the value thereof . . ."
1. The Department of Commerce oversees the nation's trade and business. In 1903 Congress passed a law establishing a Department of Commerce and Labor. In 1913 Commerce and Labor became separate departments.	1.
2. In 1829 Congress passed a law establishing the Department of the Post Office. This department served the nation from 1829 to 1971. In 1971 Congress removed this department from the executive branch and made it an independent agency — the United States Postal Service.	2.

Laws Passed by Congress	Expressed Constitutional Powers
3. In 1940 Congress passed the Selective Service Act — a law that required all men to register for the military draft within five days of their eighteenth birthday.	3.
4. In December 1941, following the Japanese attack on Hawaii, Congress declared war on Japan.	4.
5. Congress has passed several laws establishing federal district and federal appeals courts throughout the United States. Congress passed the first major judiciary act in 1801.	5.

★★★★★★★★★★★

Expanding Power: The Expressed and Implied Powers of Congress

The last paragraph of Article I, Section 8 establishes the principle of the implied powers of Congress. This paragraph is known as the "elastic clause." It stretches the powers of Congress to permit it to pass any laws necessary to perform its expressed powers. The elastic clause establishes Congress's implied powers.

The implied powers of Congress have been necessary to meet changing times and needs. For example, Congress is given power "to raise and support Armies," and Congress is ordered "to provide and maintain a Navy." Review the expressed powers on page 222. Are there any expressed powers in Section 8 for Congress "to provide and maintain an Air Force"? The thought of flying armadas was beyond the imagination of most people two hundred years ago. But today many believe a strong air force is just as important as a strong navy. The power of Congress to create an air force has been implied from the power "to provide for the common Defense."

The implied powers have allowed Congress to pass many laws to "provide for the common Defense and general Welfare of the United States." Can you name or describe at least one federal law that provides for the "common Defense" and/or the "general Welfare"?

YOUR TURN: Contemporary Problems and Congressional Powers

Examine the following pictures and commentary. After studying each, answer the following:

1. Does Congress have the constitutional power to deal with this problem? What is the source of this power? Give a quote from Article I, Section 8.

2. In your opinion, should government be concerned about this problem? Briefly explain your answer.

3. If yes, which level of government — federal (Congress), state, or local — do you think can best deal with this problem? Briefly explain your answer.

Picture 1

Each year more than fifty thousand people are killed and over two million are injured in traffic accidents in the U.S. The National Safety Council and the Department of Transportation's National Highway Traffic Safety Administration (NHTSA) claim that half of these deaths and many serious injuries are caused by drunk drivers.

Picture 2

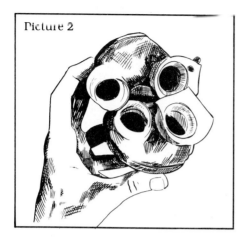

"The Model T of artificial hearts" and the patient who received it represent a giant step forward in the effort to conquer heart disease.

Dr. Barney Clark, the first recipient of an artificial heart made of polyurethane and aluminum, lived for 111 days with the artificial heart. His ordeal and extended life represented a great advance for scientists striving to conquer heart disease. The health costs for these 111 days, however, amounted to more than $1 million.

Scientific success in this field and medical advancement in organ transplants make it possible to save lives. Such achievements can improve the health of millions of people. Yet the medical treatment has high costs. Many patients cannot afford to pay for artificial hearts and organ transplants.

Picture 3

Courtesy of Chrysler Corporation

Thousands of assembly line workers in auto, steel, and related industries have been replaced by robots. Many of these laid-off workers have not been trained for jobs in new industries. These workers remain unemployed. Some say that without additional job training, the unemployed workers will add to the ranks of the permanently unemployed.

Public Problems — Whose Responsibility?

The Preamble of the United States Constitution states:

> We, the People of the United States, in order to form a more perfect union, establish justice, insure domestic tranquility, provide for the common defense, promote the general welfare, and secure the blessings of liberty to ourselves and our posterity, do ordain and establish this Constitution for the United States of America.

Today, "we, the People of the United States" refers to over 225 million people. Great public concern and commitment can help in solving a particular problem. But 225 million people cannot reasonably and practically discuss or resolve any problem. For this reason, the Constitution has established a representative form of government. "We, the People" elect representatives to examine problems and to pass laws to resolve the problems. State and local governments also have established representative forms of government to address and resolve public problems. It is not always clear which level of government — federal, state, or local — should resolve public problems. Sometimes more than one level of government acts to resolve public problems. Then conflicts among the levels of government often result.

Federal Lawmaking — The People and the Process

"We, the People" participate in the problem-solving process by helping to choose representatives for Congress. Every person living in one of the fifty states is represented by two U.S. Senators and a member of the U.S. House of Representatives elected from his or her congressional district. An average of ten thousand **bills** are introduced in Congress every year. Some of these bills become laws. These laws affect everyday life. It is important, therefore, to know the names of the congressional representatives who are making federal laws that govern your life.

ON YOUR OWN: Know Your Congressional Representatives

1. With the help of your teacher, a librarian, or the telephone directory, find out who represents you in Congress.

THE U.S. SENATORS WHO REPRESENT ME IN CONGRESS ARE:

a. U.S. SENATOR:

b. U.S. SENATOR:

THE U.S. REPRESENTATIVE WHO REPRESENTS ME IN CONGRESS IS:

c. U.S. REPRESENTATIVE:

2. Randomly select five adults and ask them:

a. To identify three problems they believe federal lawmakers (members of Congress) should solve.

b. For each problem identified, determine whether Congress has the power to solve such problems (refer to Article 1, Section 8).

How a Bill Becomes a Law
At the Federal Level

Bill is introduced in either the House of Representatives or the Senate.

The bill is . . .

REFERRED TO HOUSE OR SENATE COMMITTEE

Referred to subcommittee for study and approval.

REPORTED BY FULL COMMITTEE

In the House, many bills go before the Rules Committee. This committee sets conditions for debate and amendments on the floor of the House. Some bills are "privileged" and go directly to the floor. In the Senate, special "rules" are not used. The Senate leadership normally schedules action on bills.

DEBATED, AMENDED, PASSED, OR DEFEATED BY HOUSE OR SENATE

If passed, the bill is sent to the other chamber to follow the same route through committee and floor stages. If the other chamber has already passed a related bill, both versions go straight to conference.

REFERRED TO CONFERENCE

Committee members of both the House and Senate meet to work out differences. A compromise version is then sent to each chamber for final approval.

APPROVED BY BOTH CHAMBERS

SENT TO PRESIDENT

President may sign the bill into law or veto and return it to Congress. Congress may override the veto with a two-thirds vote in both houses. The bill then becomes law without the president's signature.

ON YOUR OWN: Congress is in the News

Use newspapers, magazines, radio, or television to identify news stories involving congressional action on contemporary problems. After investigating each news story, answer the following questions:

1. What need or problem is being addressed?

2. What congressional action has or may be taken?

3. Using the chart on page 29, "How a Bill Becomes a Law at the Federal Level," identify the location of the Congressional action on the flow chart. Is it in the House or Senate, at what committee level, or what stage of action?

4. What constitutional power is Congress exercising in this action?

5. In your opinion, what should Congress do about this problem(s)?

With the help of your teacher you may wish to use this information to develop a bulletin board — "Congressional Action Affects Us."

National Environmental Policy — An Idea Becomes Federal Law

Air and water pollution were common in highly populated areas throughout the United States in the 1950s and 1960s. The effects of this widespread pollution could be seen, tasted, and smelled even in rural areas. By the late 1960s many people expressed strong support for laws to combat pollution. In 1969 Congress passed the National Environmental Policy Act to prevent and eliminate damage to the environment and to encourage respect for the environment.

Since the passage of this major act in 1969, Congress has passed a series of laws requiring federal action to protect the nation from poisons in the air, in the water, and on the land. Among the major statutes enacted by Congress were the following:

Clean Air Act, passed in 1970;
Clean Water Act, passed in 1972;

Marine Resources, Research and Sanctuaries Act, passed in 1972;

Safe Drinking Water Act, passed in 1974;

Solid Waste Disposal Act, passed in 1976;

Toxic Substances Control Act, passed in 1976;

Surface Mining Control and Reclamation Act, passed in 1977;

Superfund Act, passed in 1980.

Clearly, Congress has made a legislative commitment to carry out the ideals of the National Environmental Policy Act. But not everyone agrees on the seriousness of environmental problems or the means to solve them. Some citizens believe antipollution laws are unnecessary. Others believe the laws are too costly and confusing. These citizens are calling for Congress to repeal or relax some of the laws. Other citizens argue that weakening the laws against pollution will cause disasters for the environment and our lives. These conflicting concerns are expressed throughout the United States.

YOUR TURN: Legislating Clean Air

A Simulated Congressional Hearing

Background information: Congressional committees sometimes schedule **hearings** in locations around the nation. They do this in order to hear from persons who may be affected by congressional actions. Imagine that your class is the site for such a congressional hearing.

Assume that you live in Hometown, USA. Since the mid-1970s many Hometowners have experienced hard times. Several factories and businesses, including the large United Motors, Inc. plant, have suffered shutdowns. Some factories have moved to other countries where labor is cheaper and regulations fewer. Other factories have moved to states with lower labor costs, less government regulation, and lower taxes. Some Hometown businesses have gone out of business as a result of the hard times. Now one out of every five workers is unemployed.

Some residents of Hometown blame the federal Clean Air Act for causing many of these problems. They complain about the Clean Air Act's requirement "that all sources of pollution (such as factories, power plants, refineries, and chemical plants) use the most effective pollution controls available." They say this requirement has created intolerable and costly standards that have destroyed or driven profitable business away from Hometown.

Several members of the House of Representatives have co-sponsored a bill to change the "most effective pollution control" requirement of the Clean Air Act. This new bill would add the following clause to the Clean Air Act:

> "that all sources of pollution (such as factories, power plants, refineries, and chemical plants) use the most effective pollution controls available based on cost-benefit analysis."

Under the new bill, a polluter would not have to install the most effective pollution control available if the costs of doing so were greater than the benefits. Costs might include the expense of pollution control equipment, losses of jobs, and price increases for products made at a factory. Only if the benefits of a particular pollution control are greater than these costs can a polluter be required to install that control.

The Speaker of the House of Representatives assigned the bill to the House Energy and Commerce Committee. The chairperson of this committee has great concern about the impact of this special cost requirement of the Clean Air Act. Recently, the chairperson received a letter from a high school student living in Hometown. The student tried to explain the town's suffering and doubts about the future. The student was called as a witness when the House Energy and Commerce Committee scheduled hearings in Hometown.

Directions: The teacher should help select six students who will testify about the revised Clean Air Act — three students for and three against. The remainder of the class will represent the members of the House Energy and Commerce Committee. One student should serve as chairperson of the committee.

Witnesses for the revised Clean Air Act:

WITNESS #1: The sad sixteen-year-old Hometown High School
                student
"I would like to read the following letter addressed to the chairperson of the House Energy and Commerce Committee:

> "The Clean Air Act is making Hometown a ghost town.
> Factories have shutdown and moved. Workers have lost
> their jobs. The unemployed cannot buy as much so

business are laying off workers and losing money. Some businesses are bankrupt. The utility companies have raised rates to pay for the required pollution control devices. Many people are moving from Hometown seeking jobs and lower living costs. There are more and more abandoned factories, businesses and houses. If my family can continue to live here for at least another year, I'll graduate from high school, but then what? Won't you help us? We don't want to live in a ghost town."

Signed,
A Sad Sixteen Year Old

WITNESS #2: President of United Motors, Inc. (UM)

"As President of United Motors, I had to make a difficult decision to recommend shutting down our plant in Hometown. As a business-person, I am responsible to UM stockholders. The stockholders want a healthy financial future for UM. The costs of installing the required pollution control devices in our old plant were too great. Closing the Hometown plant was a decision I had to make. Within three years, we plan to open a new plant to replace the Hometown plant. The new plant will be in Newtown. Newtown has passed building bonds and tax abatement legislation that will make our move more profitable. Our new plant will be highly automated, like the Japanese models. The installation costs will be much less than trying to convert the old plant in Hometown.

"If the Clean Air Act is revised, corporations like UM would not have to make such distressing, shutdown decisions. It should be obvious that the costs of installing the pollution control devices would far exceed the benefits to the community and the corporation."

WITNESS #3: Chair of the Board of Directors, Pollyana Power & Light Company

"Pollyana Power & Light provides electrical power to the Hometown area. Pollyana's main powerplant uses industrial coal-fired boilers. These boilers and our large, tall smokestacks produce pollutants from the sulphur emissions. In order to obey the Clean Air Act's requirements, it was necessary to install smokestack scrubbers. These pollution control devices were very costly. The high costs were passed on to consumers. Hometowners' utility bills are higher than those in areas with more modern powerplants.

"The proposed change in the Clean Air Act would permit Pollyana to gradually replace the costly pollution control devices with less costly, more reasonable devices. As a result, utility bills will not rise as rapidly.

"You can be assured that Pollyana will continue to do everything possible to maintain a healthy environment for Hometown."

Witness AGAINST the revised Clean Air Act:

WITNESS #1: Professor of Environmental Science and President of Citizens for Clean Air and Jobs

"The proposed change in the Clean Air Act would be a devastating blow to the nations's goal of clean air. The current Clean Air Act has saved thousands of lives. It has prevented millions from suffering the ill effects of dirty air. Two teams of economists recently reported 'that the attainment of Clean Air Act goals would save 125,000 lives per year.' Making these goals dependent on 'cost-benefit analysis' may jeopardize these life-saving benefits. Is any cost too great if it saves lives or prevents cancer and heart and lung illnesses?

"The argument that the Clean Air Act leads to losses of jobs is misleading. According to a study by the National Academy of Science, for every job loss due to environmental controls, thirty jobs are created in the pollution control industry. Therefore, I urge the committee to vote against the proposed change. Please maintain the high standards of the current Clean Air Act."

WITNESS #2: Assistant Director, National Public Opinion Poll, Inc.

"An opinion survey in 1981 indicated that 80 percent of the population of the United States opposed weakening the Clean Air Act. As pollster Lou Harris told another congressional hearing, 'the deep desire on the part of the American people to battle pollution is one of the most overwelming and clearest we have ever recorded in our twenty-five years of surveying public opinion. You mess around with the Clean Air Act and the Clean Water Act and you are going to get into the deepest kind of trouble.' Those were Lou Harris's conclusions. Our polling shows that the people support the present Clean Air Act. Even in Hometown, a clear majority of the people favor keeping the high standards of the Clean Air Act."

WITNESS #3: A sixteen-year-old student at Hometown High School

"Like my classmate, I am concerned about my future and the future of Hometown. But changing the Clean Air Act is not our answer. Having clean air and water, both now and in the future, is worth the price. The professor has testified that many jobs could be provided in the pollution control industry. I suggest that you consider funding pollution control industries in depressed areas like Hometown. I am sure the federal budget has some money to support industries trying to achieve the goals of the Clean Air Act. Hometown even has empty factory space where such industries could be located. I know that students would pitch in to help convert these factories and save Hometown. For the sake of saving lives and promoting a healthy environment, I urge you to help save Hometown by supporting the creation of pollution control industries right here in Hometown."

PROCEDURE FOR A SIMULATED CONGRESSIONAL HEARING:

1. Each witness should read the given testimony. The testimony is provided as an informational resource. Students should testify in their own words, while maintaining their respective arguments for or against the revised Clean Air Act bill.

2. While witnesses prepare to testify, the remaining students should meet in small groups (2–3 students per group). Each group should be assigned one witness whom they will question as members of the House of Committee on Energy and Commerce. Each group should then read the witness's testimony and develop a list of at least five questions to ask its respective witness based on the given testimony.

3. After the witnesses have reviewed their testimony, and the small groups prepared their questions, the formal congressional hearing may begin. The following steps are recommended:

    a. Call the three witnesses for the revised Clean Air Act bill.

    b. Each witness should state his or her name and occupation and give an opening statement to the class (the members of the congressional committee).

    c. The members of the small groups assigned to question a particular witness should then ask their witness the questions they have developed. Members of the group may have to adjust their questions as the witnesses give their opening statements or answer questions.

    d. After all three witnesses for the bill testify, call the three witnesses against the bill, and follow the procedures in steps b and c.

e. After all witnesses have testified, students should ask for any other questions or comments regarding the proposed legislation. Allow approximately 10 – 15 minutes for this closing discussion and/or debate.

f. The chairperson should ask the committee members (all classmates except witnesses) to vote for or against the proposed new Clean Air Act legislation. The chairperson should record the votes on the chalkboard as they are cast. The chairperson should then tally the votes and announce whether the bill passed or failed.

★ ★ ★ ★ ★ ★ ★ ★ ★ ★ ★

3

STATE AND LOCAL LAWMAKING

STATE LAWS MAKE HEADLINES:

"Mandatory Sentencing for Armed Criminal Action Approved by State Legislature"

"State Legislature Passes Bill Raising Minimum Age Requirements for Driver's License from 16 to 18"

"General Assembly Increases Minimum High School Graduation Requirements in the Basics"

"General Assembly Passes Joint Resolution Calling for a Federal Constitutional Convention"

State and Local Governments — Sources of Power

The above headlines represent actual news stories about legislation passed in various states. These headlines identify state laws

37

that currently affect millions of people. Do states have the power to pass such legislation? If so, where does this power come from?

One source of power for states is the United States Constitution. The Tenth Amendment to the Constitution states:

> The powers not delegated to the United States by the Constitution, nor prohibited by it to the States, are reserved to the States respectively, or to the people.

These powers are commonly known as the *reserved powers*. Reserved powers belong only to the states and to local governments created by the states.

Article IV of the Constitution describes the relation of the federal government to the governments of the states. The Constitution guarantees each state a republican form of government — the same as the federal government. Among other things, Article IV makes sure that states do not have monarchies.

States establish their republican form of government through their state constitutions. The state constitutions vary in content, but all provide for a similar structure of government. Each constitution establishes legislative, executive, and judicial branches of government. In forty-nine states there are two lawmaking bodies, or bicameral legislatures. Bicameral legislatures have one body similar to the U.S. Senate and another like the U.S. House of Representatives. Only the Nebraska constitution provides for a single body of legislators, or a unicameral legislature.

State legislatures have enormous power to pass laws that affect daily life. State laws govern many actions. For example, state laws govern the minimum number of days children are required to attend school. State laws establish requirements for drivers, teachers, doctors, nurses, barbers, beauticians, and other occupations. State laws define crimes and set punishments.

Under the Tenth Amendment, states have the power to establish and to charter cities. A **charter** is a written document issued by a state government to establish and organize a local government. The charter is like a constitution. It defines the purpose, powers, and boundaries of a local government. Under these powers, local governments enact ordinances that affect people within their jurisdiction. Examples of ordinances are laws setting curfews for juveniles, laws requiring people to take care of their houses, and laws requiring licenses for video arcades. States can set up other necessary forms of local government such as county government, school districts, and fire protection districts.

State Regulation of Education — School Laws Affect You

> There is no doubt as to the power of a State, having a high responsibility for education of its citizens, to impose reasonable regulations for the control and duration of basic education. . . . Providing public schools ranks at the very apex of the function of a State. . . . No one can question the State's duty to protect children from ignorance.
> *Wisconsin v. Yoder,* 406 U.S. 205 (1972).

The federal, state, and local governments all have laws regulating education. Public education, however, is primarily a state responsibility. State responsibility has been acknowledged in a number of U.S. Supreme Court decisions. The following are illustrative of these decisions:

> The right and power of the state to regulate the method of providing for the education of its youth at public expense is clear.
> *Gong Lum v. Rice,* 275 U.S. 78 (1927).

> It is, of course, quite true that the responsibility for public education is primarily the concern of the States, but it is equally true that such responsibilities, like all other state activity, must be exercised consistently with federal constitutional requirements as they apply to state action.
> *Cooper v. Aaron,* 358 U.S. 1 (1958).

Simply put, state governments, acting within constitutional guidelines, have the primary responsibility to provide schooling.

Laws begin with needs. Throughout the nation's history community needs have varied from state to state. As a result, school regulations also varied. For example, in the mid-1800s people living in crowded crime-ridden cities in the eastern states called upon their state legislatures to take action to get children off the streets. People also demanded that children learn three basic subjects — reading, writing, and arithmetic. These demands led the state legislature of Massachusetts to pass the first compulsory attendance law in 1851. This was the first time that a state law required children to go to school.

Many educators called for mandatory schooling from grades 1–12. Not all state legislatures agreed with this idea. However by 1980, all fifty states had passed compulsory attendance laws. Why do you think all states now have compulsory attendance laws?

Reports by highly recognized public or private commissions can also lead state legislatures to consider new state laws for education. For example, in 1983 the National Commission on Excellence in Education recommended that state and local high school graduation requirements be strengthened. The commission recommended that all students be required to pass four years of English, three years of mathematics, three years of science, three years of social studies, and one-half year of computer science. As a result of these recommendations, state legislatures and local school boards have begun to revise their high school graduation requirements.

In the following activity you will have the opportunity to study some proposed changes in school laws that would affect you and your schooling.

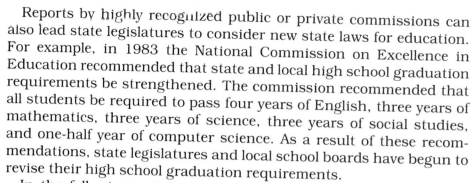

YOUR TURN: S.O.S.: Strengthen our Schools — The State's Response

Assume the role of a state legislator on the state legislature's Education Committee. Your committee is assigned one of the following bills to examine. Imagine that each of these bills has already been introduced (read aloud and assigned a number) in your state legislature.

YOUR COMMITTEE ASSIGNMENT — Each small group should prepare a report to the class on its bills by completing the following steps:

1. Read the bill carefully. Find out the meaning of any words or phrases that you do not understand.

2. List and discuss at least two reasons to vote *for* this bill and at least two reasons to vote *against* this bill.

3. Debate the bill in your small group and then vote to "Pass" the bill as read; or
   "Do Not Pass" the bill as read; or
   "Change the bill and then vote to pass."

4. If a majority of your group votes "Pass," then the bill should be recommended to your entire class. If a majority of your group votes "Do Not Pass," then your group should recommend defeat of the bill to your class. If a majority of your group votes to change

the bill, rewrite the bill and read the amended bill to the entire class. Each member of the group should have at least one reason in support of his or her vote.

Before beginning your group activity, review the following sample:

> SAMPLE bill for a small group:
> HB 1188 (H = House of Representatives; B = Bill; 1188 = Number assigned to this bill after it was introduced and read in the imaginary House)
> Proposed bill:
> "All children between the ages of six and eighteen are required each year to attend an educationally recognized public, private, or parochial school."

1. What does "educationally recognized" mean? This means a public, private, or parochial school that has been approved by the State Department of Education.

2a. Two reasons to support HB 1188:
   (1) This law will make sure that all children have an opportunity to have an elementary and high school education. A good education will help young people succeed.
   (2) This law will greatly reduce the number of young people who are dropping out of school at sixteen under the current compulsory attendance ages of six to sixteen.

2b. Two reasons against HB 1188:
   (1) This is another example of the state ordering people around. Abe Lincoln and Thomas Edison did not need complusory attendance laws to make them productive and successful citizens. This law is not needed.
   (2) This law would cause more problems for high schools. Making someone attend school does not necessarily mean that person will learn. A sixteen or seventeen year old who is forced to attend school will probably resent being there and may cause trouble. Besides, this law would prohibit a sixteen year old from having a full-time job.

3. Group vote.

4. Each member gives at least one reason to explain his or her vote.

Assignment:

The following bills are assigned. When your group receives a bill, follow the appropriate steps.

HB 101 — In order to qualify for a high school diploma, students will be required to take and pass the following, plus any additional requirements of the local school district:
4 years of English;
3 years of mathematics;
3 years of social studies (including successful passage of a state and U.S. Constitution exam);
3 years of science;
1 year of computer science.

HB 102 — In order to receive a high school diploma, all students must successfully pass the required subjects plus successfully pass a basic essential skills test. This basic essential skills test measures a student's ability to apply basics to common experiences — things to know in order to survive, such as accurately balance a checkbook, properly complete a job application, and identify the basic steps in lawmaking.

HB 103 — In order to increase instructional time for students, the state requires all students from the age of five through seventeen to attend an educationally recognized school a minimum of seven hours a day, at least two hundred days of each year.

HB 104 — In order to give students a chance to represent themselves, the Boards of Education of all public school districts are required to appoint two nonvoting student members to their respective boards — one student to represent grades nine and ten and another student to represent grades eleven and twelve.

The teacher will ask each group to make its report and recommendation to the entire class.

ON YOUR OWN: State and Local Lawmakers Affect Daily Lives

Using newspapers, magazines, radio, and/or television, identify stories concerning legislation being considered by your state and local lawmakers. After identifying each story, answer the following questions and discuss your findings with the class.

1. In your own words, describe the legislation or proposed legislation discussed in the news story.

2. Which level of government is involved — state or local?

3. In your opinion, does your state or community need this legislation? Why or why not?

4. How might this legislation affect you?

5. Would you vote for or against this legislation? Why?

Local Governments — Increased Demands, Expanding Services, and Limited Powers

Often, news media and public awareness focus on national and state stories (for example, foreign policy, federal and state budgets, and changes in criminal codes). Yet, the greatest growth in government has been at the local level. The power to establish local governments is defined and described by state statute and/or state constitution. Local governments are not even discussed in the U.S. Constitution.

Increasingly, people are turning to state and local government to meet their needs. In recent years local governments have passed many laws that affect us everyday. Local laws may control handguns, ban the storage or passage of toxic waste, control what is shown at theatres, regulate cable television, regulate rent increases, and establish curfews. Local governments have even passed laws declaring their areas to be nuclear-free zones.

Local governments need more revenue to administer and enforce these new laws. They have raised more money by increasing the fees for services, licenses, and business permits. They have doubled or tripled the fines for violating municipal ordinances that control parking or traffic. Local governments have also increased sales, property, and earnings taxes. In some communities, these increased costs have sparked taxpayer revolts. Some citizens want to lessen the power and services of their local governments.

The growth of local government and the resulting rise in taxes have caused many citizens to question the limits of power of local governments. One limit is the Constitution. The U.S. Constitution is the highest law in the nation. All lawmakers, therefore, must make every effort to enact laws that are constitutionally acceptable. The lawmaking powers of local governments are further restricted by state legislatures and state constitutions. In fact, the very existence of local governments depends on grants of charters by legislatures. In some states, the state legislatures grant very limited powers to local governments. In other states, municipal and county governments possess greater power, sometimes called home rule. The next activity focuses on lawmaking in your community.

YOUR TURN: What is, and What Should be, the Power of Local Governments?

Read each of the following laws. After reading the laws, review each one and answer the questions in each column by writing "yes," "no," or "undecided." Explain your answers. Then refer to the Bill of Rights of the U.S. Constitution on page 228. Decide whether the law raises constitutional issues (for example, freedom of expression) and whether it is constitutional. Be able to explain your answers.

Does your community have a law like this?	Should your community have a law like this?	Is the law constitutional?	Local Law
1_____	_____	_____	A curfew law requires all persons under the age of eighteen to be off the streets by 11:00 P.M. Sunday through Thursday, and by 12 midnight on Friday and Saturday.
2_____	_____	_____	An anti-litter law states that any person found guilty of littering will be fined from $10 to $500.

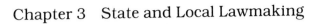
Does your community have a law like this?	Should your community have a law like this?	Is the law constitutional?	Local Law
3_____	_____	_____	A law regulates smoking. It bans smoking in all public places. It also requires employers to provide separate work spaces for smokers and nonsmokers.
4_____	_____	_____	A law regulates video arcades. It prohibits minors from playing video games during school hours.
5_____	_____	_____	A law bans the use of listening devices (for example, Walkman radios) while jogging or walking across streets, or while operating a moving vehicle.
6_____	_____	_____	A law requires all pet owners to control and properly supervise their pets, and to be responsible for properly disposing of their pet's excrement.
7_____	_____	_____	A law prohibits noise pollution. Anyone found guilty of producing decibel levels of beyond the legal limit may be fined and/or jailed.

★★★★★★★★★★★★

The Costs of State and Local Government

Taxpayers have to pay most of the costs of the services provided by state and local governments. Lawmakers often face the difficult decision of whether the government should provide services at the cost of increased taxes or whether to do without certain services. If a state or community becomes known as a "high tax" area, businesses and individuals may move away to "low tax" areas. As a result, state and local lawmakers pass laws that grant tax credits, exemptions, or tax-free bond programs to attract businesses to their areas. Areas with low tax revenues cannot afford many government services.

YOUR TURN: Dividing up the Tax Bill

In 1980, people paid $745.2 billion as follows:

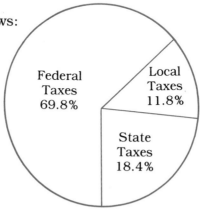

Using your mathematical skills, calculate the dollar amount actually paid to each level of government.

State and local governments are supported by a variety of revenue sources. Among these sources are:

—local earnings tax and state income tax (taxes on amounts earned by individuals)

—corporate profit tax (tax on profit of corporations)

—sales tax (tax on purchase of goods)

—excise tax (special tax on the sale, manufacture, or use of luxury goods)

—business registrations and license fees (For example, a local government may require all vending machines within its jurisdiction to have a local vendor's permit or stamp. The operators or distributors of the vending machines must pay the local government a certain fee for the permit.)

—personal property tax (usually a tax on valuable property other than real estate, such as automobiles, boats or recreational vehicles, furniture, and jewelry)

—real property or real estate tax (tax on land and the buildings on the land)

—bonds (certificates that local governments sell to raise revenue. The local governments promise to pay back the bond buyer, with interest, over a period of time.)

—inheritance tax (tax on amount inherited by individual)

—revenue sharing (federal funds to state and local governments to pay for local projects and services)

—licenses and permits (for example, hunting permits and marriage license fees)

—fees for services (for example, bus fares or museum admissions)

—lottery (state run game of chance)

In one way or another, you the taxpayer must help to pay for government services.

ON YOUR OWN: Your Taxes Support Local and State Government

Review the sources of revenues for local and state governments. Identify which taxes or fees you or your family pay. For example, you probably pay sales tax on most goods and services. You may pay some taxes indirectly. For example, a vending machine operator or distributor may include the fee for the machine's operating license in the cost of the service provided by the machine. Then, one cent of every fifty-cent video game may be included to offset the distributor's fee.

For one week make a list of how much money you contribute to local and state government. Make a list of how much you pay in sales taxes or any indirect taxes. You may be paying a local earnings tax or state income tax if you have earned income. Begin recording your revenue contributions on Friday after school and report your totals to the class the following Friday.

State Laws Affect Youth

Numerous state laws provide for the health, safety, and well-being of young people. Historically, the age limits for various activities have been decided by state law. Although some adult rights have been extended to teenagers, many laws continue to establish limits on the behavior of young people. These laws classify people into two major classes: "children," who are considered too young to assume a particular right or responsibility, and "adults," who are old enough to assume such rights and responsibilities.

YOUR TURN: From Childhood to Adulthood: Changing Legal Status

Read each action and then identify the legal age for this action in your state. In the last column, indicate what you believe should be the legal age for this action. Explain your answers.

Legally Acceptable Actions for Adults	What is the Legal Age?	What Should be the Legal Age in Your State?
Get married without parental permission		
Get married with parental permission		
Legally consume alcoholic beverages		
Legally qualify for a driver's license for autos		
Make legal contracts		
Be **certified to stand trial** as an adult		
Serve on a jury		

Legally Acceptable Actions for Adults	What is the Legal Age?	What Should be the Legal Age in Your State?
Qualify to vote in state elections		
Legally stop attending school		
Make a will		
Choose where to live		
Choose hours to come home		

QUESTIONS FOR GROUP AND CLASS CONSIDERATION:

1. Review your answers in the two columns. How many differences are there between the two columns?

2. Identify at least one reason why there is a legal age for each of the actions you have examined.

3. If you could choose two legal ages to change, which two would you change? What age change would you make, and why?

NOTE: The teacher will share information regarding your state's majority age laws for each of the listed actions.

ON YOUR OWN: From Childhood to Adulthood: Majority Age Laws Vary From State to State

Using the library, research and identify the legal age in the states bordering your state for some of the actions in YOUR TURN on pages 48-49. Several reference books have this information, such as *The Book of the States.* After locating a resource with this age of majority information, do the following:

1. Identify the states that border your state.

2. Locate the legal age limits in the states bordering your state for several "legally accepted actions." (See Column 1, YOUR TURN on pages 48-49.)

3. Compare your state's majority age laws with those of the bordering states. Are there any differences in the ages of "adulthood"?

4. How might these differing majority age laws affect the young people in these states?

5. Identify the state with the youngest age of majority for the actions. For example, which state has the youngest majority age for marrying with parental consent?

6. You may wish to research the legal age for other actions such as:
   being employed to work at any gainful occupations;
   consenting to medical treatment;
   owning a handgun;
   filing a suit in Small Claims Court;
   purchasing cigarettes; and
   serving as an elected state official.

Share your answers with the class.

The Reason for State and Local Lawmaking

Laws vary from state to state and from community to community. In one state a person may be eligible for a driver's license at age sixteen while in another state a person must be eighteen. Why do laws vary throughout the United States? One reason for these differences is found in the U.S. Constitution.

The representatives who attended the Constitutional Convention in 1787 were determined to preserve as much power as possible for their own states. They recognized the need for cooperation among the states. But they also wanted to keep state power over most matters. Article IV and Amendment X emerged as a result of the conflicts and compromises made by these representatives. Together these two constitutional provisions reserve power to the states and make sure the states exercise these powers through a republican form of government.

State and local lawmaking have many advantages over federal lawmaking. State legislatures provide greater proportional representation than the U.S. Congress. Local lawmaking bodies are even more representative. A member of the U.S. House of Representatives represents approximately 520,000 people in each congressional district. A state representative represents far fewer people. A local lawmaker represents even fewer. Therefore, a citizen probably has a better chance of knowing state and local lawmakers than U.S. representatives. After all, the U.S. House of Representatives is in Washington, D.C. But the state legislature is in the state's capital city. For most people, the state capital is closer to home than is Washington, D.C. Many state lawmakers say, "We can serve the needs of our people better than someone in Washington. We know our state and our needs. We are closer to our people." Similarly, local lawmakers believe they know the needs of their communities better than lawmakers in the state capital.

The following analogy might better explain the advantages of state and local lawmaking. For example, imagine that your school has fifty classrooms. Each room elects one student to serve on the Student Council. The Student Council recommends rules for the entire school, plans schoolwide activities, and considers suggestions from the students about matters affecting the entire school. Each room also has a Room Council consisting of five elected students. The Room Council primarily focuses on concerns affecting each room. If you had an idea for improving class discussions in your room, would it be better to take the idea to the Student or the Room Council? In most instances, it would be easier, more effective, and more practical to approach the Room Council with your idea.

If you lived in a state where there had been an increase in cattle rustling, would you take your ideas for increasing the punishment of cattle rustlers to the U.S. Congress in Washington, D.C. or to your state legislature? Generally, you could expect the state legislature to be more interested in a local cattle rustling problem than Congress would be. Similarly, if an intersection near your school were dangerous, would you ask your local lawmakers for a traffic light, or would you ask your state legislature or Congress? Local lawmakers are likely to better informed of this need.

YOUR TURN: Are State Laws Better Than Local or Federal Laws?

Review the actions described in the YOUR TURN activity on pages 48-49. After reviewing the actions and your answers, answer the following question: In your opinion, is a state law better than a local or federal law in each of these actions? Briefly explain your answer for each action.

YOUR TURN: Contemporary Problems and Legislative Proposals

Examine the proposed laws below. Answer the following questions and be prepared to report to the class.

1. What problem(s) does this proposed law address?

2. Does your community already have this law?

3. What are some arguments against this law?

4. What are some arguments for this law?

5. If you were voting on this proposed law, how would you vote and why?

PROPOSED LAW #1: Beverage Container Deposit Ordinance

The proposed ordinance bans the sale of throwaway bottles and cans. All beverages must be sold in returnable containers. A five-cent deposit is required on the purchase of each container. Containers may be returned and deposits refunded. The purpose of the law is to reduce litter and trash.

PROPOSED LAW #2: Good Samaritan Statute

The proposed statute requires that bystanders must give aid during an emergency to any person who has suffered serious physical harm or who has been exposed to serious physical harm. The "good samaritan" must either call the police or get medical help for the person. If the bystander fails to give aid, then he or she may be charged with a **misdemeanor.**

ON YOUR OWN: Know Your State and Local Government

I. LOCAL

Using information available in the library, attempt to answer the following questions about local governments in your community:

A. County Government
   1. In what county do you live?
   2. Briefly describe the type of government at your county level (for example, county executive - county council, board of commissioners, or county administrative judge).
   3. Identify at least two services provided by your county government.
   4. When was your county chartered? Has the charter been changed in the last ten years?
   5. Approximately how many people are employed by the county government? What is your county government's annual budget?
   6. What are the major sources of revenue for your county government?

B. Municipal Government (complete if you live in a city, town, or village). Answer the same questions as those asked about county government, only substitute "city," "town," or "village" for "county" in each question.

C. Special District Governments
   Place a check mark in the space before each of the types of special districts (sometimes called "authorities") governing your community:

   ____ Fire Protection District
   ____ School District
   ____ Soil Conservation District
   ____ Water District
   ____ Library District
   ____ Housing District
   ____ Parks and Recreation District
   ____ Highways and Streets District
   ____ Health and Hospital District
   ____ Cemetery District
   ____ Public Transportation District
   ____ Flood Control District
   ____ Other types of Special Districts (identify any others)

Review the list. For each checkmark, answer the following:

1. How is the special district governed?

2. What is the purpose of the district? What services does the district provide?

3. Approximately how many people are employed by this special district? What is the district's annual budget?

4. How does this special district pay for itself; in other words, what are the district's sources of revenue?

As you find the answers to these questions, share them with the teacher. The teacher may wish to create a bulletin board highlighting this information: "Our Local Governments."

II. STATE

Using information in the library, or information provided by a state legislator, or from the League of Women Voters, answer the following questions:

1. When was your state constitution adopted? Does your state constitution provide for a legislative branch of government?

2. Is there a Bill of Rights in your state constitution? If so, how does it compare to the Bill of Rights in the U.S. Constitution?

3. List or describe some of the powers granted your state legislature by the state constitution.

4. Does your state legislature have one or two houses?

5. How are representatives chosen to serve in your state legislature?

6. What are the constitutional qualifications for serving in your state legislature?

7. How many members are in your state legislature? If there are two houses, how many members are in each house and what is the total number in both houses?

8. Name the members of the state legislature or general assembly who represent the area where you live.

9. How would you contact your senator or representative? (Identify address and telephone number.)

4

CONFLICTS OF POWER: FEDERAL, STATE, AND LOCAL LAWMAKING

Who Has the Power to Solve Public Problems?

People in need often seek help from the government. Yet when they do, government officials sometimes claim that "we would like to help but we lack the authority. This is really a problem for someone else to handle."

Which level of government — federal, state, or local — should have the power to solve public problems? The representatives from the thirteen original states who met in 1787 recognized the need to answer this question. Their answer, expressed in the Constitution, establishes a **federal system** of government. A federal system is a compromise between an extreme concentration of power in one central government and a loose association of independent states. The Constitution establishes a strong national government to handle the problems involving the entire nation. The national government, therefore, has the power to control interstate trade, a monetary system, national defense, and foreign relations. At the same time, the Constitution reserves other powers to the states and the people.

Reprinted with permission from the Minneapolis Star and Tribune Company.

The Constitution describes the powers of the national government and the state governments. Local governments, however, are not mentioned in the Constitution. State governments have the power to establish local governments. Every state legislature has exercised this power by establishing counties and granting charters to cities, towns, and special districts (for example, school districts, fire protection districts, water districts, and sanitation districts). Each state government has **jurisdiction,** or power to act, over affairs within the state's borders. Similarly, each local government has jurisdiction over affairs within its borders (for example, police protection, fire protection, parks and playgrounds, and zoning and building codes).

The following chart lists some of the lawmaking powers under the federal system:

Federal Lawmaking Powers (Exclusive Powers)	Powers Shared by Federal and State Governments (Concurrent Powers)	State lawmaking Powers (Reserved Powers)
— Regulating foreign trade and commerce between the states — Coining and printing money — Conducting foreign relations with other nations — Establishing post offices and roads — Raising and supporting armed forces — Declaring war and making peace — Governing American territories and admitting new states — Regulating naturalization and immigration — Making all laws "necessary and proper" to carry out the powers of the federal government	— Collecting taxes — Borrowing money — Establishing courts — Prohibiting crimes and punishing lawbreakers — Providing for the health and welfare of the people	— Establishing local governments — Regulating wills, contracts, and family relations — Regulating trade within the state — Conducting elections — Determining qualifications of voters — Establishing and supporting public schools — Licensing professional workers — Keeping all the "reserved powers" not granted to the federal government nor prohibited to the states

Which Law is Supreme?

What happens when Congress passes a law that contradicts a state law? What happens when a state passes a law inconsistent with a federal law? In other words, when there is a conflict between federal and state law, which law controls? For example, Congress passes a law prohibiting the manufacture, sale, and possession of tobacco. But the state has a law permitting the manufacture and sale of tobacco. Which law should the people obey?

The framers of the Constitution answered the question in Article VI:

> This Constitution, and the laws of the United States which shall be made in Pursuance thereof; and all Treaties made, or which shall be made, under the Authority of the United States, shall be the supreme Law of the Land; and the Judges in every State shall be bound thereby, any Thing in the Constitution or Laws of any State to the Contrary notwithstanding.

This clause is known as the Supremacy Clause.

Under the Supremacy Clause, the Constitution is the highest, most powerful law in the country. Any law — whether a statute, an ordinance, a regulation, or a common law principle — that conflicts with the Constitution is invalid. Similarly, no act of any government official or department — whether at the federal, state, or local level — is valid if it conflicts with the Constitution. For example, a school board cannot fire a coach for writing a letter to the newspaper criticizing the school board for cutting athletic activities. That action would violate the First Amendment guarantee of freedom of speech. Likewise, a federal statute cannot take away the citizenship of a person in order to punish him or her. That law would violate the Eighth Amendment protection against cruel and unusual punishment.

YOUR TURN: Laws in Conflict With the Constitution

The following laws and government actions are invalid under the Supremacy Clause because they conflict with the Constitution. Read each law or government action. Using the Constitution in the appendix of this book, identify the amendment or section of the article of the Constitution with which the particular law or government action conflicts. The reference to amendment or specific article is provided to assist in locating the appropriate constitutional section.

1. A state statute requires voters in federal elections to be twenty-one years old. (Amendment)
2. A state court refuses to give a jury trial to a person accused of a crime. (Amendment)
3. The president issues an order naming her husband to succeed her in office. (Amendment)
4. A state agency prints the money needed to pay state workers. (Article I)
5. A municipal judge sentences any person convicted of three or more traffic violations to death by hanging. (Amendment)
6. A federal statute creates a second Supreme Court. (Article III)

★ ★ ★ ★ ★ ★ ★ ★ ★ ★ ★ ★

The Supremacy of Federal Statutes

When Congress passes a law, that statute becomes part of the supreme law of the land — higher than all laws except the Constitution. People in every state must obey federal statutes.

Prior to the 1960s, several states enacted what were known as "Jim Crow" laws. These laws required segregation of the races in public places. For example, drinking fountains were labeled for "whites only" or "colored only."

Library of Congress

Many persons worked to change these state laws. They also tried to persuade Congress to pass a law forbidding racial discrimination. In 1964 Congress passed a major civil rights law that included the following:

CIVIL RIGHTS ACT OF 1964
Title II
Section 201. (a) All persons shall be entitled to the full and equal enjoyment of the goods, services, facilities, privileges, advantages, and accommodations of any place of public accommodation, as defined in this section, without discrimination or segregation on the ground of race, color, religion, or national origin. [The law goes on to define public accommodations as hotels, motels, restaurants and other eating establishments, gasoline stations, theaters, concert halls, sports arenas, or other places of exhibition or entertainment.]

Does the 1964 Civil Rights Act apply to persons in every state? What do you think happened to state "Jim Crow" laws as a result of the 1964 Civil Rights Act?

YOUR TURN: Case Study on a Clash of State and Federal Laws

Read the section of the federal civil rights law and the case summary below. Then answer the questions that follow:

CIVIL RIGHTS ACT OF 1964
Title VII
Section 703. (a) It shall be an unlawful employment practice for an employer —

(1) to fail or refuse to hire or to discharge any individual, or otherwise to discriminate against any individual with respect to his compensation, terms, conditions, or privileges of employment opportunities or otherwise negatively affect his status as nation origin; or

(2) to limit, segregate, or classify his employees in any way which would deprive or tend to deprive any individual of employment opportunities or otherwise negatively affect his status as an employee, because of such individual's race, color, religion, sex, or national origin.

Section 703(a) appears to prohibit all discrimination based on sex. But, section 703(e) permits an employer to refuse to employ persons of a particular sex when sex is a qualification reasonably necessary to the normal operation of that particular business.

The Case of Rosenfeld v. Southern Pacific Company

Leah Rosenfeld, an employee of the Southern Pacific Company, applied for a promotion to agent-telegrapher. The job of agent-telegrapher required heavy physical effort. Southern Pacific would not consider her for the job because she was a woman. Only men were allowed to apply for the job. The company said that "women, in general, are not physically or biologically suited for such work." The company claimed that being male was a necessary qualification for the job. Also, Southern Pacific claimed that hiring Ms. Rosenfeld would violate California law. According to the company, the repeated lifting of weights greater than twenty-five pounds would violate the state law protecting women from doing heavy lifting. The company also said that agent-telegraphers are sometimes asked to work over ten hours a day. The California Labor Code prohibited women from working more than eight hours a day.

Ms. Rosenfeld filed a lawsuit against Southern Pacific. She claimed that the refusal to promote her violated Section 703 of the 1964 Civil Rights Act. The state of California joined the lawsuit to defend its laws. *Rosenfeld v. Southern Pacific Company*, 444 F.2d 1219 (9th Cir. 1971).

YOU BE THE JUDGE — Answer the following questions:

1. What are the important facts in this case? Who are the parties involved? What is the problem?
2. What is the legal issue in this case?
3. How is the state of California involved in this case?
4. How does the 1964 Civil Rights Act apply to this case?
5. What are the major arguments for each party (Leah Rosenfeld, Southern Pacific Company, and California) in this case?
6. If you were the judge hearing this case, what would you decide and why?

★★★★★★★★★★★★

Relationship Between Federal and State Levels of Government

Concurrent powers are powers shared by the federal and state governments. This means that both federal and state governments have power to pass laws and take action on certain problems. For example, both the federal government and state governments have laws to control pollution, prevent unfair business practices, investigate crimes, and protect natural resources.

The exercise of these concurrent powers sometimes raises difficult questions. Many citizens and elected officials believe it is better to rely on state and local government for public services. They believe these governments have a better understanding of their needs. Also, they prefer to keep their tax money closer to home. There they can keep an eye on how the government uses the money. Others believe the federal government can better solve problems that affect people in many states. The same kinds of conflicts can occur between state and local levels of government. Following are examples of conflicts that may occur between the different levels of government.

YOUR TURN: Who Controls?
Conflicts of Power

A. State vs. Federal

Examine the section of the Constitution and the cartoon below. Then answer the questions that follow:

> Article I, Section 8. The Congress shall have the Power . . . To regulate Commerce with foreign nations, and among the several States, and with the Indian tribes.

1. According to the cartoon, who had the idea that the Missouri legislature consider allowing bigger trucks on the highways?

2. What does the cartoon say about the relationship between state government and the federal government?

Dictator Of The Road

©1983 Engelhardt in the St. Louis Post-Dispatch — reprinted with permission

Read this news summary, and then answer the questions below:

States Protest Bigger Trucks

Leaders of state governments spoke out against the federal government's big truck legislation, the new Surface Transportation Assistance Act. States in the East and West stood united in defense of states' rights and control of their own roads as the Federal-State Assembly of the National Conference of State Legislatures unanimously adopted a resolution saying the trainlike tandem trailer trucks are a deadly menace. These state officials believe that they can best decide what size trucks can safely travel their highways.

The Surface Transportation Assistance Act was passed by Congress to open all interstate highways to larger trucks. In other words, with the new legislation trucks would not have to travel around states that had limits on the size of trucks permitted on their highways. For example, if a double-rigged tractor trailer were traveling from Indiana to Kansas, the truck would now be able to travel through Illinois and Missouri, whereas before Illinois and Missouri prohibited single tractors pulling two trailers. Congress and the president have stated that the new law will reduce shipping costs for consumers. The new law is also hailed as a jobs bill. The act raises the federal tax on gasoline by five cents per gallon and the new money is to be spent for road repairs and other transportation needs.

Since the new law was enacted and signed by the president, several states have gone to court to fight the big trucks. Thirty-seven states already allowed the double trailers, but most states had restrictions that were erased under this new law. (Compiled from News Services.)

1. What congressional act opened all interstate highways to the larger trucks?
2. Explain at least one reason why many state legislatures oppose this congressional act.
3. Explain at least one reason why Congress passed this new law.
4. If you were asked to vote on the new Surface Transportation Assistance Act, how would you vote?
5. Who should be responsible for regulating the size and weight of trucks? Why?

B. Local vs. State

Examine the editorial and answer the questions that follow:

Shooting Down All Local Gun Laws

The Local Government Committee of the state House of Representatives has approved a bill that could prevent local governments in Missouri from trying to protect their citizens by regulating guns. For no apparent reason other than to please the gun lobby, the bill would set aside all existing local ordinances on firearms and prohibit any political subdivision in the state from enacting a law dealing in any way with firearms.

Rep. Charles Troupe, one of the co-sponsors of the bill, is from St. Louis, where some 160 homicides a year are committed with handguns. Given that fact, why would Mr. Troupe want to prevent St. Louis from enforcing a gun law designed to protect its citizens from a threat that is greater in the city than perhaps anywhere in the state? St. Louis can hardly be accused of acting on firearms in a way that threatens state sovereignty.

The real push for House Bill 572 (to ban local gun laws) seems to be coming from groups like the National Rifle Association, which wants to head off legislation like that of Morton Grove, Ill., where a law was passed to ban the sale and possession of handguns, except for antique-gun collectors, licensed gun clubs and military and police personnel. Similar legislation has been introduced, so far without success, in Manchester, Mo.

But surely no evidence has been advanced to justify so thorough a state intrusion into local affairs as that represented by HB 572, which would bar any ordinance ''concerning in any way the sale, purchase, delay, transfer, ownership, use, keeping, possession, bearing, transportation, licensing, permit, registration, taxation, or other controls on firearms, components, ammunition, and supplies.'' The authors of the bill seem to have covered all of the possible rights of guns but not the right of people to protect themselves against being shot.

St. Louis Post-Dispatch

1. How would the **bill** approved by the Local Government Committee of the Missouri House of Representatives restrict the power of local governments?
2. Briefly explain the editorial's position on the bill.
3. Write an editorial in favor of the bill.

4. In your opinion, should the state government have the power to restrict local governments from regulating handguns within their jurisdiction? Briefly explain your answer.
5. Should federal lawmakers (Congress) have the power to pass a similar law to restrict the power of state governments? Briefly explain your answer.

Coexistence and Pre-emption

What happens when federal and state laws try to solve the same problem? The existence of a federal law does not automatically mean that the state cannot also have a law on the same subject. No state law can give less rights than does federal law. State laws, however, can grant more rights than federal law. For example, a state law could lower the voting age to seventeen for state elections. But a state law that raised the voting age to twenty-five for all elections would be unconstitutional. In other words, state laws can grant *more* rights than federal law but not less. If the state law directly conflicts with the federal law, the state law is invalid.

Congress may decide that its law is compatible with existing state laws on the same subject. In this case both the federal and state laws are valid. For example, when Congress set up the Equal Employment Opportunity Commission to investigate complaints of employment discrimination, Congress expressly stated that complaints should be considered first at the state level.

On some subjects, Congress may pass laws that deal with only part of a problem. The states can then make laws on other parts of the problem. For example, there are both federal laws and state laws on issues such as telephone rates, minimum wages, and car safety requirements.

In some cases Congress completely pre-empts a certain area of the law. When Congress pre-empts a subject, it decides that is the *only* lawmaking body that should make laws on the subject. For example, Congress has pre-empted lawmaking in the areas of radio and television advertising and drug and cosmetic labelling. This means that states cannot pass any laws on these subjects. Sometimes Congress does not make it clear whether it wants to pre-empt a subject or whether states can still make laws on that subject. When this happens, the federal courts usually have to decide the issue.

YOUR TURN: Case Study on State Versus Federal Lawmaking Power

Read the case below and answer the questions that follow:

Pacific Gas & Electric Company v. State Energy
Resources Conservation & Development Commission
103 Sup. Ct. 1713 (1983)

In 1976 California enacted a law prohibiting nuclear power plant construction until there was a federally approved plan for disposing of nuclear waste. Pacific Gas & Electric Company and several other utility companies, along with the federal government, challenged this law. The United States Supreme Court heard the case.

The utility companies and the federal government argued that the California law conflicted with the federal Atomic Energy Act. The Atomic Energy Act gives the federal government authority to regulate the development and use of nuclear power. California argued that the Atomic Energy Act only applied to regulation of nuclear power and not to nuclear wastes. Therefore, California claimed it had the right to protect its citizens from hazardous radioactive wastes.

YOU BE THE JUDGE — Answer the following questions:

1. What are the important facts in this case? What is the major problem? What parties are involved in this case?
2. What is the legal issue?
3. What are the major arguments for both sides?
4. If you were one of the Supreme Court justices hearing this case, what would you decide and why?

Relations Among States

Our Constitution establishes the powers and relations between the federal government and state governments. In Article IV it also provides guidelines for relations among the fifty states. Article IV states that "full faith and credit shall be given in each state to the public acts, records and judicial proceedings of every other state." In other words, while each state has the power to govern the affairs within its own boundaries, the states should recognize and respect the laws of every other state. For example, each state has its own laws governing divorce. One state may allow divorce for reasons not recognized in other states. Without the requirement that each state give full faith and credit to the laws and judgments of other states, a person could be legally divorced in one state and still be legally married in another. What kind of problems could this cause?

Another important guideline requires each state to give citizens of other states all the "privileges and immunities" to which citizens of that state would be entitled. That means that states may not discriminate against each other's citizens. As a result, people can move from one state to another without losing basic privileges like driving a car, purchasing property, or holding a job. A state, however, can require citizens of other states to meet special conditions. For example, a state cannot keep citizens of other states from attending its public universities. But the state can require out-of-state students to pay tuition even though its own citizens pay no tuition. States can refuse to give some privileges to citizens living in other states, for example, voting in state elections, holding public office, and being on a jury. Why do you think states keep these privileges only for their own citizens?

A third guideline in the Constitution requires states to extradite persons accused of a crime who flee from another state. In other words, the state must return the accused person to the state accusing the person of crime. Yet, states sometimes block extradition of a person to another state if there is controversy about the crime or claims of unfair or prejudicial treatment. For example, the governor of California refused a South Dakota request to extradite a leader of the American Indian Movement charged with attempted murder. The California governor claimed the Indian leader's life would be endangered if he were returned to South Dakota.

Some people believe that even with these guidelines, there are too many conflicts among state laws. They think that we should have more federal laws so there will be more uniformity. Others say that such action would be a violation of the states' reserved powers and, therefore, unconstitutional.

YOUR TURN: There Ought to be a Law?

Read each of the proposed laws below. Answer the questions that follow. Be able to explain your answers.

1. What do you think is the purpose of this proposed law?
2. Should this proposed law be passed? Briefly explain your answer.
3. Which level of government (federal, state, or local) do you think should pass this proposed law? You may list more than one level of government as possible lawmakers. Be able to give reasons to support your choice.
4. Which three proposed laws do you think are most important? Why?

Proposed Laws

1. All persons convicted of driving drunk shall be sentenced to a mandatory minimum sentence of forty-eight hours in jail or forty hours of community service.
2. All drivers and their front seat passengers shall use seat belts for safety.
3. All young men shall register for the draft when they reach the age of eighteen.
4. All persons under the age of eighteen shall be off the streets by 11:00 P.M. Sunday through Thursday, and by 12 midnight on Friday and Saturday.
5. All bystanders shall give help (like calling the police or getting medical help) to persons exposed to or suffering serious physical harm.
6. Abuse of a spouse or a child shall be a crime.
7. No company shall manufacture nuclear weapons.
8. All boxers must wear protective headgear.
9. No individual or company shall hire an illegal immigrant.
10. All businesses with coin-operated amusement devices (like video games or pinball machines) shall get the signatures of approval from at least five hundred residents in the neighborhood where the business is located before the business will be granted a license for the devices.
11. The government shall sponsor a program to give unemployed youth (aged sixteen to twenty-five) jobs working in public parks.
12. Landlords shall not refuse to rent to families with children.

13. Pollution control equipment on cars shall be tested as part of an annual safety inspection in order to get license plates.
14. There shall be established a government operated lottery to increase money for public schools.
15. No hazardous waste materials shall be transported on public roads.
16. There shall be established a government owned and operated health care program to provide low cost or free health care to all.

All of the proposed laws are now law or are being considered as proposed laws by various local, state, and federal lawmakers.

Review your answers on the proposed laws. How many of these proposals did you think should be a law? Which level of lawmakers did you choose most often to pass the proposed laws? Be prepared to discuss and compare your answers with those of other students in the class. For every law you think should be passed, consider how much the law will cost and who will pay the cost.

ON YOUR OWN: There Ought to be a Law-Survey

Identify at least two members of the community (relatives, friends, neighbors) and have them respond to the previous YOUR TURN activity. Record their answers in columns, identifying them as Community Respondent #1, #2, and so on.

Students should tally their responses as a class project. Compare the responses from the community to the responses in your class. After surveying the community, invite a lawmaker to class to discuss the survey results.

Community Respondent #1		Community Respondent #2	
SHOULD THERE BE A LAW?	WHO SHOULD PASS THIS LAW?	SHOULD THERE BE A LAW?	WHO SHOULD PASS THIS LAW?
1. _____	_____	1. _____	_____
2. _____	_____	2. _____	_____

5

IMPACT OF PRESIDENTIAL DECISION MAKING

> There's never been an office — an executive office — in all the history of the world with the responsibility and power of the president of the United States. That is the reason in this day and age that it must be run and respected as at no other time in the history of the world because it can mean the welfare of the world or its destruction.
>
> President Harry Truman, 1954

President Truman would probably be even more convinced of the truth of this statement if he were alive today. The first atomic bomb was dropped on Hiroshima in 1945. Since then United States presidents have been on the brink of nuclear warfare many times. In each case, one individual — the president — has had to determine the fate of the world. In 1950, for example, President Truman warned that nuclear weapons might be used against the Chinese who surrounded U.S. troops during the Korean conflict. In 1954 President Eisenhower offered the French the use of atomic weapons in the French-Indochina conflict. In 1962 President Kennedy faced a number of dramatic decisions that could have led to nuclear war as he responded to the presence of Soviet nuclear weapons in Cuba. In 1969 President Nixon sent an ultimatum to the North Vietnamese that the United States would use nuclear weapons against them if they did not agree to settle the Vietnam conflict. In 1980 a national security study during President Carter's administration concluded, "To prevail in Iran, we might have to threaten or make use of tactical nuclear weapons." Since 1945 each president has known that he commands the nuclear weapons that could destroy the world.

The Source of Presidential Power

What powers allowed President Truman to order the atomic bomb dropped on Japan? By what right can any president consider the use of nuclear warfare? Like the power of lawmakers and the courts, the source of presidental power is the United States Constitution. Article II of the Constitution describes the executive branch of the federal government. It provides for the following presidential powers:

— To be commander in chief of the armed forces, including the militias of the states;

— To conclude treaties with foreign nations (with approval by two-thirds of the U.S. Senate);

— To nominate and appoint ambassadors, federal judges, and other principal officials with the advice and consent of the Senate;

— To receive ambassadors from other countries;

— To grant **reprieves** and **pardons**;

— To present to Congress his or her views on the state of the union and recommend legislative measures;

— To call extraordinary sessions of Congress and adjourn Congress if the House and Senate cannot agree on a time of adjournment;

— To veto legislation passed by Congress; and

— To "take care that the laws be faithfully executed."

These presidential powers can be grouped into five general areas of responsibility:

COMMANDER IN CHIEF — The president is in charge of all American armed forces. On any given day, more than two million uniformed soldiers are under his or her command. The president is responsible for the nation's security. All military officers take their orders from the president. The president has the power to decide how weapons and troops will be used. The president is responsible for the day-to-day duties of the armed forces, but only Congress has the power to declare war.

CHIEF OF STATE — The president is in charge of relations with foreign powers. He or she negotiates treaties and executive agreements. The president decides to recognize new governments and nations, selects and supervises the nation's diplomatic staff, directs the nation's policy in the United Nations, and communicates with foreign leaders. Presidents have enormous power in the area of foreign affairs. As one president said, "I make American foreign policy."

LEGISLATIVE LOBBYIST —The president has legislative programs that he or she wants Congress to pass. The president recommends proposed laws in the annual State of the Union address. Congressional supporters of a president introduce these proposals in the Senate and/or House of Representatives. Then the president, the president's staff, and leaders of the various executive departments and agencies try to persuade Congress to support these proposals. The president also makes public speeches in support of his or her

The Executive Branch

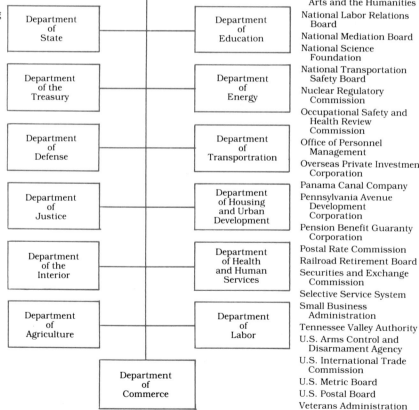

The President
Executive Office of the President

White House Office
Office of Management and Budget
Council of Economic Advisors
National Security Council
Office of the Special Representative for Trade
Negotiations
Council on Environmental Quality
Domestic Policy Staff
Office of Science and Technology Policy
Central Intelligence Agency

ACTION
Administrative Conference
  of the U.S.
American Battle
  Monuments Committee
Appalachian Regional
  Commission
Board of International
  Broadcasting
Canal Zone Government
Civil Aeronautics Board
Commission on Civil Rights
Commission on Fine Arts
Commodity Futures Trading
  Commission
Community Services
  Administration
Consumer Products Safety
  Commission
Environmental Protection
  Agency
Equal Employment
  Opportunity Commission
Export-Import Bank of the
  U.S.
Farm Credit Administration
Federal Communications
  Commission
Federal Deposit Insurance
  Corporation
Federal Election
  Commission
Federal Emergency
  Management Agency
Federal Home Loan Bank
  Board
Federal Labor Relations
  Authority
Federal Maritime
  Commission
Federal Mediation and
  Conciliation Service
Federal Reserve System,
  Board of Governors
  Federal Trade
  Commission
Foreign Claims Settlement
  Commission of the U.S.
General Services
  Administration
Inter-American Foundation

Department of State
Department of the Treasury
Department of Defense
Department of Justice
Department of the Interior
Department of Agriculture
Department of Commerce

Department of Education
Department of Energy
Department of Transportration
Department of Housing and Urban Development
Department of Health and Human Services
Department of Labor

International
  Communication Agency
Interstate Commerce
  Commission
Merit Systems Protection
  Board
National Aeronautics and
  Space Administration
National Credit Union
  Administration
National Foundation on the
  Arts and the Humanities
National Labor Relations
  Board
National Mediation Board
National Science
  Foundation
National Transportation
  Safety Board
Nuclear Regulatory
  Commission
Occupational Safety and
  Health Review
  Commission
Office of Personnel
  Management
Overseas Private Investment
  Corporation
Panama Canal Company
Pennsylvania Avenue
  Development
  Corporation
Pension Benefit Guaranty
  Corporation
Postal Rate Commission
Railroad Retirement Board
Securities and Exchange
  Commission
Selective Service System
Small Business
  Administration
Tennessee Valley Authority
U.S. Arms Control and
  Disarmament Agency
U.S. International Trade
  Commission
U.S. Metric Board
U.S. Postal Board
Veterans Administration

legislative proposals. The president often asks citizens to contact their legislators to urge them to support new laws. The president also has the power to veto legislation passed by Congress. Congress can override this veto by a two-thirds vote of both houses.

PARTY LEADER — The president is usually the leader of one of the major political parties. Since 1860 presidents have been either Democrat or Republican. The president is elected as the candidate of a political party. Members of that party work hard to elect their candidate. The president then tries to help other party members seeking public offices such as senators, representatives, governors, and mayors. This mutual assistance is very important as the president tries to carry out his or her duties. The president can usually achieve more legislative proposals when his or her political party controls both the U.S. Senate and the U.S. House of Representatives.

CHIEF EXECUTIVE — The president is the leader of the executive branch. The president is responsible for carrying out the laws passed by Congress. He or she must make sure the federal government functions properly. The chief executive is in charge of the cabinet-level departments, the federal agencies and bureaus, and the several million civilian employees responsible for the day-to-day duties of the executive branch. The president nominates ambassadors, federal judges, and other principal officials of the federal government. These officials influence public policy for years. The president appoints about fifteen hundred high-ranking officials who represent the wishes of the president to their departments. The chart on the previous page illustrates the number of executive offices, cabinet-level departments, agencies, and bureaus that the president must manage.

YOUR TURN: The Roles and Influence of Presidents

Study the following examples of presidential power. After each example, answer the following:

1. Which of the following role(s) is the president using?
   COMMANDER IN CHIEF, CHIEF OF STATE, PARTY LEADER, LEGISLATIVE LOBBYIST, CHIEF EXECUTIVE

2. How might people be affected by the actions of the president in this role?
3. How could the president's actions affect your life?

Example 1

UPI/Bettmann Newsphotos

Left to right, seated: British Prime Minister Winston Churchill, President Franklin D. Roosevelt, and Soviet Premier Joseph Stalin.

As World War II ended, the victorious Allied leaders (Churchill, Roosevelt, and Stalin) met at the city of Yalta in the Soviet Union in February 1945. The leaders negotiated and issued a declaration describing plans to bring peace and representative government throughout Europe. The leaders also discussed the organization of the United Nations. The leaders agreed that a United Nations conference should be held in San Francisco in April 1945. Leaders of nations throughout the world would be invited to prepare the permanent **charter** of the United Nations.

The Premier of the Union of Soviet Socialist Republics, the Prime Minister of the United Kingdom and the President of the United States of America . . . jointly declare their mutual agreement to . . .

— the right of all peoples to choose the form of government under which they will live — the restoration of sovereign rights and self-government to those people who have been forcibly deprived of them by the aggressor nations.

To foster the conditions in which liberated peoples may exercise these rights, the three governments will jointly assist the people in any European liberated state . . . (a) to establish conditions of internal peace; (b) to carry out emergency mea- *sures for the relief of distressed peoples; (c) to form interim governmental authorities broadly representative of all democratic elements in the population and pledged to the earliest possible establishment through free elections of governments responsive to the will of the people; and (d) to facilitate where necessary the holding of such elections.*

When, in the opinion of the three governments, conditions . . . make such action necessary, they will immediately consult together on the measures necessary to discharge the joint responsibilities set forth in this declaration.

From Declaration on Liberated Europe, Yalta Conference, February 1945.

Example 2

CBS news reporter Bill
Moyers.

AP/Wide World Photos

AP/Wide World Photos

Director of the Central Intelligence Agency, Stansfield Turner; and President Jimmy Carter.

In June 1977 President Carter watched Bill Moyer's CBS report on the Central Intelligence Agency (CIA). After watching the report, President Carter called Stansfield Turner, the head of the CIA. Carter ordered Turner to get a tape of the report and watch it. Carter told Turner to find out if the charges of CIA spying on citizens within the United States were true. Carter wanted a complete report regarding these charges. Carter told Turner if the charges were true, he wanted to know it, and he wanted the CIA to stop such spying.

Example 3

Reagan, O'Neill In Tug-Of-War Over Immigration Legislation

Compiled From News Services

WASHINGTON — A tug-of-war between President Ronald Reagan and House Speaker Thomas P. O'Neill Jr. has begun over immigration legislation.

Although Reagan favors it, O'Neill says the president could veto the measure to curry favor with Hispanic groups.

O'Neill said Tuesday that Hispanic legislators had told him they indirectly had been given "a promise of veto" from the White House, despite previous indications of administration support for such a measure.

O'Neill then said that the legislation "won't go to the (House) floor this year."

"Do I think the president is political enough to veto the bill to get more votes for his party? Yes," O'Neill said.

In response, White House spokesman Larry Speakes said Reagan had first proposed an immigration bill more than two years ago.

Speakes said Reagan was "naturally disappointed" to learn of O'Neill's remarks and still hoped O'Neill would allow the House to vote on the bill.

"The president sent the original immigration reform legislation to the Congress more than two years ago." Speakes said. "He supported it then. He supports it today.

"This is not a political issue," Speakes continued. "It is not a partisan issue. It is an issue that concerns all Americans, and it is in the best interests of all Americans to have the nation regain control of its borders."

But privately, the administration has expressed strong reservations about the version of the bill pending in the House. Justice Department documents made available Tuesday by administration officials and members of Congress detailed those objections.

The administration says the House bill would be too costly, is overly generous in granting amnesty to illegal aliens and goes too far in protecting the civil rights of permanent resident aliens living legally in the United States.

The administration estimates that the bill, in the form approved by the House Judiciary Committee, would cost $11.5 billion over five years. Amendments requested by the administration would reduce the five-year cost to $3.6 billion.

Congress has tried several times in the last decade to rewrite the immigration laws by forbidding employers to hire illegal aliens. The House passed legislation in 1972 and 1973 to penalize employers for hiring illegal aliens, but the Senate did not act on the bill.

In 1977, then-President Jimmy Carter proposed such penalties and appointed a bipartisan study commission that made a similar recommendation. Reagan sent his proposals to Congress in July 1981.

Hispanic-Americans, including some members of Congress, contend that if employers were subject to civil and criminal penalties for hiring illegal aliens, the employers would be more likely to discriminate against American citizens of Hispanic descent.

O'Neill said he would not bring the bill to the floor unless it were acceptable to Hispanic members of Congress, even if Reagan changed his mind and decide to support the House bill. "It has to be acceptable to the Hispanic Caucus," O'Neill said.

The speaker said that, so far as he could determine, the bill was supported only by a handful of legislators and a few "liberal newspapers." On the other hand, he said, there was a clear constituency against the bill. O'Neill said Hispanic-Americans had told him that the bill, if passed, would be "the most devastating thing that could happen to them."

Example 4

Fleet Off Lebanon Set To Aid Marines

ABOARD THE USS EISENHOWER (AP) — An American fleet bristling with warplanes, missiles and big guns is assembling just off the Lebanese coast in case U.S. Marines in Beirut call for help.

The White House announced Tuesday that President Ronald Reagan had authorized commanders of the 1,200-man Marine force in the Lebanese capital to ask the Navy for air strikes if necessary to defend the multinational peacekeeping force.

The U.S., French, Italian and British troops who make up the force have come under artillery fire from Druse and Shiite Moslem militias in the latest round of fighting in Lebanon. Four Marines have been killed.

The conditions set by Reagan may be wide enough to permit U.S. support also for the Lebanese army in a major battle. The only significant piece of territory controlled by the army is Beirut.

"The U.S. is co-deployed with the Lebanese army and it is likely that if the Lebanese army comes under attack, it will endanger the lives of the Marines," said a State Department official, who insisted on anonymity.

If a call for help comes from the Marine commander, Col. Timothy J. Geraghty of St. Louis, the Navy ships off shore will be able to supply air strikes or bombardments within minutes.

As the fighting in Lebanon has escalated in recent weeks, the Navy has amassed about a dozen warships off the coast, including the aircraft carrier Eisenhower, with more than 90 warplanes.

The Marines also are backed up by sea-based Cobra helicopter gunships and six Marine Harrier jets on the Tarawa, an amphibious assault ship that arrived Monday from the Indian Ocean as part of a task force with 2,000 more Marines who will remain with the fleet.

The French have a 2,000-man contingent that has suffered more casualties than any of the other three nations. The French have 40 planes on the aircraft carrier Foch; among the aircraft are Super Etendard fighters.

Italy keeps two frigates within sight of Beirut's beaches. The British dispatched six Buccaneer fighter-bombers to Cyprus — only 10 minutes by air from Beirut.

The U.S. flotilla has gone into action only once so far. The frigate Bowen fired four rounds from its five-inch guns into the hills east of Beirut on Thursday after the Marines were shelled.

If the Marines request an air strike, fleet commanders probably would use either Harriers from the Tarawa or planes from the Eisenhower, which patrols between 35 and 50 miles off the coast. The Harriers fire air-to-surface Zuni missiles. Any planes from the Eisenhower probably would be A-6 Intruders or A-7 Corsair IIs.

Naval officers praise the Harrier, which the British used effectively in the Falklands War. One officer, who asked not to be named, said pilots can hit targets no more than 10 feet wide about 80 percent of the time.

Harriers are originally of British design, but an advanced version is made by McDonnell Douglas Corp. in St. Louis.

The Intruders and Corsairs carry an array of missiles and up to 15,000 pounds of bombs. That is only about 2,000 pounds less than the load carried by a B-17, the heavy bomber of World War II fame.

Used by permission of the Associated Press

★★★★★★★★★★★★★

Presidential Decisions:
Their Long-lasting Effects

The actions of the president affect our lives daily. Anyone who watches TV or reads the newpaper will find examples of presidental actions that could affect the welfare of the world. Many presidential decisions have a direct or indirect impact on your life or the lives of others. The exercise of presidential power can lead to a president being seen in dramatically different roles, as the following news photo demonstrates:

UPI/Bettmann Newsphotos

President Lyndon Johnson, Martin Luther King, Jr., and other congressional and civil rights leaders attend the signing of the Civil Rights Act of 1964. President Johnson's achievements included programs to end poverty and racial discrimination.

Presidents Eisenhower, Kennedy, Johnson, Nixon, and Ford made decisions during the Vietnam conflict that had long-lasting effects. Congress never officially declared war in Vietnam, but these commanders in chief sent over a million troops to Vietnam. They increased the size and strength of the armed forces. As a result of these decisions, more than fifty thousand U.S. troops were killed in Vietnam, hundreds of thousands were injured, and families were torn apart.

YOUR TURN: Presidential Decisions ★ ★ ★ ★
                Have Serious Consequences

Read the following article. Answer the questions that follow.

The death of one veteran

By Robert L. Tecklenburg

Yesterday another Vietnam war veteran killed himself. I write this in his memory because he was my friend.

More than 50,000 veterans of our longest war and only military defeat have chosen to end their lives this way, continuing the American tragedy of Vietnam.

While experiencing only one-twenty-fifth of the psychological breakdowns of troops during World War II, soldiers in Vietnam met their problems after they had returned home. Many experienced delayed-stress reaction, or as it is called Post Traumatic Stress Disorder, shortly after returning from Nam. For others, years passed. And for many the clock continues to tick away without incident, but they live under the fear that it will strike them tomorrow or the next day.

The stress disorder is often characterized by a growing apathy, alienation, depression, mistrust, cynicism, expectation of betrayal, difficulty in concentrating, insomnia, restlessness, nightmares, uprootedness and impatience with almost any situation or relationship.

Dr. Chaim F. Shatan, founder and coordinator of Vietnam Veterans Working Group, in his discussion of the plight of Vietnam veterans, said: "Unable to forget, unable to endow their Vietnam experiences with meaning, they live through some things forever. Often they find inner peace only through creating a dead place in their souls — a file where memories live on, divorced from their unending emotional impact. The price of peace is alienation from feelings in general and relative inability to form close relationships."

The war veterans returned to a restive American society that was not inducive to forming the type of close, meaningful relationships they needed. Values and concerns had changed rapidly in this highly mobile society.

They also returned to a society badly divided by the war they had just fought. At first, they were greeted by peer hostility. Later Americans wanted to forget the war and soon forget its warriors as well.

As a period of high inflation, recession and declining job opportunites set in, many vets were left behind. Lack of employment opportunities complicated by inadequate training and education benefits (GI Bill) made it increasingly difficult to compete for jobs.

Any unusal behavior such as anxiety, disillusionment and listlessness, went unnoticed because it was not uncommon among those unemployed for long periods times. Their "odd" behavior was dismissed if it was nonthreatening to the community. In any event, access to quality mental heath care for veterans was difficult to obtain, and these vets simply became the walking wounded.

In 1974, two years after the American withdrawal from Vietnam, 55,000 of the 2.8 million men and women who served there were receiving compensation from the Veterans Administration for service connected psychiatric disorders. Dr. Cherry Cedarleaf, former psychiatrist at the VA Hospital in Minneapolis, estimated that "50 percent of the returnees need some professional help in adjusting to civilian life."

In that same year, 25 percent of the 800,000 Vietnam vets who were seeking admission to or who had been sent to VA hospitals attempted suicide, and by the end of the decade more than 50,000 Vietnam veterans had succeeded in taking their own lives — more than were killed by hostile fire in Vietnam.

A pamphlet distributed by Vietnam Veterans of America in 1980 stated: "The suicide rate was 25 percent higher for Vietnam veterans than among their nonveteran peer group; their divorce rate was double the national average; unemployment was twice as high . . ."

The Argus of Fremont-Neward, Calif., ran a story about one veteran of Vietnam on June 6, 1978. It told of how he could no longer live with his memories of war.

"I can't sleep anymore. When I was in Vietnam, we came across a North Vietnamese soldier with a man, woman and a 3- or 4-year-old girl. We had to shoot them all. I can't get the little girl's face out of my mind. I hope that God will forgive me. I hope the people in this country who made millions of dollars off of the men, women and children that died in that war can sleep at night (I can't, and I didn't make a cent)," he wrote, and after writing this — 12 years after returning from Vietnam — the young ex-GI quietly ended his life.

I am not certain what was troubling my friend, but I am certain of one thing — he will not be forgotten.

Chicago Tribune

1. How did the presidential decisions on Vietnam affect the veterans who are the subject of the article? What effect did these decisions have on the veterans' families and friends? What positive impact did these decisions have on these veterans and/or others?

2. What presidential powers did the presidents exercise in the Vietnam conflict?

YOUR TURN: Exercising Presidential Power Has Shaped the Course of History

Read each of the following situations that describe important decisions made by presidents. Working with a partner or in a small group, answer the following questions about each situation:

1. What impact did this presidential decision have on people when the decision was made? Who was affected by the decision?

2. How might this decision affect people today?

3. What area of power did the president use in making this decision? (For example, the president was using his power as commander in chief when he sent troops there.) More than one area of power may be involved.

SITUATION 1

President Van Buren ordered that no person should work more than ten hours a day on federal public works projects. This was one of the first efforts by a president to regulate working conditions for federal employees.

SITUATION 2

When President Lincoln was elected in 1860, seven southern states seceded from the Union. They formed the Confederate States of America. Soon after, Confederate forces fired on Union troops at Fort Sumter in Charleston Harbor, South Carolina. President Lincoln asked Congress to declare war on the Confederacy in order to bring these states back into the Union. Then four more southern states seceded. This action led to the Civil War, 1861–1865.

SITUATION 3

During the Great Depression in the 1930s, President Roosevelt urged Congress to pass his proposed Social Security Act. This act provided government assistance to people who could no longer work. It also provided old-age and survivors' assistance to millions of needy people throughout the nation.

SITUATION 4

Presidents Truman, Eisenhower, Kennedy, and Johnson refused to exchange ambassadors with the People's Republic of China, a communist nation. Each of these presidents recognized the island of Taiwan as the government of China. Taiwan's government was fiercely anti-communist. The vast majority of Chinese, however, lived in the People's Republic of China. In 1972 President Nixon initiated a new China policy. He made a trip to the People's Republic of China. The president established diplomatic relations and sent an ambassador to the People's Republic of China. Nixon also signed several trade and foreign exchange agreements with the leaders of the People's Republic of China. The new China policy led to many changes. Military tensions have been reduced. Goods made in the United States are now sold in China and vice versa. Educational, cultural, and athletic exchanges have also occurred.

SITUATION 5

On October 14, 1962, a U.S. spy plane found definite evidence that the Soviet Union was installing nuclear missiles in Cuba. The missiles were aimed at the United States. For six days President Kennedy and a small group of advisors debated how to get the Soviet missiles out of Cuba. On October 22, the president told the public about the Soviet missiles in Cuba. Kennedy announced several steps to force their removal. He ordered a naval quarantine of all shipments into

Cuba. He issued a stern warning to Cuba and the Soviet Union that "any nuclear attack launched from Cuba would be regarded as an attack by the Soviet Union on the United States, requiring a full retaliatory response upon the Soviet Union." In other words, he warned of all-out nuclear war if the missiles were not removed. By October 28, the Soviet Union ordered the missile bases dismantled and the missiles sent back to the Soviet Union. Soviet leaders vowed never to have to back down from the United States again. The United States and the Soviet Union have since spent billions of dollars on their militaries to make sure that they are as strong as one another.

SITUATION 6

President Johnson urged Congress to enact the Civil Rights Act of 1964. This law aims at eliminating certain forms of discrimination based on race, color, religion, or natural origin. It prohibits discrimination in places of public accommodation such as hotels, motels, restaurants, cafeterias, lunchrooms, soda fountains, retail stores, gas stations, theaters, and sports arenas. The act also prohibits discrimination in employment based on race, color, religion, sex, or natural origin and other forms of discrimination.

SITUATION 7

After Vice-President Agnew resigned, President Nixon appointed Congressman Gerald Ford as vice-president. Vice-President Ford became president after President Nixon's resignation. One of Ford's first actions was to pardon President Nixon for any crimes that he may have committed while he was president.

SITUATION 8

To protest the Soviet Union's invasion of Afghanistan, President Carter announced that the United States would boycott the 1980 Olympic Games scheduled to be held in Moscow, capital of the Soviet Union. The President also ordered an embargo on the sale of grain that was to be shipped to the Soviet Union from United States farmers.

SITUATION 9

In 1981 and 1983, President Reagan issued **executive orders** to censor communications from civilian and military employees of the federal government. All federal employees with access to certain secret government information must sign censorship agreements. The employees agreed to submit for government review any speech, article, or book they produce that concerns the secret information. The agreements are in effect for the rest of their lives. By early 1984, more than 120,000 federal employees had signed the censorship agreement. President Reagan said the order will help protect national security. He said the order will make it more difficult for enemies of the United States to receive secret information.

ON YOUR OWN: Presidential Actions Affect Everyday Lives

Using newspapers, magazines, radio, or television, identify news stories that describe presidential decisions. The decisions can be those made by the president directly or decisions made by persons or departments acting on behalf of the president. For example, an article on the Environmental Protection Agency investigating asbestos poisoning would, in some way, reflect presidential decision making. After reading each news story, answer the following:

1. What presidential decision(s) was involved in the news item?

2. How does this decision(s) affect people?

3. What is the area of power used by the president or the executive department in making this decision(s)? (See pp. 73-75.)

Presidential Duty: Enforcing the Laws of the Nation

Article II of the Constitution expresses the general outline of presidential power and responsibility. These powers have allowed presidents to be flexible in acting as chief executive. The presidents themselves have put life into the words of the Constitution by their actions and decisions. This has increased the power of the presidency.

The Constitution states that the president must "take care that the laws be faithfully executed." In other words, the president has the duty to enforce the law. This duty refers to more than just enforcing the laws passed by Congress. The president also has the duty to enforce court decisions and the Constitution.

President Eisenhower's response to the school desegregation crisis in Little Rock, Arkansas, illustrates this important presidential duty. In 1954 the United States Supreme Court ruled in the case of *Brown v. Board of Education, 347 U.S. 483 (1954),* that public schools that separated white and black students were violating the Constitution's guarantee of **equal protection of the laws.** Within a year, the Supreme Court declared that such **segregated** schools would have to be **desegregated** "with all deliberate speed." Some school districts, however, resisted this order.

In 1957 Arkansas Governor Faubus ordered the Arkansas national guard to block nine black students from enrolling in Little Rock's Central High School. After a face-to-face discussion with President Eisenhower, Governor Faubus withdrew the Arkansas national guard. When the black students attempted to enter Central High, however, they were mobbed by crowds of angry whites opposed to school desegregation. Governor Faubus took no steps to protect the black students. As a result, President Eisenhower ordered federal troops to Little Rock to restore order and protect the black children who attended Central High. The president was enforcing a court order, not an act of Congress.

YOUR TURN: Recognizing Presidential Power

Review the Little Rock public school desegregation situation and answer the following:

1. What were two areas of power President Eisenhower used in the crisis at Central High?

2. How did President Eisenhower's actions affect the black students? the other children? the nation?

3. What are some other ways that President Eisenhower could have acted in response to the crisis at Central High? (For example, could the president have decided to take no action?)

Presidential Power: Immense, but Not Absolute

Presidents have enormous power and influence. The president's power in foreign relations is superior to that of any other branch of government. This supremacy of the president's power has even been recognized by the Supreme Court. In the 1936 case of *U.S. v. Curtiss-Wright Export Corporation, 299 U.S. 304,* the Supreme Court declared, "The president alone has the power to speak . . . as a representative of the nation. He makes treaties with the advice and consent of the Senate; but he alone negotiates. Into the field of negotiation the Senate cannot intrude."

The president's power to negotiate and manage foreign relations goes far beyond treaties. To avoid possible rejection of treaties by the Senate, recent presidents have relied more on executive agreements for making foreign policy. Executive agreements are compacts with other nations made by the president in the name of the United States. Recent presidents have said that executive agreements are part of their implied powers to "take care that the laws be faithfully executed." Between 1949 and 1970, presidents negotiated 310 treaties and signed 5,653 executive agreements with foreign countries. This trend continues today.

Yet even in the field of foreign affairs a president's power is not absolute. The people, the Congress, and the federal courts can influence presidential decisions. For example, unpopular wars in Korea and Vietnam influenced the decisions of Presidents Truman and Johnson not to seek re-election.

The ultimate limits of presidential power are set forth in the Constitution. For example, the Constitution prevents presidents from appointing ambassadors without the advice and consent of the Senate.

YOUR TURN: What Are the Constitutional Limits to Presidential Power?

Read the following historical cases.

CASE #1

President Andrew Jackson enforced a plan, approved by Congress, to relocate all Indian tribes on lands west of the Mississippi River. In enforcing the plan, some native Americans were driven from their homes by military force. The Cherokee Indians of Georgia tried to resist this removal plan by filing a lawsuit. The Cherokees took their case all the way to the U.S. Supreme Court. They claimed that the state of Georgia and the United States had no **jurisdiction** over the Cherokees. Therefore, Georgia and the United States had no claim to the Cherokee lands.

In the case of *Worchester v. Georgia*, 31 U.S. (6 Pet.) 515 (1832), the Supreme Court agreed with the Cherokees. The Court ruled that Georgia had no jurisdiction over the Cherokees and no claim to their lands. But Georgia officials simply ignored the decision and seized the Cherokee land. President Jackson also ignored the Supreme Court and continued with his Indian Removal policy. President Jackson would not agree that the Supreme Court had the final word on matters of dispute. He believed that the president's oath bound him to support the Constitution "as he understands it, and not as it is understood by others." Jackson felt the president had a duty to enforce the laws as he interpreted them and as he believed the people wanted them enforced.

CASE #2

In 1973 and 1974, two branches of the United States government clashed during the **Watergate** crisis. A special investigating committee of the United States Senate concluded that several high-ranking officials in the executive branch had misused their powers. The investigation revealed that President Nixon had taped conversations of most meetings held in the president's Oval Office. The Senate asked the president to turn over the tapes as possible evidence in their investigation. The president refused. President Nixon claimed that the tapes belonged to the executive branch. He claimed **executive privilege.** Therefore, in his opinion, the tapes were not subject to congressional investigations. The federal courts resolved this dispute over presidential power. In the 1974 case of *U.S. v. Nixon*, 418 U.S. 683 (1974), the Supreme Court struck down President Nixon's claim of executive privilege. The court ordered him to turn the tapes over to the investigating committee. At first it appeared that the president might ignore the Supreme Court ruling. But he soon complied with the Court's order. In August, 1974, President Nixon resigned as president of the United States.

After reading these two cases, answer the following:

1. How did President Andrew Jackson's decision affect the Cherokee

Indians? How did President Jackson's decision to ignore the Supreme Court's decision affect the state of Georgia? How might Jackson's actions have affected the decisions of future presidents?

2. How did President Nixon's decision to follow the Supreme Court's order affect his presidency? What effect, if any, do you believe the Watergate crisis had on the powers of the presidency?

3. In your opinion, why did President Nixon decide to abide by the Supreme Court's decision while President Jackson ignored the Court's decision?

4. Examine Article II of the Constitution and identify what, if anything, can be done to a president who refuses to obey a ruling of the Supreme Court. Remember: a ruling of the court is law.

5. Are there any limits to how many times a president may be elected? Briefly explain your answer.

★ ★ ★ ★ ★ ★ ★ ★ ★ ★ ★

Influencing Presidential Decisions

A former secretary of state and National Security Council advisor for two presidents recently described his view of the process influencing presidential decisions. He said, "There are three main levers of power in the White House: the flow of paper, the president's schedule, and the press." In some ways, presidents make decisions much like you do. Many decisions are made during daily routines. Most decisions are influenced by personal beliefs, by those around us, and by the formal and informal rules governing everyday life.

Presidents receive volumes of reports to read and study. It is impossible for one person to examine all of this information effectively. Very often presidents rely on senior White House staff to select and interpret what they believe to be the most important reports. This control of the "flow of paper" often influences presidential decisions.

Senior staff also determine the president's schedule. A president's day could begin with a senior staff breakfast meeting to discuss overnight news developments, to prepare responses for the news media, and to discuss the president's agenda for the day.

After breakfast, the president might meet with the National Security Council. This council consists of the vice-president, the secretaries of defense and state, the chair of the Joint Chiefs of Staff, the director of the Office of Emergency Preparedness, and the advisor to the National Security Council. The National Security advisor has an office next to the White House. This council discusses foreign affairs.

The president might then meet with the head of the Office of Management and Budget (OMB). The OMB prepares the executive budget. This budget describes the president's spending priorities. The OMB head could use this meeting to persuade the president to include funding for a special project in the executive budget. The president might then greet a foreign dignitary visiting the United States, pose for pictures, and briefly discuss improving relations between the dignitary's nation and the United States.

From here the president could have a luncheon meeting with members of Congress from the president's political party. They might discuss ways to increase party support for the president's legislative proposals.

The president would have an afternoon schedule as busy as the morning schedule. By late afternoon or early evening, the president might travel to another part of the nation to address a political or business meeting. But the president even continues his or her duties while in flight.

All persons meeting with the president realize they must make the most of the limited time. This is a valuable opportunity to share their views with the president. Those who receive the president's closest attention can often strongly affect executive decisions. President Reagan's Chief of Staff during his first administration James A. Baker III said, "Anytime the president's friends — members of the **kitchen cabinet** — want to see him, we put them on the schedule."

A president's beliefs in the role of government often determines the direction of public policy. For example, Franklin D. Roosevelt believed that the federal government should have broad powers in solving social problems. In establishing support for his programs during the Great Depression, President Roosevelt said, "Better the occasional faults of a Government that lives in a spirit of charity than consistent omission of a Government frozen in the ice of its own indifference." President Ronald Reagan believed that the federal government should exercise limited powers, leaving private citizens and state and local governments to solve many social problems. In calling for a reduction of federal programs, President Reagan said, "My administration seeks to limit the size, intrusiveness and cost of Federal activities . . . and to aid State and local governments in carrying out their appropriate public responsibilities." These differences in outlook led public policy in different directions.

Presidents are also sensitive to public opinion. The president is aware of public opinion expressed in news media reports and actions of individual citizens. Citizens can write letters to the president, attend meetings called by representatives of the executive branch, or take part in demonstrations. Presidents often urge citizens to write and express their opinions on various issues.

More and more citizens appear to be sharing their views with presidents. Between 1856 and 1860, President Buchanan handled all of the letters written to him with the assistance of only one secretary. President Cleveland often answered phone calls to the White House. But today the president has a large staff to perform such routine duties. The White House now receives thousands of letters and an average of twenty thousand telephone calls a day. Presidential staff provides the president with reports of the opinions expressed by these letters and calls. Some presidents have made special efforts to hear from citizens. On Dial-A-President Day, President Carter and the White House communications staff received more than nine million calls from concerned citizens.

The president and presidential advisors pay special note to how the news media present governmental issues. Realizing that the news media both reflect and influence puplic opinion, the president and presidential staff closely listen to and read national, state, and local news stories reported by the media. In fact the president may watch four news telecasts simultaneously. The president knows that public opinion can affect decisions by Congress.

ON YOUR OWN: Presidential Advisors Are Influential

Review the chart of the Executive Branch on page 74. Using the library and/or other reference resources, answer the following:

1a. Select two **cabinet**-level departments and give the names of the current secretaries (heads). For example, who is the secretary of state?

1b. Which president appointed each of these department heads?

2. Who is the president's press secretary?

3. What did each of these persons do before being appointed to this position? How might the person's background help him or her in this position?

★ ★ ★ ★ ★ ★ ★ ★ ★ ★ ★

Presidents and International Problems

The world is constantly changing. Presidents have to respond to new needs and different demands. Space stations, satellites, computers, and improved communication systems bring presidents almost instant information about national and world problems. The problems of overpopulation, food supplies, dangerous weapons, and control of natural resources in other parts of the world require the president's attention. Even problems of drug abuse go beyond the nation's borders.

Presidents can use the powers and expertise of the executive branch to help study and solve problems. For example, the people of the United States and other industrialized nations depend on oil for economic survival. Some nations receive more than half of their oil from the Middle East. War among some of the oil-exporting nations such as Iran, Iraq, Kuwait, and Saudi Arabia could cause the amount of oil being shipped to the United States, Japan, and Western Europe to decline. Then gas stations would soon run out of gas and the price of gas would skyrocket. This gas shortage would halt driving and shut down factories, resulting in loss of jobs.

A president could use his or her powers to try to solve this problem. As commander in chief, the president could order armed forces into international waters in the Middle East. The navy and air force could be ordered to escort oil tankers in and out of the Middle East. As chief of state, the president could use diplomatic skills to try to persuade the nations at war to negotiate a cease fire and/or peace. As a lobbyist, the president could ask Congress to pass legislation approving military and economic aid to Middle East nations. This aid would help the oil exporting nations defend their oil fields, refineries, and ports. The president could also lobby for legislation to conserve energy, like imposing the fifty-five-mile-per-hour speed limit. As chief executive, the president could confer with the secretaries of state and defense, review background information on the problem, and discuss ways to end the conflict. The president could also ask the Central Intelligence Agency and the National Security Council to provide detailed information about the conflict, the amount of military power of the nations involved, and the impact the conflict may have on the flow of oil. These executive departments could assist the president in reaching a diplomatic solution to the conflict. As leader of his or her political party, the president could call upon other party leaders to support his or her efforts to resolve this conflict. Presidents often use a variety of powers to solve complex problems.

YOUR TURN: Using Presidential Powers to Solve an International Problem

Read and study the problem below. Then answer the following:

1. How does this problem affect people in the United States?

2. Does the president have any powers to try to solve this problem? What are these powers?

3. How might the president use his or her power to solve this problem? Be specific, like the example regarding the oil shortage.

4. What are some ways that you and others might use in order to persuade the president to use his or her powers to solve this problem?

According to the latest United Nations report, international drug consumption has reached its highest level ever. More people around the world are using addictive illegal drugs than ever before. Western Europe is experiencing its worst heroin problem ever. The United States leads the world in the number of heroin addicts. More than 500,000 persons are addicted to heroin. The U.S. Department of Justice estimates that Italian organized crime has made more than $800 billion in profit from sales to sellers in the United States since 1976. Afghanistan, Pakistan, and Southeast Asia are major producers and suppliers of opium and heroin.

The use of cocaine also increased dramatically in recent years. About seventy percent of the illegal cocaine coming into the United States is refined in Columbia, South America. It is grown in Peru and Bolivia. Cocaine is processed out of the coca plant. Coca cultivation is legal in Peru. Growing and selling cocaine is big business. Billions of dollars are involved in the cocaine trade. The U.S. ambassador to Columbia recently estimated Columbia's cocaine trade to be worth $3 billion a year.

Heroin, cocaine, and other illegal drugs have become major cash crops for some nations. The illegal drug trade provides a source of income for thousands of people. The drug trade results in increased drug addiction and death.

★ ★ ★ ★ ★ ★ ★ ★ ★ ★ ★

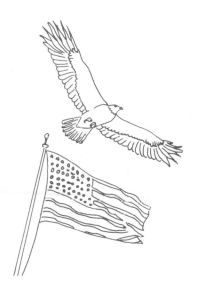

6

THE REGULATORS: ADMINISTRATIVE AGENCIES

Administrative Agencies — The Hidden Lawmakers

How much DDT residue should be allowed on cranberries?
How much noise may a truck make on an interstate highway?
How many seals may be killed or seriously injured in Alaskan waters?
What ingredients may be included in canned cherries?
How much should a phone call cost?

The answers to these questions are now law. The questions were not answered by legislative bodies — by Congress, by the state legislature, or by a local council or board of aldermen. The laws that answer these questions were made by administrative agencies. These agencies were given power by legislators to decide questions like those above. Administrative agencies are part of the executive branch of the government. The executive branch has the job of putting laws into effect. The federal government, each state, and most local governments have administrative agencies. These agencies may be known as agencies, departments, bureaus, boards, commissions, authorities, or offices. Another word for administrative agencies is bureaucracy.

Administrative agencies sound like alphabet soup:

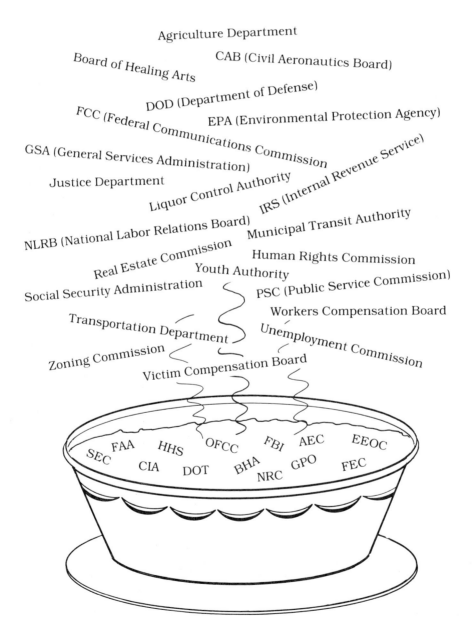

How Administrative Agencies Make Law

Usually legislatures only deal with problems in very general ways. If this were not true, legislatures might spend full time on one problem and never get to other problems. To enforce the law, administrative agencies make the law more specific so that people can understand how the law affects them. They do this by making **rules** and **regulations.** Rules and regulations have the force of law and must be obeyed by everyone affected by them.

A regulation can become a law without going through all the steps that a bill must follow to become a law in a legislature. The regulation does not go through committees, votes, and legislative hearings in the same way that a bill does. But agencies do give the public an opportunity to support or oppose a proposed regulation. Often agencies hold **public hearings** to learn the views of people who might be affected by proposed rules. Proposed federal regulations must be published in a special newspaper called the the *Federal Register.* This allows people to find out about proposed rules and make comments. The Office of the Federal Register also gives information on regulations and proposed regulations by telephone. When an agency adopts a regulation after considering the comments, the regulation must be published again in its final form. Some states have similar publications.

Below is a page from a notice in the *Federal Register.*

40004 Federal Register / Vol. 44. No. 131 / Friday, July 6, 1979 / Proposed Rules

DEPARTMENT OF AGRICULTURE

Food and Nutrition Service

[7 CFR Parts 210 and 220]

National School Lunch Program and School Breakfast Program

AGENCY: Food and Nutrition Service USDA

ACTION: Proposed Rule.

SUMMARY: This proposed rule would amend the regulations for Part 210, National School Lunch Program and Part 220, School Breakfast Program to implement the amendment of section 10 of the Child Nutrition Act of 1968 by section 17 of Public Law 95-168, respecting the sale of foods in competition with meals served under the National School Lunch Program and the School Breakfast Program. This proposed rule would establish minimum nutritional standards for foods sold in competition with meals served in the School Breakfast and National School Lunch Programs. It would identify foods of minimal nutritional value and would restrict their sale until after the last lunch period. In publishing this proposed rule, we are not suggesting that these foods should never be eaten by students. Rather, we are restricting their sale during certain hours of the school day in order to preserve the nutritional integrity of federally subsidized school meals.

DATES: To be assured of consideration comments must be received on or before September 6, 1979.

ADDRESSES: Comments should be

sent to Margaret O.K. Glavin, Director, School Programs Division, USDA. FNS Washington, D.C. 20250 (202) 447-8130. Comments will be available for review and inspection during regular business hours (8:30 a.m. to 5:00 p.m.) Monday through Friday in Room 4300 Auditors Building at the address as listed above

FOR FURTHER INFORMATION CONTACT: Margaret O.K. Glavin, Director School Programs Division, USDA. FNS Washington, D.C. 20250 (202) 447-8130.

Appendix B — Foods of Minimal Nutritional Value

(1) SODA WATER as defined by 21 CFR 165.175 Food and Drug Administration Regulations except that artificial sweeteners are an ingredient that is included in this definition.

(2) WATER ICES as defined by 21 CFR 135.180 Food and Drug Administration Regulations except that water ices which contain fruit or fruit juices are not included in this definition.

(3) CHEWING GUM flavored products from natural or synthetic gums and other ingredients which form an insoluble mass for chewing.

(4) CERTAIN CANDIES processed foods made predominantly from sweeteners or artifical sweeteners with a variety of minor ingredients which characterize the following types:

(a) HARD CANDY — a product made predominantly from sugar (sucrose) and corn syrup which may be flavored and colored is characterized by a hard brittle texture and includes such items as sour balls, fruit balls, candy sticks, lollipops, starlight mints, after dinner mints, sugar wafers, rock candy, cinnamon candies, breath mints, jaw breakers and cough drops.

(b) JELLIES AND GUMS — a mixture of carbohydrates which are combined to form a stable gelatinous system of jelly-like character, are generally flavored and colored and include gum drops, jelly beans, jellied and fruit-flavored slices.

(c) MARSHMALLOW CANDIES — an aerated confection composed of sugar, corn syrup, invert sugar, 20% water and gelatin or egg white to which flavors and colors may be added.

(d) FONDANT — a product consisting of microscopic-sized sugar crystals which are separated by a thin film of sugar and/or invert sugar in solution such as candy corn, soft mints.

(e) LICORICE — a product made predominantly from sugar and corn syrup which is flavored with an extract made from the licorice root.

(f) SPUN CANDY — a product that is made from sugar that has been boiled at high temperature and spun at a high speed in a special machine.

(g) CANDY COATED POPCORN — popcorn which is coated with a mixture made predominantly from sugar and corn syrup. (Sec 17. Public Law 95-156. 91 Stat. 1345 (42 U.S.C. 1779).

YOUR TURN: Introduction to the Federal Register

Answer the following questions after reviewing the sample page from the *Federal Register:*

1. What is the proposed rule?

2. Which agency is proposing the rule?

3. According to the summary, what would the proposed rule do?

4. On what date was the proposed rule published in the *Federal Register?*

5. Where can you send comments on the proposed rule?

6. What is the deadline for sending comments?

7. Looking at Appendix B (following "FOR FURTHER INFORMATION" on the previous page), listing the Foods of Minimal Nutritional Value, identify two items by brand name sold at your school that may be affected by the proposed rule.

8. What are your comments on the proposed rule? For example, how would the rule affect you? Do you favor it or oppose it?

9. The Department of Agriculture Food and Nutrition Service has authority to set minimum nutritional standards for school lunches. Do you think the proposed rule fits that responsibility? Explain your answer.

Use the comments to debate the pros and cons of the proposed rule or to rewrite the proposed regulation.

ON YOUR OWN: Using the Federal Register

1. At your public library look in the *Federal Register* for proposed regulations that might affect students your age. Use the questions in the Your Turn activity above to get all the information about the regulation. Then write a letter to the agency stating your comments about the regulation. Be sure to let the agency know whether you favor the proposed regulation or are against it and the reasons why.

   You can put together a news bulletin for other students informing them about the proposed regulation and explaining how they can express their views on proposed regulations to agencies.

2. Find out if your state or community has a register for proposed agency rules and regulations. Those students doing this assignment as a group should contact the Secretary of State's office. Use this state register to find out about proposed state regulations. You can then write letters and news bulletin articles. If your state does not have a register, find out how the public can learn about proposed rules and regulation before they go into effect.

3. If you know about a problem you think an agency might be able to solve with a regulation, write a proposed regulation and send it to the agency with your comments.

★ ★ ★ ★ ★ ★ ★ ★ ★ ★

How Far Can Administrative Agencies Go in Making Law?

Legislatures create agencies. They can also abolish any agency that does not do the job intended. Agencies can only do what the legislature authorizes them to do. If any agency goes further than the legislature intended, the legislature can take away power from the agency. Or, a court might stop the agency from acting outside of its authority. As long as the agency acts within the authority given it by the legislature, an agency has a lot of power to decide how the law really works. Sometimes the way an administrative agency interprets the law seems to change the law itself. If an agency dislikes a particular law or thinks it is not important, it might enforce the law in a way that makes the law ineffective.

For example, in 1980 Congress enacted a law to help prevent kidnapping by parents who are not given custody of their children in divorces. The law is known as the Parental Kidnapping Prevention Act. Under the law, the U.S. **Justice Department** and its **Federal Bureau of Investigation** (the FBI) are responsible for helping to find children kidnapped by their parents. But the Justice Department did not consider child snatching to be a criminal matter. Instead, it looked at child snatching as a family problem in which the FBI should not get involved. The Justice Department, therefore, adopted a regulation that the department would not look for children kidnapped by their parents unless it received information that the child was being abused or was in serious danger. That information had to come from someone other than the parent looking for the child.

YOUR TURN: The Regulation vs. the Statute

Review the information about the Parental Kidnapping Prevention Act and the regulation adopted by the Justice Department.

1. What do you think is the purpose of the act?

2. What do you think is the purpose of the regulation?

3. What do you think are the likely effects of the regulation?

4. Where do *you* stand on the following lines? Be able to support your position.

Against the regulation	*For* the regulation

The regulation *defeats* the purpose of the statute.	The regulation *promotes* the purpose of the statute.

In part because of the way that the Justice Department administered the law, many members of Congress thought a stronger law to help prevent kidnapping by parents was required. They proposed that child snatching by parents be a federal crime. Where do you stand on that proposal?

Child snatching by parents is a family matter and the federal government should not be involved.	Child snatching by parents should be a crime and the FBI should have the power to arrest parents who kidnap their children.

ON YOUR OWN: Administration of the Parental Kidnapping Law Today

Write a letter to the U.S. Justice Department, the chairperson of the U.S. House and Senate Judiciary Committees, the regional office of the Federal Bureau of Investigation, or the U.S. Attorney's office to inquire about the Parental Kidnapping Law today. The teacher will assist you in choosing one of the officials to write.

Among the questions you should ask are:

1. What are the current Justice Department regulations on child snatching?

2. How has Congress changed the Parental Kidnapping Prevention Act since 1980?

Administrative Agencies —
The Law Enforcers

Administrative agencies make rules and regulations that apply to many people. They also enforce the rules and regulations in individual situations. For example, suppose you would like to be a barber, a real estate salesperson, a school teacher, a psychologist, or a nurse. Most likely, those professions are regulated by state administrative agencies that can approve or reject you for a license to practice the profession.

Would you instead like to run a restaurant that sells your favorite food or run a video game center? If so, you would probably need a license from an administrative agency at the state level, the local level, or maybe both. If someone in your family applies for welfare, social security, or unemployment benefits, an agency decides if that person is entitled to get the benefits. If the rate on your utility bill increases, that increase probably had to be approved by an agency. For example, if the gas or electric company wants to increase rates, that company must get the approval of an agency often called the Public Service Commission.

Administrative agencies enforce other regulations too. For example, if a bus company, railroad, or airline wants to drop or add service to a particular town, the company cannot do so without the permission of an agency. If your family owns any property, the local tax authorities will decide how much property tax your family has to pay. If you want a driver's license, a pilot's license, or a work permit, an administrative agency will decide if you are qualified.

ON YOUR OWN: Regulation of Occupations in Your State

Choose an occupation or profession — one of those listed on the previous page or another — and, with the assistance of your teacher, find out what administrative agency regulates that occupation. Your teacher will assign you, or your group, an agency to write or call to find out what a person must do in order to get a license for that occupation or profession, including answers to the following questions:

1. What are the qualifications for that occupation or profession?

2. What is the minimum age?

3. What kind of test, if any, must a person take?

4. How much is the fee that a person must pay to get a license?

5. How does the agency decide who gets a license and who does not?

The job of the administrative agency in enforcing the laws over which it has authority is varied. The agency considers applications of persons or businesses regulated by the law. For example, agencies would consider applications of persons who want to be real estate agents or who want to receive disability benefits. An agency also has the power to receive and investigate complaints about persons and businesses regulated by the agency. It can also investigate persons who do not have licenses but who do things related to a regulated occupation. For example, someone might complain that a person was in the business of cutting hair without being licensed as a barber.

If the alleged misconduct of the person or business is serious enough, the agency may hold a hearing, similar to a trial. The hearing would determine whether the person acted illegally and, if so, what the punishment should be. In these cases, the administrative agency acts as both accuser and judge. For example, a state fair employment commission might hold a hearing to determine if a business has discriminated against a woman by not hiring her. Or, the state real estate commission might hold a hearing to determine if a real estate salesperson cheated a home buyer and whether the real estate license of the salesperson would be suspended as a result.

Also, a person who disagrees with a decision by an administrative agency can request a hearing to review whether the decision was correct. For example:

— a public school teacher who is fired may request a hearing to review whether the school acted properly in dismissing the teacher;

— a taxpayer may request a hearing to question the tax imposed by the state or local authority on the taxpayer's property;

— a person rejected for disability benefits may request a hearing to question whether he or she is eligible for the benefits.

In these cases, the administrative agency acts as both the **defendant** and the judge.

Why does the administrative agency act as a judge even when it is a party to a dispute? This is because the agency usually has so much special knowledge about the subject area that it can make more informed and quicker decisions than a court could. Usually the person from the administrative agency who acts as judge is not one of the people actually involved in the dispute.

YOUR TURN: Simulation of a Housing Authority

You have been appointed to the housing authority. This agency takes care of public housing in your community. Over the years there have been problems with pets ruining the apartments, making noise, and scaring some of the older tenants. You issue a rule prohibiting pets in the apartment complex. Some people have applied to the housing authority for special permission to bring animals into the complex. Your job is to decide whether the housing authority should give that permission for each of the following:

1. Mrs. Nicholls has a seeing-eye dog that helps her get around.

2. Mr. Robinson has a parrot that he has owned for many years and does not want to give away.

3. Ms. Ford's relatives are traveling across the country with their dog and are visiting her for about two hours.

4. Ms. George lives in a garden apartment on the ground floor and wants to keep a few chickens so she can have fresh eggs.

5. Miss Curry lives alone and wants to keep a guard dog to protect her because of recent break-ins at the apartment complex.

6. Mrs. Carl wants to keep a tape recording of a barking dog that she will play when she goes out at night.

7. Susie won a pair of goldfish at a school fair.

8. Mrs. Franklin is planning a carnival for the apartment complex and wants to have an organ grinder with a monkey for entertainment.

9. Michael keeps a big bowl of bird seed on his window ledge and lots of wild birds stay there all day long.

10. Rita is doing a science experiment and wants to bring home a guinea pig for two months.

Which of these requests will you permit? Do you need a new rule? What should the rule be? What helped you make your decisions? Be prepared to explain your answers.

★★★★★★★★★★★

A Closer Look at One Administrative Agency — The Federal Trade Commission

The Federal Trade Commission, known as the FTC, is a federal agency. It was established by Congress in 1914 to prevent unfair methods of competition between businesses. Since 1914, Congress has passed more than a dozen new laws changing the powers and responsibilities of the FTC.

For example, in 1938 the Wheeler-Lea Act gave the FTC the job of protecting consumers from unfair or **deceptive business practices,** including unfair or deceptive advertising. The law does not define "unfair or deceptive practices" because Congress could not predict all the different ways unfair or deceptive practices might occur. In part, this is because new developments change how businesses operate. If the law had listed the illegal, unfair, or deceptive practices in 1938, think what would have been left out: business practices relating to television, computers, and credit cards, none of which existed then. The broad term "unfair or deceptive practices" in the law allows the

FTC flexibility in enforcing the law as times change, without the law being constantly amended by Congress.

But what are unfair or deceptive practices? For businesses that have to obey the law, it is especially important to understand what "unfair or deceptive practices" are. In some situations, what one person thinks is fair, another person may think is unfair and vice versa. How can business make sure they obey the law if they are not sure what is considered an unfair or deceptive practice?

YOUR TURN: Are these Unfair or Deceptive Practices?

Read the following situations. For each of the following examples, decide whether the business is doing anything unfair or deceptive. Explain your answers.

1. A company sells shampoo and hair coloring. Its advertisement states that use of its hair color product gives a permanent color. Obviously the product cannot color hair that has not yet grown out. Is the ad unfair or deceptive?

2. A company sells iron supplement pills. It runs an ad telling consumers to use the pills when weary, tired, run-down, or just dragging around with no ambition left. The pills have little benefit except for people with iron-deficiency anemia. Is the ad unfair or deceptive?

3. A company makes paper towels and toilet paper with a red cross and the words "Red Cross" printed on it. The company has no connection with the Red Cross. Is the practice deceptive or otherwise unfair?

4. A company is a record club that sells records by mail. Its advertisment offers a free record to new members who agree to buy four records in the next year. If they do not buy four records, the company bills members for the price of the free record. Is the ad unfair or deceptive?

It is difficult to obey the law when what is forbidden is unclear. To help businesses understand what practices are illegal, the FTC makes regulations. The regulations have the force of law even though Congress did not pass them. In several recent situations, Congress disapproved a regulation proposed by the FTC and passed a law to prohibit the FTC from making the regulation. This happened when the FTC wanted to make a regulation to require ads promoting sugary foods on children's television programs to also give information about health and nutrition. Congress thought the FTC was trying to regulate more than unfair or deceptive practices.

The FTC cannot do more than Congress permits it to. When Congress tells the FTC not to make a regulation about a certain kind of business practice, the FTC cannot do it. The FTC only has power to do what Congress has said it can do. The Federal Trade Commission Act says that the FTC may make rules and regulations to carry out the law against unfair or deceptive practices.

FTC regulations say that it is an illegal, unfair or deceptive practice —

1. For a door-to-door seller not to give both a full receipt and a notice that the buyer has three days to cancel the contract;

2. For a store to constantly run out of advertised specials;

3. For a mail-order seller not to deliver ordered merchandise within thirty days or refund the buyer's money if it cannot deliver in thirty days;

4. For eye doctors to require patients to buy glasses from them or to not give the patients their prescriptions so they can shop around for eyeglasses;

5. For television ads on children's programs to promote sugared food products without also giving information about health and nutrition (proposed regulation as of the writing of this book);

6. For an appliance (stove, refrigerator, washing machine, and the like) not to have a label describing the energy costs of using the machine.

Do you agree that these practices are unfair or deceptive? Do you think these practices should be illegal? Or do you think the FTC went too far in any of the regulations?

Like other administrative agencies, the FTC enforces the laws over which it has authority. That means that the FTC tries to prevent businesses from using unfair or deceptive practices and stop businesses that do. The FTC finds out about violations by businesses through letters from consumers, business competitors, consumer organizations, the Better Business Bureau, trade associations, and state and local officials. When it finds out that business is using a unfair or deceptive practice, the FTC asks the business to stop. If the business will not stop the practice, the FTC may hold hearings and order the business to stop. If the business still does not stop, the FTC may ask a court to order the business to pay a fine.

Some of the practices the FTC has stopped include the following:

— Television ads for Campbell Soup showing a bowl of soup that had marbles in it to make the vegetables stick out;

— Television ads showing a man wearing a white coat recommending Rolaids, giving the impression the man was a doctor;

— Ads for Morton Lite claiming that there is a relationship between eating sodium and high blood pressure (Morton Lite is low in sodium);

— Television ads for Tomy's dollhouse showing a furnished dollhouse when customers had to buy the furniture separately.

ON YOUR OWN: Finding Out More About Administrative Agencies in Your Community

1. Look in the newspaper for an article about an administrative agency and answer the questions below. Be sure that the agency you choose is an administrative agency. Sometimes private organizations call themselves agencies, for example, modeling agencies or advertising agencies. Administrative agencies are public or government agencies.

   a. What is the name of the agency? Does the article also use an abbreviation of the agency's name? What abbreviation?

   b. What does the agency do?

   c. Is the agency a federal, state, or local agency?

   d. What does the article discuss about the agency?

   e. What is the impact of the agency on people's lives?

2. Find out about an administrative agency in your community or state by writing a letter for information, interviewing someone that works at the agency or inviting someone to class. Does your state or community have a agency like the FTC? What does it do? What are some of the rules and regulations it has issued? What are some of the practices it has stopped?

3. Read the newspaper for notices of public hearings by administrative agencies. If one is scheduled to take place in your community, arrange a field trip to attend the hearing. Before going to the hearing, be sure to find out more about the issues that will be discussed so that you will understand what people are talking about. Ask someone from the agency conducting the hearing to contact you later to let you know what the agency decided.

★★★★★★★★★★★

7

IMPACT OF JUDICIAL DECISION MAKING

The Judiciary — Decisions Affecting Everyday Life

Millions of people throughout the United States influence the judicial branch of government. They ask our courts to resolve an increasing number and variety of disputes. The National Center for State Courts recently reported that state courts process some ninety million cases each year. The **chief justices** of the fifty state courts reported a 10 to 25 percent increase in the number of cases being processed each year. In addition to the state courts, hundreds of thousands of cases are filed yearly in federal courts. The many actions of the courts affect people every day, even people who are not in court. Daily examples of court actions are reported in the news media.

YOUR TURN: Whose Orders?
By Order of the Court . . .

Each of the following news summaries describes one or more court action. Read the news summaries. Then answer the following questions concerning each court action:

1. What is the court action(s)? For example: "A judge sentenced a man to serve thirty years in prison for first degree murder."

2. How does the court action affect the individuals involved? For example: "As a result of the judge's order, the defendant will spend the next thirty years of his life behind bars, the defendant will lose some of the constitutional rights we take for granted (such as the right to privacy) and many of the defendant's relations with family and friends will end."

3. How could this court action affect your life? For example, you realize that the consequences of crime may be the loss of freedom for a long time. Also, you are protected from being a victim of this man while he is in prison.

News Summary 1

On Friday the Illinois Supreme Court upheld the death penalty sentence of two men: Andre Jones and Luis Ruiz. Jones was convicted of murdering a letter carrier and two other people in 1979. Luis Ruiz of Chicago was convicted in the gang slayings of three teenagers. An execution date of March 16, 1983, was set for Ruiz; an execution date of May 18, 1983, was set for Jones.

News Summary 2

A judge found Eleanor Davis in **contempt of court.** The judge had ordered her forcibly evicted from her seven-room apartment in the Carr Housing Complex. Ms. Davis and six of her children refused to move to another apartment despite a court order that she move. Ms. Davis ignored the court order and has now been found in contempt of court. The judge ordered that her eviction take place tomorrow.

News Summary 3

After a six-week **civil** trial, the McSurelys were awarded $1.6 million by a Kentucky **jury.** The trial was held thirteen years after the McSurelys first filed their lawsuit. The jury agreed that the McSurelys' constitutional rights of free speech and protection against unreasonable searches had been violated by former high-ranking government officials: Kentucky **prosecutor** Thomas Ratliff, the late United States Senator John McClellan, and two deceased Senate staff members, John Brick and Jerome Alderman. Following the jury verdict, the judge ordered the high-ranking officials to pay the McSurelys the $1.6 million.

News Summary 4

A state court judge ordered 5 more prisoners released Tuesday to prevent overcrowding at the City Jail and Workhouse. These 5 prisoners bring the current total to 101 prisoners released early in order to prevent overcrowding. The state court judge is acting as a result of an order from a U.S. district judge. The U.S. district judge recently ruled that the jail and workhouse prison populations must be kept within the limits set by an earlier federal court order.

News Summary 5

A federal district judge issued an order blocking the broadcast of part of the CBS television show "60 Minutes." The judge acted after attorneys for seven police officers accused of brutality requested that the judge ban the showing of the "60 Minutes" segment concerning this case. The attorneys for the police told the federal judge that the program would hurt their clients' cases. A CBS attorney said the court order amounted to a nationwide blackout of the program. CBS said it would cost thousands of dollars to replace the banned segment with another. CBS immediately appealed the federal judge's order. Within hours, a federal **appeals court** ruled that CBS could broadcast the banned segment as scheduled.

News Summary 6

The U.S. Supreme Court upheld the right of students to wear black armbands to express their opposition to the war in Vietnam. A majority of the Supreme Court ruled that students cannot be deprived of their First Amendment rights. The decision ruled that public school officials had violated the free speech and due process rights of Mary Beth Tinker, John Tinker, and Christopher Eckhardt. All three students had been suspended for wearing the black armbands to their schools.

News Summary 7

The U.S. Supreme Court ruled that public school students facing suspension or expulsion are protected by the Constitution. According to the Court, students facing suspension should be given oral or written notice of the charges against them. The students should also be given an opportunity to tell their side of the story. The Court said students qualify for **due process** protection.

The Court cautioned, however, that if a student "poses a continuing danger to person or property or an ongoing threat of disrupting the academic process," then school authorities may suspend the student immediately. In such cases, the student must be given notice of the charges and an opportunity to have a hearing as soon as is practical.

News Summary 8

The U.S. Supreme Court upheld the authority of public school teachers and administrators to use corporal punishment in disciplining students. The Court ruled that Florida school officials had acted with proper authority when they disciplined James Ingraham, a junior-high student, by swatting him with a wooden paddle. The court stated, "The prevalent rule in the country today privileges such force as a teacher or administrator reasonably believes to be necessary for the child's proper control, training, or education."

News Summary 9

The U.S. Supreme Court upheld a New York state law allowing authorities to keep juveniles in detention for up to seventeen days before trial to protect both society and the juveniles from the potential consequences of crimes they might commit. Justice Rehnquist wrote the majority opinion calling the New York law a "regulatory" statute, serving "the legitimate state objective, held in common with every state in the country, of protecting both the juveniles and the society from the hazards of pretrial crime."

News Summary 10

The U.S. Supreme Court ruled that public school officials can conduct "reasonable" searches of students without search warrants. The ruling said teachers and administrators do not need a search warrant or have to show "probable cause" to search a student suspected of violating a law or a rule of the school. The majority opinion said that a search of a student and his or her possessions is justified if school authorities have reasonable grounds for believing a law or rule is being broken.

ON YOUR OWN: Did You Read What the Supreme Court Said Today? . . . Did You Hear What the Court Ruled? . . . Does the Decision Affect You?

A. Using newspapers, magazines, radio, and/or television, make a list of news stories involving court actions. Include the following information for each news story:

   1. Headline or brief summary of the court action (for example, "Court Orders School District to Change Spanking Policy");

   2. Briefly describe how the court action affects people.

You may wish to record your stories in a notebook or scrapbook. You may wish to share your stories with the teacher and other students by discussing them in class or creating a bulletin board for "Court Decisions Affect Our Lives."

B. Review the news summaries of decisions of the U.S. Supreme Court on pages 113-115. Select at least one case that you would like to examine in detail. Your teacher will show you how to research a Supreme Court case using a law library. After examining the case you selected, answer the following questions.

   1. Identify the parties in the case: Who is the plaintiff? Who is the defendant?

   2. What are the facts in the case? What problem(s) led to the suit? What is the court being asked to do in the case?

   3. What are the legal issues in this case?

   4. What is the majority opinion in this case?

   5. Were there any dissenting opinions in this case? If yes, briefly explain the dissenting opinion(s).

6. If you were asked to be a judge in this case, how would you have decided and why?

Court Orders: What To Do?

Courts have the power to order many things. Some court orders follow a trial or other court **hearing.** Other court orders occur before a trial and tell the person to appear in court. A **summons** is a court order to appear in court. For example, you might receive a summons to serve on a jury. A **subpoena** is a court order commanding a person to testify as a witness or to produce certain documents or other evidence. No one should ever ignore a court order. In some cases, people can be evicted from their homes or made to pay money when they ignore a court order. Under some circumstances, they can be arrested for ignoring a court order. Any person who receives a court order should consider consulting with an attorney.

Anyone may receive a court order at some time. Many people do not know how to respond to such orders. First and foremost, carefully read the order. After reading the order, review it and answer these questions:

1. Who issued the order? Identify the court and the name of the judge or clerk.

2. Does the order require a response from you?

3. What action are you ordered to take?

4. Are any dates mentioned in the order? If yes, what are the dates and what are you asked to do on each of the dates?

5. Are there any terms in the order that you do not understand? If yes, make a list of these terms.

6. Do you need an attorney to help you respond to the court order?

YOUR TURN: Examining a Court Order

Read the following court order. It is a summons to appear in **Small Claims Court.** It also explains the consequences of failing to appear in court. Examine the summons and attempt to answer the six questions above as if you were James Justin.

SMALL CLAIMS COURT

In the Circuit Court, Associate Division
of Clay County, Missouri

Terry Tort
Plaintiff

999-2001
Case Number

vs.

James Justin
Defendant

SUMMONS

The State of Missouri to Defendant,

James Justin

the Associate Circuit Court, Assignment
Division

You are summoned and required to appear in person in Room 100 of the Court building, located at Freeburg, Missouri, on the 19th day of Nov. 1985, at the hour of 9 am.

If you fail to appear, a judgment may be entered against you for the amount asked in the attached petition but not to exceed $1,000, plus interest and costs.

THIS ACTION HAS BEEN FILED UNDER THE SMALL CLAIMS COURT ACT. RULES OF EVIDENCE DO NOT APPLY AND YOU MAY DEFEND THIS ACTION WITHOUT OR WITH THE ASSISTANCE OF AN ATTORNEY.

Given under my hand this 30th day of Sept., 1985.

Sharon Metzger
Clerk of Court

Read carefully instructions on reverse side
RETURN

_____
_____
_____
_____
_____

INSTRUCTIONS TO DEFENDANT

1. If you do not wish to oppose plaintiff's claim you may:
   a. Contact plaintiff and make an out-of-court settlement with the plaintiff before the hearing date and file with the clerk of the court a dismissal of the case signed by the plaintiff or
   b. Make no appearance at the hearing. In that case the plaintiff may be given a default judgment against you.
2. If you wish to oppose the claim:
   a. You must appear on the date and at the time set for hearing.
   b. You should bring with you all books, papers, witnesses, and evidence you have to establish your defense.
   c. At your request the clerk will issue a subpoena for any witness you may need (you must order the subpoena as soon as possible and before the hearing date).
3. If you have a claim against a plaintiff, it is a counterclaim.
   You may file a counterclaim.
   NOTE: Forms and assistance are available from the clerk of the court which issued this summons.
4. If the counterclaim did not arise out of the same transaction or occurrence as plaintiff's claim against you, and if you desire to file such a counterclaim, then:
   a. You must file your counterclaim with the court within ten days after receive this summons.
   b. To do this you must personally appear before the clerk of the court.
   c. The clerk will assist you in preparing the counterclaim.
5. If you are a member of the Armed Services of the USA, please advise the court immediately upon receipt of this summons.
6. Rules of evidence do not apply and you may defend this action with or without the assistance of an attorney.
7. A pamphlet explaining the small claims court may be obtained from the clerk of the court issuing the summons.

117

What will happen to the defendant if he ignores this summons and fails to appear in Small Claims Court at the required time and date?

★ ★ ★ ★ ★ ★ ★ ★ ★ ★ ★

Court Action: By Request Only

Often people respond with outrage to news stories about court actions. Some common reactions to the news stories on pages 112-115 might be, "Did you read where that judge threw a lady and her six children out of their home?" Or "Can you believe the court awarded that couple $1.6 million for violations of their constitutional rights? Did the judge have some kind of grudge against those officials?" Or "Those judges are releasing prisoners faster than they lock them up — the streets will never be safe!" Or "Banned '60 Minutes' — why don't judges mind their own business?" These are common reactions but they are based on misconceptions about the role of courts.

cases. Courts do not act unless people ask them to act. Individuals or organizations **petition** the courts to help resolve legal problems.

Civil cases begin when a person files a **suit** in court seeking relief for an injury to his or her rights. The person filing the suit is known as the **plaintiff** or **complainant** or **petitioner.** The term varies depending on the nature of the suit and the court in which the petition is filed. Court actions are also begun by prosecutors. The prosecutor is a public official who begins legal proceedings against persons accused of committing crimes. Civil and criminal courts only act when people ask them to act.

People can ask courts to order actions that will affect people's lives far beyond the courthouse doors. Examine the following news articles for further examples of the impact of actions of courts.

YOUR TURN: Who Started it?

Carefully read each of the news articles below. Then answer the following questions:

118

1. Who started this court case?

2. What is the court being asked to do?

3. What action, if any, did the court take in this case?

4. How could the possible actions by the court affect the lives of others?

ARTICLE 1

Children Harassed, Agnostic Testifies

MOBILE, Ala. (UPI) — An agnostic father says his children were unable to understand why they were being harassed for refusing to pray in school, so he told them it was because they lived in the conservative South.

Ishmael Jaffree testified Tuesday in a federal court test of the school-prayer law enacted in Alabama last year. He said he had found it difficult to explain to his three pre-adolescent children why local officials had been ignoring the 1962 ban on such prayer by the U.S. Supreme Court.

"You're living in the South. You're living in a conservative area," he said he told them. He said he was trying to stop the prayer, Jaffree testified.

Jaffree, a black lawyer from Mobile, filed a suit to do just that. He asked a federal judge to grant him $115,000 in damages because his children had been allegedly ridiculed for refusing to participate in devotionals, the Lord's Prayer and grace before lunch.

He named three public school teachers and their superiors in the suit. He asked U.S. District Judge W. Brevard Hand to declare the law unconstitutional.

The law sets aside one minute each school day for silent meditation or voluntary prayer.

Testimony was to resume today.

Jaffree is also challenging a prayer law enacted by the Alabama Legislature last summer. The law allows teachers to lead willing students in prayer and even includes a "suggested prayer" written by Gov. Fob James' son, a lawyer. That law will be tested in a separate trial before Judge Hand. A date has not been set in that case.

A parade of witnesses has been brought to Mobile by about 650 intervening advocates of school prayer. The witnesses began testifying Tuesday. Their testimony was expected to continue through the end of the trial.

One witness, R.J. Rushdoony, a Californian introduced as an expert on religion and education, called public schools a "church for humanism" because of the ban on religion.

He linked humanism to agnosticism, saying its followers have no interest in God and see no need to learn about him.

"This is why humanism has made the school its church," he said.

Reprinted with permission of United Press International, Inc.

ARTICLE 2

Son, 43, Gets The Message: Get Out Of The House

PITTSBURGH (UPI) — A jury needed only 10 minutes to decide that a retired couple living on pension benefits had a right to evict their 43-year-old son from their home.

The couple and their son have not spoken to each other since 1981.

An Allegheny County Common Pleas Court jury said Friday that Andrew Zarna Jr. must leave his parents' home in suburban McKees Rocks and pay $7,269.83 in back rent and utility bills.

"You raise your children and do the very best you can," said Angeline Zarna. "It's just a shame that by the time you see the results, it's too late to do anything about it."

Mrs. Zarna, 66, said she and her husband, Andrew, had tried every way possible to entice their son to leave the house. The younger Zarna, earning $27,000-a-year as a computer programmer, refuses.

"I spoiled him," she said. "I fixed his plate, I did everything for him for so many years. I think a lot of this is my fault — it just took me a while to realize he's nothing but a chiseler."

According to testimony at the trial, the son stopped paying room and board three years ago when his parents increased his monthly payment to $200. The son, however, said he had contributed a one-third share toward major home improvements over the years because he thought he would always live there.

Mrs. Zarna had taken the case before a district judge twice — and won both times. But the younger Zarna appealed both times, which led to Friday's trial before Judge Emil Narick.

The Zarnas live on pension benefits of $884 a month. Not speaking to their son has done little to remedy the situation. "I hate to say this, but he doesn't exist," Mrs. Zarna said. "I've replaced him. I got a puppy."

Reprinted with permission of United Press International, Inc.

ARTICLE 3

Wounded Burglar Sues Homeowner Who Shot Him

SEATTLE (UPI) — A man who wounded a fleeing burglar with a shotgun has become a folk hero, but he also is the defendant in a civil suit. He's being sued by his victim.

"I can't figure it out," says Jim Cain. "Here I am, having to pay $4,000 to $7,000 in legal fees to defend myself against someone who wrecked my home. How can he sue me? There's got to be something wrong with the system."

Cain, 38, an auto accessories sales manager, arrived at his home Dec. 29 to find a young man and a teen-age girl tearing things apart and splattering the inside of his house with food and glass.

He says the girl fled but he held the

man at gunpoint. The man, James Keith, 20, tried to run, and Cain fired, wounding him.

Keith is recovering from surgery to remove birdshot. He was being tried this week on an unrelated stolen-vehicle charge and is being investigated for several other buglaries.

He is suing Cain for unspecified damages because of "great pain and suffering, permanent scarring and internal injury, future pain and suffering, lost earnings, loss of earning capacity and medical expenses" due to the birdshot wound.

Cain has countersued, asking for $5,500 to pay for damage done to his belongings and for "severe emotional distress." He says what bothers him most is "why he did this to me in the first place. I didn't know the kid or have any connection with him."

Reprinted with permission of United Press International, Inc.

ARTICLE 4

Jordache Sues K mart; Says Jeans Are Fake

TROY, Mich. (AP) — The makers of Jordache jeans have filed a $100 million suit against K mart Corp., accusing it of selling jeans under a counterfeit Jordache label.

K mart, the nation's second-largest retailer, denies the allegation. Bernard M. Fauber, company chairman, said Tuesday that the company would file a counterclaim against Jordache.

He accused Jordache of trying to block discounters — such as K mart — from selling the jeans in order to protect their prices and distribution.

"We believe Jordache's tactics raise questions of restraint of trade in violation of the federal antitrust laws," he said.

Melissa Parker, vice president with Jordache, said Tuesday that the company had purchased a pair of phony Jordache jeans from a K mart store in Staten Island, N.Y. "When we put them on the scale they weighed 8 ounces less (than the real thing)," she said.

Last week, U.S. marshals seized Jordache jeans at three K mart stores in Los Angeles.

The company has pulled all Jordache jeans from its shelves.

"Jordache has claimed that some men's denim Jordache jeans sold by K mart are not genuine," Fauber said. "K mart suppliers say they are genuine. A federal court will decide the issue."

Fauber said that at K mart's request, a federal court in California has dissolved the seizure order obtained by Jordache and required the jeans manufacturer to post a $250,000 bond.

Ms. Parker said the jeans were not bought from Jordache.

"I don't know if they bought them knowingly, but they didn't purchase them directly," she said.

"K mart is able to buy Jordache jeans from reputable sources that supply genuine Jordache merchandise," Fauber responded.

Used by permission of the Associated Press

ARTICLE 5

Trucker Fired Because Of Epilepsy Wins Out Against Federal Regulation

By Howard S. Goller
Of the Post-Dispatch Staff

After eight years of trying, Sam Costner, 48, of St. Louis, has won the right to a truck-driving job. A federal judge in St. Louis ruled last week that a regulation disqualifying epileptics does not apply to Costner.

The ruling may have a far-reaching impact on epileptics and other handicapped people because it says that regulatory agencies must, at some point, decide whether federal regulations apply to particular cases.

Costner, who takes anti-convulsant medication, has been seizure-free since 1959. He had driven trucks for 15 years — and without an accident — when in 1974, an embittered former girlfriend wrote his employer that Costner was epileptic. The firm, Slay Transportation Co., fired him.

The company cited a regulation of the Department of Transportation that prohibits trucking companies from hiring persons suffering epileptic seizures as drivers. In his suit against the government, Costner challenged the regulation as it applied to his case.

Last week, in a 10-page order, U.S. District Judge Clyde S. Cahill wrote that persons suffering epileptic seizures may generally be prohibited from driving in interstate commerce for the sake of highway safety. But the judge ruled that Costner must be considered for a job on the basis of his own medical and physical characteristics, "not barred by the application of a generic restriction."

The judge ruled also that the government may require Costner to submit to tests from time to time and to submit proof that he is taking anti-convulsant medication prescribed for him.

"It's a relief in a way," said Costner, who is now a driving instructor. He said his case had proved that "there's an exception to everything." But he acknowledged that the victory was bittersweet. "I would've liked to be compensated for the difference between the way I lived before I lost the job and the way I've lived since," he said.

Stuart R. Berkowitz, the attorney who took Costner's case at the request of the American Civil Liberties Union, said that Costner was trapped in a legal quagmire that precluded his seeking damages from the federal government or his former employer.

This story begins when, at age 11, Costner suffered a fractured skull. At 15, he began to have epileptic seizures. At 24, he began taking medication. The following year, he began driving trucks. That was 1959, and he has been seizure-free since. He's now 48.

Costner worked for Slay Transportation in 1974, driving heavy transport vehicles carrying chemicals. He was on the job little more than three months when Slay suspended him. He was told he needed the approval of a company doctor to drive. But Slay's doctor refused to certify Costner because the federal regulation said that anyone with a medical history of epilepsy was physically unqualified to drive. Costner looked for another job.

In 1975, Costner filed a complaint with the Office of Federal Contract Compliance Programs. He accused Slay of discrimination. Five years later, in 1980, he got an answer. The office said it would take no action, citing the regulation, public safety and its own review of literature about epilepsy.

The next year, Costner went to court. He accused the Transportation Department of violating his constitutional rights and the Rehabilitation Act of 1973. The act prohibits federal contractors from discriminating against the handicapped.

Three doctors said that Costner was qualified to drive. One, Dr. William M. Landau, was referred to extensively by Judge Cahill in his order. Dr. Landau is professor and head of neurology at Washington University School of Medicine and neurologist-in-chief at Barnes Hospital.

Costner is pleased enough with the decision not to send a four-page letter he wrote to President Ronald Reagan.

But he still feels bad about the loss of his job eight years ago. He once owned his own house, a nice car and could buy what he liked. Now he, his wife and three children live in Section 8 public subsidized housing in Soulard; he owns a '68 Chevy. His wife works part-time.

He teaches others how to drive cars and specializes in teaching the handicapped, people with cerebral palsy, paraplegics. Many have special devices that enable them to accelerate and brake using hand rather than foot controls. "I like what I'm doing. But there's just no pay in it and no future in it," he said.

St. Louis Post-Dispatch

ON YOUR OWN: Judicial Information Survey — The Impact of the Courts

Interview persons in the community (relatives, friends, or neighbors) and ask them the following questions about the judicial system and the impact of courts on their lives. Explain to each person that the information is for a class project and individual responses will remain confidential.

Ask each person you interview the following questions:

1. Have you ever received an order from a court (for example, a subpoena, a jury summons, or any type of summons)?

2. Have you ever been directly affected by a court decision?

3. Can you think of any court decisions that have influenced your life in some way? Briefly explain.

4. Can you recall at least one court case you have heard or read about in recent news stories? If yes, briefly describe the court case and identify the source of the story (for example, newspaper, television, radio, "friend told me").

5. How are judges chosen to serve in our community?

6. How should judges be chosen? Should they be elected by the voters or appointed by government officials (for example, appointed by governors)?

7. In your opinion, does the public need to know more about the judicial system? If yes, what should be done to increase the public's knowledge (for example, televise more trials live; teach more about the judiciary in schools)?

Be ready to share your survey findings in class. If several students complete these interviews, you should consider sharing your results with the local bar association. Ask a representative of the bar association to comment on the survey, the results, and what can be learned from the the survey.

★★★★★★★★★★★★★

The Court Rules: Precedents in Judicial Decision Making

Precedents are a major source of information courts use to make decisions. A precedent is a previous court decision on the same legal question. It guides decisions on cases involving similar questions. For example, what would a judge decide if a defendant accused of armed robbery informed the judge that he could not afford an attorney? Based on the precedent established by the United States Supreme Court in *Gideon v. Wainwright*, 372 U.S. 335 (1963), the trial judge would have to provide the defendant with an attorney at the state's expense.

Court decisions on legal issues are usually written. These written decisions serve as precedents in future cases. When cases come to court, judges refer to the precedents set in earlier cases to help them decide the case before them. Because there are thousands of precedents, judges must determine which precedent best applies in a particular case.

YOUR TURN: Applying the Right Precedent — You Decide

Each of the answers (Precedents A, B, and C) is based on an actual court decision but only one of the decisions is the correct precedent in this case. Read the following cases. Then decide which of the precedents that follow it best applies to the case. Be prepared to explain your answer.

CASE #1

The police received information from a reliable informant that Peter Pusher was selling narcotics. The police then went to the building where Pusher lived. The police forced open the door to Pusher's bedroom. On a nightstand beside Pusher's bed, the police saw two capsules. Pusher grabbed the capsules and swallowed them. The police jumped on him and tried to get the capsules out of his mouth. When that failed, Pusher was handcuffed and taken to city hospital. At the direction of the police, the emergency room doctors pumped Pusher's stomach. Among the substances pumped out of Pusher's stomach were two capsules containing morphine (a drug that is prohibited by state and federal law). Pusher was charged with illegal drug possession. Based on the evidence introduced during Pusher's trial, including the morphine capsules, Pusher was convicted of illegal drug possession and sentenced to prison.

Pusher **appealed** his conviction. He claimed that the morphine capsules should not have been used as evidence in his trial because they were taken from his body against his will. Pusher said this was a violation of his constitutional right to be free from self-incrimination. Pusher asked the appeals court to reverse his conviction.

Read each of the following precedents and identify the one that you believe best applies in this case:

PRECEDENT A

The right to freedom from self-incrimination applies to confessions that a suspect makes after being beaten up by a law enforcement officer. The government cannot use this confession as evidence because the person was forced to testify against himself or herself.

PRECEDENT B

The right to freedom from self-incrimination does not apply to fingerprints, photographs, and other evidence taken off the body of a suspect. The government can use fingerprints, photographs, and other evidence of the body because the suspect was not forced to testify against himself or herself.

PRECEDENT C

The right to freedom from self-incrimination applies to evidence taken by forcible invasion of a suspect's body. The government cannot use evidence taken by forcible invasion of the body because the suspect was forced to testify against himself or herself.

CASE #2

Ward Wanderer was charged with breaking and entering into a pool room with intent to commit petty larceny. These charges were **felonies** in Florida where Wanderer lived. Unable to afford an attorney, Wanderer asked the trial judge to appoint an attorney to represent him. The judge refused, informing Wanderer that state law only permitted court-appointed attorneys to represent a defendent when that person was charged with a capital crime (that is, crimes that are punishable by the death penalty or life imprisonment). Wanderer was left to conduct his own defense in his trial. The jury returned a verdict of guilty. Wanderer was sentenced to serve five years in the state prison.

While in prison, Wanderer appealed his case. He claimed that the state's refusal to appoint an attorney was a violation of the due process clause of the Fifth, Sixth, and Fourteenth Amendments of the Constitution. He also claimed that due process included the right to the assistance of an attorney for his defense. Wanderer requested the appeals court to reverse his earlier conviction. He asked that the court order a new trial with an attorney appointed to represent him.

Read each of the following precedents and identify the one that you believe best applies in this case:

PRECEDENT A

The right to an attorney for persons sued in a civil case is not guaranteed. Each state is free to follow its own interpretation of the need for an attorney for persons involved in civil cases.

PRECEDENT B

Persons who are suspected of committing serious crimes have the right to consult an attorney while being questioned by police. For defendants too poor to hire an attorney, the state must provide the defendant with an attorney at the state's expense.

PRECEDENT C

Persons accused of any crime, including a **misdemeanor** where a jail term may be imposed, have the right to an attorney. If the defendant cannot afford to hire an attorney, the state must appoint an attorney to represent the defendant at the state's expense.

CASE #3

Carla, a five-year-old child, was in a serious accident. She lost a lot of blood. Witnesses to the accident brought her to the nearest hospital. The doctors at the hospital agreed that Carla would die in a few hours unless she was given blood. Carla's parents were called, but they refused to give their permission for a blood transfusion because blood transfusions were against their religious beliefs. The doctors asked a judge to issue a court order giving the hospital temporary custody of Carla. This would allow the doctors to give Carla a blood transfusion and other medical treatment necessary to save her life. The parents told the judge that they were Carla's legal guardians and that only they could decide how to properly care for her. The parents believed their religious faith would provide for Carla. The doctors insisted that Carla needed immediate medical treatment in order to save her life.

Read each of following precedents and identify the one that you believe best applies in this case:

PRECEDENT A

Freedom of religion includes the freedom to refuse a certain medical treatment because of religious beliefs about treatment, except where the treatment is necessary to protect the rest of the community from a disease.

PRECEDENT B

Freedom of religion includes the freedom of a parent to refuse medical treatment for a minor child because of religious beliefs about treatment, except where the treatment is necessary to save the minor's life or to treat a serious medical condition.

PRECEDENT C

Freedom of religion does not include the freedom to give a minor drugs for religious purposes where the use of the drugs is dangerous to the minor's health.

★★★★★★★★★★★

United States Supreme Court Decisions: Causes and Consequences

Decisions by the United States Supreme Court set precedents for federal courts and, in some cases, state courts. On May 17, 1954, Chief Justice Earl Warren delivered the Supreme Court's decision in the landmark school desegregation case, *Brown v. Board of Education*, 347 U.S. 483 (1954). The following passage highlights this decision:

> Today, education is perhaps the most important function of state and local governments. Compulsory school attendance laws and the great expenditures for education both demonstrate our recognition of the importance of education to our democratic society. It is required in the performance of our most basic public responsibilities, even service in the armed forces. It is the very foundation of good citizenship. Today it is a principal instrument in awakening the child to cultural values, in preparing him for later professional training, and in helping him to adjust normally to his environment. In these days, it is doubtful that any child may reasonably be expected to succeed in life if he is denied the opportunity of an education. Such an opportunity, where the state has undertaken to provide it, is a right which must be made available to all on equal terms.
>
> We come then to the question presented: Does segregation of children in public schools solely on the basis of race, even though the physical facilities and other "tangible" factors may be equal, deprive the children of the minority group of equal education opportunities? We believe that it does.
>
> . . . .
>
> We conclude that in the field of public education the doctrine of "separate but equal" has no place. Separate educational facilities are inherently unequal. Therefore, we hold that the plaintiffs and others similarly situated for whom the actions have been brought are, by reason of the segregation complained of, deprived of the equal protection of the laws guaranteed by the Fourteenth Amendment.

Within a year, the Supreme Court issued a second opinion on this case. The second opinion, *Brown v. Board of Education*, 349 U.S. 294 (1955), established guidelines for desegregating schools. The Supreme Court said that school desegregation must occur under the supervision of the district courts "with all deliberate speed." The *Brown* decisions have had a profound impact on the lives of millions of children.

Who started the *Brown* case and how did the Supreme Court reach this landmark decision? The *Brown* case has deep historical roots. For most of our nation's history, our school systems were racially segregated—black children were required to attend one set of schools, and white children were required to attend another set of schools. State laws requiring school segregation were common throughout the nation. In the early 1950s, most children in the United States attended segregated schools.

Linda Brown, an eight-year-old black student, wanted to attend the elementary school nearest her home. She could not do so, however, because the school nearest her home was for white children only. Instead, Linda Brown had to attend an elementary school twenty-one blocks away from her home. Linda Brown's home was in Topeka, Kansas where segregated schools for black and white children were required by law. Linda's parents filed a lawsuit claiming that their daughter was being denied the equal protection of the laws promised in the Fourteenth Amendment. The Browns argued that the law requiring segregated schools was unconstitutional. They said segregation had a harmful effect on black children because it made black children feel inferior and denied them an educational opportunity equal to white children.

The Topeka Board of Education argued that the separate schools were equal in terms of buildings, courses of study, and quality of teachers as required by law. In addition, the school board argued that under the *Plessy v. Ferguson* case, the Supreme Court had ruled that "separate but equal" treatment did not violate the Constitution.

The justices of the United States Supreme Court decided the *Brown* case in 1954. The justices had to base their decision on the facts as well as the precedents applying to this case.

Precedents Leading to the *Brown* Decision:

★★★ In 1896 the Supreme Court upheld a Louisiana law requiring separate but equal train cars for black and white passengers. The Supreme Court ruled that this segregation was not unreasonable and therefore not unconstitutional. This famous decision, *Plessy v. Ferguson*, 163 U.S. 537 (1896), established the doctrine of "separate-but-equal" in public policy.

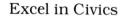

★★★ In 1899 the Supreme Court ruled in the case of *Cumming v. Richmond County Board of Education*, 175 U.S. 528 (1899), that the federal courts had no role in deciding if the school board of Richmond County, Georgia, should provide a public high school for black children. The Supreme Court acknowledged that there was no public high school for black children in Richmond County. The Supreme Court concluded, however, that education was solely a state concern. Therefore, such school-related decisions should not be determined by the Court. Thus, school boards were not required to provide high schools for black children.

★★★ In 1908 in *Berea College v. Kentucky*, 211 U.S. 45 (1908), the Supreme Court upheld a Kentucky law that prohibited private schools from teaching black and white children simultaneously unless the classes were conducted twenty-five miles apart. The Supreme Court said such a law was in keeping with the "separate-but-equal" doctrine and was therefore constitutional.

★★★ In 1938 in *Missouri ex rel. Gaines v. Canada*, 305 U.S. 337 (1938), the Supreme Court decided that a Missouri law prohibiting black students from attending the University of Missouri Law School while providing no other public law school for blacks was unconstitutional. The Supreme Court ruled that the law was a violation of the "equal protection of the laws" clause of the Fourteenth Amendment.

★★★ In 1950, the Supreme Court ordered the University of Texas Law School to admit black students after finding that the only public law school for blacks was inadequate. In *Sweatt v. Painter*, 339 U.S. 629 (1950), the Supreme Court said the state law school for blacks "could never hope to be equal in reputation of the faculty, experience of the administration . . . standing in the community, tradition, and prestige." To provide "substantial equality in the educational opportunities offered white and Negro law students by the State," the Supreme Court ordered the University of Texas Law School to admit black law students.

★★★ Also in 1950, the Supreme Court ruled that the segregated practices of the University of Oklahoma were unconstitutional. In *McLaurin v. Oklahoma State Regents for Higher Education*, 339 U.S. 637 (1950), the Supreme Court said that the University of Oklahoma's requirement that black students sit and study in separate sections of the cafeteria, classrooms, and library was unconstitutional. The Supreme Court ruled that this form of segregation violated the black student's right to equal protection of the laws. The court said special requirements of segregation "impair and inhibit his [the black student's] ability to study, to engage in discussions and exchange of views with other students, and, in general, to learn his profession."

YOUR TURN: Precents Change . . . But Not Overnight

1. Reread the summaries of Supreme Court cases on pages 129-131. Individually, or in small groups, make a chart of these precedents with two columns: in column 1, write the date and name of the cases; in column 2, summarize what this decision said.

   EXAMPLE:

U.S. SUPREME COURT PRECEDENTS	SUMMARIZE WHAT THIS DECISION SAYS ABOUT SEGREGATION AS PUBLIC POLICY
1954 — *Brown v. Board of Education of Topeka, Kansas*	Segregated education is inherently unequal and therefore unconstitutional.

2. Briefly describe the change in Supreme Court decisions regarding schools and segregation between 1896 and 1954.

YOUR TURN: School Segregation — It's Not the Law, But it is a Fact of Life . . . Applying the Brown Precedents

Read the following case, based on *Dayton Board of Education v. Brinkman*, 433 U.S. 406 (1977). Then answer the questions that follow:

Segregated public schools have been prohibited by Ohio state law since 1888. But in 1954 Dayton, Ohio, still operated what was basically a dual school system, one white and one black. By 1964, a decade after the first *Brown* decision, the Dayton public school system remained basically segregated. Fifty-seven out of sixty-four schools had student populations which were 90 percent one race. Only one out of every ten students attended schools with both black and white students. By 1972 total school enrollment was decreasing. And white student enrollment was decreasing even faster than black student enrollment. This resulted in even greater school segregation. Almost twenty years after the *Brown* decisions, the white and black children in Dayton continued to attend separate public schools.

In the years between 1954 and 1972, the Dayton Board of Education did not take steps to eliminate the racial segregation in the public schools. Public schools remained segregated because neighborhoods were segregated. Dayton school board members said children were attending segregated schools because of housing patterns not because of any laws — blacks just lived in separate neighborhoods. During this period, the school board approved construction of schools in locations that resulted in continued segregation. The board even designed "optional pupil attendance zones" (for example, "permissive transfers" permitting white children to transfer to predominately white schools) that had the effect of continuing segregation. During the 1971–72 school year, a group of black parents and students filed a lawsuit to end the racial segregation in the Dayton public schools in keeping with the precedents established by the *Brown* decisions.

1. What are the important facts in this case? Who are the important parties? Who started the court suit? What court action are they seeking?

2. What law applies to this case?

3. Briefly explain the precedent referred to in this case. In other words, what did the precedent state in regard to similar cases?

4. Based on the facts and the legal precedents, if you were asked to decide whether there was illegal racial segregation in the Dayton schools, what would be your decision and why?

5. If you were asked to decide how to end segregated public schools in Dayton, what would you recommend and why?

8

THE JUDICIAL PROCESS

Before the Trial

Everyday throughout the country, courts decide who is responsible for injuries to others — from traffic accidents to injuries in the workplace. They decide whether persons convicted of crime will go to prison. They decide which of two parents will have custody of children. What led to these decisions? They each resulted from cases taken to court. How can one understand what happens in a case taken to court?

To understand a case it is important to know whether the case is **civil** or criminal. The answers to the following three questions will indicate if a case is civil or criminal: (1) Who are the **parties** in the case? (2) What are the major questions raised in the case? (3) What relief is the court asked to give? Or what relief did the court give?

THE PARTIES: In civil cases, the disputes is between private individuals or groups. The party who brings the lawsuit is called the **plaintiff**. The party being sued is called the **defendant**. Cases have the names of individuals or groups, like *Pierre LaBouche v. Horace Taylor* or *Sylvia Rodriguez v. Embassy Corporation*. In these examples, Pierre LaBouche is the plaintiff who is suing Horace Taylor, the defendant. Also, Sylvia Rodriguez is the plaintiff suing Embassy Corporation, the defendant. The *v.* stands for *versus* which means *against*.

In criminal cases, a government (local, state, or federal) files suit against an individual believed to have committed a crime. The parties in the suit are known as the prosecution and the defense. Cases have the names of the government and the accused, for example, *State v. Albert Lee* or *United States v. Henrietta Purcell*. In these examples, the state is prosecuting Albert Lee, the defendant, for a violation of state law. The United States is prosecuting Henrietta Purcell for a violation of federal law.

THE QUESTIONS: Many, many different kinds of questions are raised in civil cases, as many as the kinds of legal problems that can occur between people. The following are some examples:

— questions of who will inherit property from a person who dies (**probate** cases)

— questions of whether employers treat their employees unfairly because of race or sex or religion (civil rights cases)

— questions of whether tenants paid their rent or landlords took care of their property (landlord-tenant cases)

— questions of whether persons did not do what they agreed to do in a contract (**contract** cases)

— questions of whether a person is responsible because of carelessness for injuries to another person (**negligence** cases)

— questions of whether a marriage should be ended or whether a father or mother should have custody of their children (domestic relations cases)

— questions of who has the right to produce or reproduce certain products (patent and trademark cases)

In criminal cases, there is basically only one question: whether a person committed a **crime** — that is, whether the person violated a law. Crimes considered to be very serious are called **felonies.** Less serious crimes are called **misdemeanors.**

THE RELIEF: In most civil cases, the plaintiff may ask the court for an order that the defendant pay **damages** — money to pay the plaintiff for the injuries, property damage, or violations of his or her rights. In some cases, the plaintiff may ask the court for an **injunction** — a court order that the defendant do or stop doing something. For example, a court might order a building owner not to tear down an historically important building. In other cases, the plaintiff may ask the court for an order determining the relationship or rights of the parties. For example, courts may be asked for an order that the plaintiff is no longer married to the defendant, or an order that the plaintiff's business is exempt under a state sales tax law.

In criminal cases, the prosecution asks the court to find the defendant guilty of a crime and then to sentence the defendant. The sentence may be imprisonment, probation, a fine, an order that the defendant repay his or her victim, or a combination of these.

YOUR TURN: Identifying Civil and Criminal Cases

Read the following articles. Analyze each case reported and answer the following questions:

1. Who are the parties?

2. What is the major question in the case?

3. What relief is the court asked to give? Or what relief did the court give?

4. Is the case a civil case or a criminal case?

Guilty Pleas in School Meat Case

Compiled From News Services.

Henry Stanko, an executive with Cattle King Packing Company, changed his plea to guilty on a charge of selling bad beef to national school programs.

Originally, Stanko and five other Cattle King executives had pleaded innocent to 21 charges of selling damaged beef. The Cattle King Packing Company is now out of business. These charges carry maximum sentences of more than 100 years in prison and $150,000 in fines.

Stanko pleaded guilty to a charge of concealing damaged or inferior meat from federal meat inspectors. That charge is a misdemeanor for which Stanko faces a maximum sentence of one year in jail and a fine of $1,000.

The U.S. attorney prosecuting the case for the U.S. Department of Agriculture agreed to drop charges on the more serious crime in exchange for Stanko's guilty plea and his promise to testify against other Cattle King executives.

Spy In The Cookie Jar, Suits Say

WILMINGTON, Del. (AP) — Three cookie companies cooked up schemes including infiltration, aerial surveillance and disguise to get their hands on a new baking process for moist, chewy cookies, Procter & Gamble Co. charges in a set of lawsuits.

The target was the secret behind P&G's Duncan Hines Ready-to-Serve Cookies, the company says. P&G says a newly developed baking process for the product results in the "ideal ready-to-eat cookie" with "a soft inside and crunchy outside."

Procter & Gamble was awarded a patent for the process Tuesday — and immediately filed separate patent infringement lawsuits in U.S. District Court against Nabisco Brands, Keebler Co. and Frito-Lay Inc.

It asked the court to forbid the companies from infringing on its patent and to award unspecified compensatory and punitive damages.

Nabisco and Frito-Lay Wednesday issued statements denying any patent infringement. A spokesman for Keebler reserved comment until seeing the lawsuit.

The suits allege that:

— A Nabisco employee illegally entered a P&G manufacturing plant and gained access to trade secrets "on or around June 1983."

— Last Nov. 9, a Keebler employee "falsely represented his identity and purpose, rented an airplane and took aerial photographs of P&G's" cookie plant then under construction in Jackson, Tenn.

— "A Frito-Lay employee on March 30, 1984, falsely represented himself as a supervisor of a potential customer to a P&G salesman and sat in on a confidential sales presentation referring to Duncan Hines Ready-to-Serve cookies." The Duncan Hines Ready-to-Serve Cookies were test marketed in Kansas City, beginning in February 1983, while the patent application was being considered by the U.S. Patent & Trademark Office.

"These companies started test markets of crisp and chewy cookies in 1983 and 1984 following the introduction of Duncan Hines cookies. We want business and individuals to know we have a patent on Duncan Hines cookies and we want others to respect it," said Patrick J. Hayes, a P&G spokesman at the company's headquarters in Cincinnati.

The cookies involved in the suit are Nabisco's Chips Ahoy, Chewy Chips Ahoy and the Almost Home Cookies; Frito-Lay's Grandma's and Grandma's Rich 'n Chewy, and Keebler's Rich 'n Chips, Chips Deluxe, Coconut Chocolate Drops, Chocolate Chips 100's, Biggs and Soft Batch.

Elliot Bloom, manager of media relations for Dallas-based Frito-Lay Inc., issued a statement saying the company "does not violate any valid patent. We intend to contest this suit vigorously."

He said Frito-Lay, a subsidiary of PepsiCo Inc., plans to continue national expansion of its product, introducing it into six additional states in the next six weeks.

Keebler Co., of Elmhurst, Ill., is a subsidiary of United Biscuits Ltd. of Middlesex, England. Keebler's general counsel, Craig Stevens, said, "We have no comment at this time. We have not received a copy of the lawsuit, therefore we have no idea of what the lawsuit contains."

Nabisco issued a statement Wednesday saying that it "categorically denies" infringing on any valid patent. It said it planned a countersuit "to establish that P&G's patent is invalid."

Used by permission of the Associated Press

PRETRIAL STEPS

Television and movies often focus on trials and courtroom drama. But in real life a trial is only the final act in a lengthy process. Some cases require lawyers to spend hours researching the law. Others require extensive investigations of witnesses and events. No two cases are exactly the same. Certain formal steps, however, are followed in all cases that go to trial. The steps are different for criminal cases or civil cases.

The formal steps that generally occur before trial are as follows:

Civil Cases	Criminal Cases
1. Filing of Complaint	*1. Arrest of the Defendant*
The plaintiff files a legal paper called a **complaint** (sometimes called a **petition**) with the court. The complaint states the plaintiff's claim against the defendant and describes the wrong or harm the plaintiff claims the defendant has done to the plaintiff. The complaint also includes a request for specific relief from the court.	A complainant (a person filing a formal complaint) or a prosecuting attorney may initiate **arrest** proceedings by signing a complaint in writing stating the name of the accused (if name is not known, describing the accused) and describing the facts of the crime. Upon the filing of a complaint and a finding by the court that sufficient facts have been stated to show **probable cause** that a crime has been committed, a warrant for the arrest of the accused (defendant) may be issued. Police take the defendant into custody and book him or her (take fingerprints and information about the defendant). Police advise the defendant of the charges against him or her. Sometimes police must arrest someone before a warrant is issued. In such cases, police will file a complaint after taking the person into custody.
2. Service of Complaint	
The sheriff, marshal, or process server delivers to the defendant a complaint and a **summons**. A summons is a paper advising the defendant in writing of the date on which the defendant must respond to the complaint or appear in court.	
3. Filing of Answer	
The defendant files a legal paper called an **answer** in the court. The answer denies the plaintiff's case and states defenses to it. If the defendant has a claim against the	

Civil Cases	Criminal Cases
plaintiff, the defendant may file a **counterclaim** against the plaintiff. A counterclaim is the same as a complaint, except that it is filed by the defendant.	2. *Initial Appearance* The defendant is taken before a judge. The judge explains the defendant's constitutional rights and advises the defendant of the charges against him or her. If the charge is a felony, the judge also explains the defendant's right to a preliminary examination. If the charge is a misdemeanor, the defendant pleads guilty, not guilty, or **nolo contendere** at this time. The judge decides whether the defendant will stay in jail until the next court date or be released on **bond.**
4. *Hearings on Motions* Either party (the plaintiff or the defendant) may file legal papers asking the court to dismiss — that is, drop — all or part of the other party's claims. The lawyers argue *for* and *against* the motions at **hearings** in court.	
5. *Discovery*	3. *Preliminary Examination (Felony cases)*
Each party may ask the other party to supply information in order to know as much as possible about the case. Parties may obtain information through these methods: a. Written questions to the other side, called interrogatories; b. Requests to see documents; and c. **Testimony** of parties and witnesses at depositions, which involve questioning a person under oath, usually at a lawyer's office. If one party refuses to supply the information requested, the other party may file a motion asking the court to order the party to supply the information. As with other motions, the lawyers may argue on the motion at hearings. *(end)*	The **prosecutor** presents evidence to the judge to show that a crime has been committed and there is reason to believe that the defendant committed it.
	4. *Grand Jury Indictment or Information* The prosecutor presents evidence to the grand jury, a panel of citizens who decide whether a person should be tried for a felony. If the grand jury believes there is probable cause to believe that the defendant has committed a crime, the grand jury issues an indictment, a legal paper formally charging the defendant with the crime. For

Criminal Cases *(cont.)*

some cases, the prosecutor does not use the grand jury indictment. Instead, the prosecutor files an information, a legal paper specifying the charges against the defendant.

5. *Felony Arraignment*

The judge reads the indictment or information to the defendant. The defendant pleads guilty, not guilty, or nolo contendere. If the defendant pleads guilty, the judge sets a date for sentencing and there is no trial. If the defendant pleads not guilty, the judge sets a trial date and reviews the defendant's bond status.

6. *Hearings on Motions*

The defendant's lawyer may file legal papers asking the court to drop the charges or to exclude evidence that the defendant thinks the police obtained illegally. The lawyers argue for and against the motions at hearings in court.

7. *Discovery*

Each party (defense and prosecutor) may ask the other party to supply information in order to know as much as possible about the case. Among the information that may be requested from each person are the names and addresses of persons, other than the defendant, whom the party

Criminal Cases *(cont.)*

intends to call as witnesses at any hearing or trial; reports or statements of experts made in connection with the case; depositions, other than the statements of the defendant; any record of prior criminal conviction of persons the state intends to call as witnesses at the hearing or trial; any other evidence except that belonging to the defendant that either party intends to introduce as evidence at the hearing or trial. The prosecutor may not request any information that may cause the defendant to incriminate himself or herself. The defendant has a constitutional protection from self-incrimination.

YOUR TURN: Identifying Pretrial Steps in Court Cases

Read the articles below about court cases and answer the following questions:

1. Is the case a criminal case or a civil case?

2. Describe the pretrial step involved (for example, complaint filed or initial appearance).

3. What will likely be the next step in the case?

Union Seeks To Void City Contract

By Margaret Gillerman
Of the Post-Dispatch Staff

The city employees union is accusing the city of "anti-labor" practices and of violating the City charter by hiring an outside contractor to provide meals at the City Jail and Workhouse and at two institutions for juveniles.

The city awarded the contract in November to Mid-America Food Service Inc. of Kansas City, Kan. Previously, city employees provided the service.

Also in dispute is Mid-America's practice of using inmate labor at the jail and workhouse to help prepare and serve the meals.

The union also is contending that Mid-America has hired six former city food-service employees at a lower scale and with fewer fringe benefits than the city had provided. About 15 of the city's food-service employees, most of them stewards and cooks, were laid off last month.

City officials say Mid-America can do the same as city employees at a lower cost to the taxpayers.

Local 410 of the Institutional and Public Employees Union has filed suit in St. Louis Circuit Court. It also has filed complaints with the city's Civil Service Commission alleging that the contract violates the city charter because it uses labor outside the civil service system.

The local represents about 800 city employees.

Charles Oldham, attorney for the union, said the contract with Mid-America showed that the administration of Mayor Vincent C. Schoemehl was anti-labor.

"Any time you take people who have worked for the city for 20, 30 or 35 years, kick them out, take away their pensions and health insurance, and then hire them back without their benefits, you definitely have a situation that is anti-labor," Oldham said.

Oldham said that "labor is always opposed to replacing regular labor with inmate labor. We also have a policy against hiring people outside the city, and the officers of Mid-America — the people getting all the dough — live in Kansas and Florida."

But Stephen P. Mullin, city budget director, denied that the move was anti-labor.

"It's an attempt to provide a service, at a time when there are scarce public dollars, as efficiently as possible. We're not the only municipality that has attempted to be cost-effective and gone to a non-conventional delivery of services. We have declining incomes and revenues in the city, and a decline in real purchasing power," Mullin said.

He added, "It's my understanding that this does not violate the city charter."

Mullin said Mid-America's bid had been 94 cents a meal. He said the city had budgeted $1.39 a meal for the same service using city employees. It later revised its estimate to $1.19 a meal.

No estimate of the overall saving to the city was available.

Oldham also charged that Mid-America had increased the amount of its contract after it was awarded to cover equipment costs. But

Mullin said the city would have had to pay for maintenance and repairs of "dilapidated equipment" in any case.

Under the contract, Mid-America prepares and serves meals at the jail, the workhouse, the Children's Study Home in north St. Louis and the Missouri Hills Home for Boys in north St. Louis County.

The three-member city Board of Standardization approved the contract in November after Mid-America outbid another contractor, Servomation Inc. Voting against the contract was City Comptroller Paul M. Berra.

Berra said Thursday that Mid-America had proposed to serve the same meals to adults and juveniles. "The younger people need a differ-ent kind of nourishment," he said. "Secondly, I didn't think the cost savings were sufficient enough to justify hiring an outside food management firm. And I didn't think we'd save enough to end up fighting a lawsuit."

Berra said he also had opposed the contract because he had been told during budget hearings that inmates could not be used for the job.

The city has filed a motion to dismiss the suit on the ground that the union has yet to exhaust all administrative remedies, Oldham said. But Oldham said Local 410 was contesting the motion and hoped to bring the suit to a speedy trial. A hearing on the city's motion is scheduled for next week, Oldham said.

St. Louis Post-Dispatch

Maplewood Man Faces Capital Charge In Slaying

Special to the Post-Dispatch

CAPE GIRARDEAU, Mo. — Curtis Cutts, 23, of the 2600 block of Big Bend Boulevard in Maplewood, was charged Wednesday with capital murder at a preliminary hearing in connection with the killing on Thanksgiving of a truck driver from Wisconsin.

Cape Girardeau County Associate Circuit Judge William S. Rader bound Cutts over for arraignment Monday before Circuit Judge A.J. Seier.

Cutts is also charged with first-degree robbery and armed criminal action. An alternate charge of first-degree murder was filed in case the capital murder charge is dropped.

A preliminary hearing for another suspect charged in the case, Melissa Wagner, 18, also of the 2600 block of Big Bend in Maplewood, was continued. Ms. Wagner is charged with first-degree murder.

A third defendant, Ray L. Bibbs Jr., 23, of the 200 block of Memphis Street in Meacham Park, an unincorporated area near Kirkwood, will be arraigned Monday on charges of capital murder, first-degree robbery and armed criminal action.

The three are charged in the killing of Kenneth M. Wood, 60, of Oconto, Wis. Wood was shot in the head Nov. 24 while attempting to fix a tire along Interstate 55, just north of Cape Girardeau.

Cape Girardeau County Prosecuting Attorney Larry Ferrell said David Warren, a member of the Southeast Missouri Regional Criminal Laboratory, had testified at Cutts' hearing that he had photographed a latent fingerprint impression on the steering wheel of the victim's truck after it was recovered in the parking lot of a Kirkwood store Thanksgiving morning. The fingerprint matched one taken from Cutts' hands.

St. Louis Post-Dispatch

★★★★★★★★★★★★

Settlement: A Process of Negotiation

> The obligation of our profession is to serve as healers of human conflicts. The notion that ordinary people want black-robed judges, well-dressed lawyers and fine courtrooms as settings to resolve their disputes is not correct. People with problems, like people with pains, want relief, and they want it as quickly and inexpensively as possible.
>
> Warren E. Burger,
> Chief Justice of the United States

Some cases do not follow all the steps just identified because the parties negotiate a settlement of the case before trial and before all the steps are taken. People settle problems by **negotiation** everyday. For example, imagine a student who is absent from school due to a serious illness. During the absence the student misses some classroom assignments and two important exams. The absent student's parents write a letter to the principal requesting that the student be permitted to make up the work missed. Upon returning to school, the principal and the student's teachers meet with the student and negotiate a reasonable make-up schedule.

In civil cases, the lawyers often negotiate to determine to what the plaintiff and the defendant will agree. For example, the parties may agree that the defendant will pay money to the plaintiff to resolve the conflict. In criminal cases, the lawyers negotiate plea bargains. In settling a case, both sides avoid the expense and uncertain outcome of a trial.

Settlements in Criminal Cases: Plea Bargaining

Most criminal **convictions** do not involve a trial. Instead, most convictions occur after the defendant pleads guilty. In about 90 percent of criminal cases a guilty plea results from negotiations between the accused and the defense lawyer, and the prosecutor. This process is known as plea bargaining. In plea bargaining, certain concessions are granted to the defendant in exchange for a plea of guilty. In a typical plea bargain, the prosecutor allows the defendant to plead guilty to a less serious offense than was originally charged. For example, if the charge is **burglary,** the prosecutor may agree to reduce the charge to **petty larceny** in exchange for a plea of guilty to petty larceny. In a plea bargain, the prosecutor may also agree to recommend that the judge order a more lenient sentence.

Defendants who plea bargain give up their right to a trial and the chance of being found not guilty. In return, they avoid the risk of a longer prison term. Plea bargaining is especially attractive for defendants accused of murder, rape, armed robbery, or other offenses that may require the judge to set a minimum sentence — crimes for which there is little chance of probation or a short prison term. Some defendants may agree to plead guilty to an offense that carries a longer sentence simply to avoid being labeled a sex offender.

Both the prosecution and the defense must agree to a plea bargain. The judge must also accept the plea. The judge questions the defendant to make sure the defendant makes the plea freely, voluntarily, and with knowledge of all the facts. Also, to avoid taking a guilty plea from an innocent defendant, the judge asks the prosecutor to state facts showing a good reason to charge the defendant with a crime.

Deciding to plea bargain involves many considerations. The prosecutor considers the defendant's record and background, the quality of the evidence, and the facts of the case. The prosecutor wants a conviction at the highest possible charges. But the prosecutor also wants to avoid the possibility that the defendant might win an **acquittal** at trial.

Much controversy surrounds plea bargaining. Supporters say it keeps courts from being overcrowded. Prosecutors and public defenders often have more cases than they can handle. Trials take many days of preparation and courtwork at great expense to taxpayers. But a plea bargain involves relatively little time or expense. Plea bargains also help ensure convictions where evidence is weak or witnesses refuse to testify. After all, no matter how strong the case is, a conviction is never guaranteed. Prosecutors also argue that plea bargaining often reveals additional information about other crimes.

Critics of plea bargaining, however, argue that it allows dangerous criminals to get off with light sentences. It also increases the criminal's disrespect for the law. Critics claim plea bargaining prevents justice for victims and for society. Other critics say that innocent defendants may be pressured into agreeing to a plea bargain for a lesser crime rather than face the risk of being convicted for a serious crime.

YOUR TURN: Plea Bargaining Role Play

A. Read the hypothetical cases below. In each case, the prosecutor and the criminal defense lawyer should meet to discuss the

possibility of a plea bargain. Role play the plea bargain negotiation with half of the class playing prosecutors and the other
half playing the defense lawyers. You may agree to a plea bargain
or you may end up with the case going to trial. Discuss the results
of the negotiations and then answer the questions that follows.

Why did you reach the decision you made in the plea bargain? What
facts influenced your decision?

State v. Mullen

Albert Mullen is charged with possession of heroin for sale. At the
time of the arrest, he threw away a briefcase. The police found heroin
in the briefcase—more heroin than an addict would keep for personal use. The prosecutor wants to get drug sellers off the streets.
But the prosecutor's office is filled with more cases than the prosecutor can handle.

Mullen claims that he is innocent and has told his attorneys that
he wants a jury trial on the charge of possession of heroin for sale.
The maximum penalty for that charge in this **jurisdiction** is 30 years
in prison. The maximum penalty for possession of narcotics is 5
years in prison. Mullen has no prior convictions.

State v. Marsha Brown

Marsha Brown is charged with armed robbery. She has a previous
conviction for armed robbery as well as several other felony offenses.
A number of witnesses are available to testify if there is a trial. The
trial is likely to take five days of preparation and three days of court
time, time that cannot be spent on other cases. As a second offender,
the court would have to sentence Marsha Brown to a minimum of 15
years in prison. The maximum sentence is 60 years. The sentence for
robbery (not armed robbery) as a second offender would be 7½ to 30
years.

State v. Jay Hatfield

Jay Hatfield is charged with fraud and bribery. Hatfield is a real
estate broker. He will lose his license if he is convicted of any crime
involving fraud. Hatfield is charged with offering a bribe to an insurance adjuster. The prosecuting attorney has a videotape of Hatfield
giving the insurance adjuster a $1000 payoff in return for the insur-
ance adjuster's agreeing to turn in a claim of $75,000 on property
that Hatfield bought for $5,000. The fraud and bribery charges are

felonies. A conviction for either could result in two to five years in the state prison. A conviction on both may mean four to ten years in prison for Hatfield.

B. Answer the following questions:

1. Who benefits from a plea bargain?

2. Who may be hurt by a plea bargain?

3. What are some of the disadvantages of plea bargaining?

4. When should plea bargaining be used? Are there any cases when plea bargaining should not be used?

ON YOUR OWN: Plea Bargaining in the News

Using the newspapers and magazines, locate articles describing cases involving plea bargaining. After locating each article, answer the following questions regarding the case:

1. Who benefits or would benefit from the plea bargain?

2. Who may be hurt by the plea bargain?

3. Should plea bargaining have been used in this case? Explain your answer.

The Trial

Trials occur if the parties are unable to reach a settlement through negotiation. In criminal cases, the prosecution must prove the defendant guilty **beyond a reasonable doubt.** In civil cases, the plaintiff's case must be proven by a **preponderance of the evidence.** In both civil and criminal trials, the burden of proof is on the plaintiff or the prosecution. If you think of the burden of proof as a scale of justice, the weight of more evidence is required in criminal cases than in civil cases. This is because the consequences of losing are more severe in criminal cases than in civil cases. A conviction in criminal cases leads to a sentence, which may be a death penalty in some states, a prison term, probation, fine, or combination of fine and imprisonment. In civil cases, the judgment will not result in a loss of life or freedom.

Not all court cases are jury trials. Some civil cases are never heard by juries because there is no right to a jury trial. These cases include divorces, child custody disputes, injunctions, and some civil rights cases. In criminal cases, many criminal defendants give up their right to a jury trial. Also, in some states, defendants charged with some misdemeanors are not entitled to jury trials. In a jury trial, the judge decides on the law and the jury decides on the facts. In a trial without a jury, the judge decides both. Except for matters involving the jury, the steps in a jury trial and a judge trial are the same.

After the selection of the jury by **voir dire,** the judge formally instructs the jury on how the trial will proceed and the jury's role in it. Because jurors are not expected to know the law, at the end of the trial, the judge also gives the jury an explanation of the law affecting the case. These are called jury instructions. Below is an actual jury instruction that might be given at the beginning of a civil trial. Read the instruction and answer the following questions:

1. If you were a juror hearing this jury instruction, would you understand what to expect at the trial and what your role as a juror would be? If not, why not?

2. What information in addition to this jury instruction would better help you understand the trial process and your role as a juror?

3. Based on this jury instruction, what are the steps in a trial?

Jury Instruction No. 1

"The trial may begin with opening statements by the lawyers as to what they expect the evidence will be. At the close of the evidence, the lawyers may make arguments on behalf of their clients reviewing the evidence presented and requesting the jury to make a finding in their client's favor. Neither what is said in opening statements or in closing arguments should be considered as proof of fact.

"After the opening statements, the plaintiff will introduce evidence. After that the defendant may introduce evidence. There may be **rebuttal** evidence after that. The evidence may include the testimony of witnesses who appear personally but whose testimony may be read to you, and exhibits such as pictures, documents, and other objects.

"After all of the evidence has been presented, and you have received the final instructions and heard the closing arguments of the lawyers, you will go to the jury room for your deliberations. At that time, your duty will be to select a foreman, to decide the facts, and to arrive at a **verdict.**

"Justice requires that you not make up your mind about the case until all of the evidence has been seen and heard. You must not comment on or discuss what you may hear or learn in the trial until the case is concluded and you go to the jury room for your deliberations.

"In considering the weight and value of the testimony of any witness you may take into consideration the appearance, attitude, and behavior of the witness, the interest of the witness in the outcome of the case, the relation of the witness to any of the parties, the inclination of the witness to speak truthfully or untruthfully, and the probability or improbability of the witness's statement.

"There will be times that a party objects to evidence offered by the other party. If I **overrule** the objection, you may consider that matter when you deliberate on the case. If I **sustain** an objection, then that matter is excluded and must not be considered by you in your deliberations."

As the instruction says, evidence may be presented as exhibits or as witness testimony. Witnesses only testify in answer to questions asked them by the lawyers and sometimes the judge. Each witness testifies first in response to the lawyer for the side on which the witness is testifying. This is called **direct examination.** Then the other lawyer questions the witness. This is called **cross examination.** On direct examination, the lawyer tries to get the witness to tell facts proving his or her client's side of the case. On cross examination, the lawyer tries to show that the witness is not believable or that the facts told by the witness do not hold together.

In addition to the steps outlined in the jury instruction, in most trials, after all of the evidence for the plaintiff or the prosecution has been presented, the defendant's lawyer will ask the court to find that the plaintiff or prosecution has no case. The defendant asks for the case to be dismissed without continuing with the trial. If the judge orders the case dismissed, the defendant wins.

YOUR TURN: Identifying the Steps in a Trial

Read the following quotes and answer the questions. To help you answer, use the jury instruction and the explanatory information following the instructions on pages 146-147.

1. "Ladies and gentlemen of the jury. As you can see, the evidence plainly showed that my client sold the computers to the defendant and that the defendant, for no good reason, simply refused to pay for the computers."

    At what step in a trial would this statement occur? Who do you think is saying it: judge, plaintiff's attorney (or prosecutor), or defendant's attorney? Why is this step necessary?

2. "Mr. Tomkins, isn't it true that you lied when you said you had never gone to the house of my client, the defendant?"

    At what step in a trial would this question occur? Who do you think is asking it: judge, plaintiff's attorney (or prosecutor), or defendant's attorney? Why is this step necessary?

3. "If you find in favor of the plaintiff, then you must award the plaintiff such sum as you believe will fairly and justly compensate the plaintiff for any damages you believe she sustained."

    At what step in a trial would this statement occur? Who do you think is saying it: judge, plaintiff's attorney (or prosecutor), or defendant's attorney? Why is this step necessary?

4. "Mrs. Tappan, you are here today to testify for my client, the defendant. What was the condition of the plaintiff when he left the party?"

    At what step in a trial would this question occur? Who do you think is asking it: judge, plaintiff's attorney (or prosecutor), or defendant's attorney? Why is this step necessary?

5. "Ladies and gentlemen of the jury, the plaintiff will show you today through her own testimony and that of her car mechanic that the defendant cheated her and sold her a car as new when the car actually was used and had been in an accident."

    At what step in a trial would this statement occur? Who do you think is saying it: judge, plaintiff's attorney (or prosecutor), or defendant's attorney? Why is this step necessary?

The final step in a jury trial is the instruction of the jury on the law. In the jury instructions, the judge tells the jury the legal rules it must follow in reaching a verdict — that is, deciding for the plaintiff or the defendant in a civil trial, the prosecution or the defense in a criminal trial. For example, in a civil suit for **battery,** the following jury instruction might be used:

Jury Instruction No. 2

"Your verdict must be for the plaintiff if you believe that (1) the defendant intentionally struck the plaintiff, and (2) the defendant thereby caused the plaintiff bodily harm."

This instruction tells the jurors to think over all the testimony they have heard and all the exhibits (for example, medical reports and photographs) that they have seen and decide three things: (1) Did the defendant strike the plaintiff? (2) Did the defendant intend to strike the plaintiff? (3) Was the plaintiff injured as a result? If all three questions can be answered *yes*, the jury must decide that the defendant is liable to the plaintiff for the tort of battery. The jury then has to go on to decide how much money in damages the defendant should pay to the plaintiff.

YOUR TURN: Following Jury Instructions

Divide the class into groups. Each group should act as a jury and attempt to reach a unanimous decision in the following case. If a unanimous decision is not possible, then they should attempt to reach a decision with which a clear majority agrees. Each jury group should do the following:

1. Read the case.

2. Review Jury Instruction No. 2 above.

3. Apply Jury Instruction No. 2 to this case and reach a decision, including how much money, if any, the defendant should pay to the plaintiff.

The Case of the Bully Boyfriend

The following is a summary of the testimony of the witnesses:

Bob is nineteen years old. Bob has been dating Rose off and on since Rose was in ninth grade. Rose had a big party on her eighteenth birthday. Rose did not invite Bob because they had not been getting along lately.

Around midnight Bob showed up at the party. He was angry and he was shouting. When he found Rose he started calling her names and said she owed him a good explanation for leaving him cold. According to several witnesses, Rose told him to leave. Bob then shoved Rose backwards. Rose fell backwards over a chair and struck her head on a stone wall. Rose had to be taken to a hospital. Tests revealed that she had a severe concussion and a broken left wrist.

Rose filed a suit against Bob claiming that Bob intentionally struck her, that she suffered a concussion and a broken wrist, and that as a result of these injuries, she would have to pay large medical expenses. She would also lose at least two months of work from her full-time job as a secretary.

YOUR TURN: Jury Instructions Make Headlines

Read the article below. After reading the article, answer the following questions:

1. Briefly describe the type of trial that is involved in this news story. Is it a state or federal trial? Is it a civil or criminal trial?

2. According to the news story, what were the general jury instructions in this trial?

3. Given the information in this news article, would you have wanted to be a juror in this case? Briefly explain your answer.

Jury in Federal Brink's Case Given Instructions Before Deliberations

By ARNOLD H. LUBASCH
The New York Times

A jury of six men and six women heard final instructions yesterday before the start of deliberations in the Brink's trial in Federal District Court in Manhattan.

Judge Kevin Thomas Duffy delivered the detailed instructions on the laws governing the case, which began almost five months ago.

"It is your function to determine the facts," Judge Duffy told the jurors, adding that they must be "guided solely by the law and the evidence."

The defendants are four men and two women who were indicted on Federal charges stemming from an investigation of the 1981 Brink's robbery in Rockland County, which involved killing a guard and two police officers.

Besides the Rockland robbery, the Federal charges include other robberies, the killing of an armored-car guard in the Bronx and the prison escape of Joanne D. Chesimard, a Black Liberation Army leader who is still a fugitive.

The four men on trial are Sekou Odinga, formerly Nathaniel Burns; Bilal Sunni-Ali, formerly William Johnson; Edward L. Joseph, and Cecil Ferguson. They are charged with participation in robberies involving murders, a charge carrying up to life in prison.

The two women on trial are Silvia Baraldini, who is charged with being a member of the robbery group, and Iliana Robinson, who is charged with helping two robbers escape. If convicted, Miss Baraldini could face up to 20 years for conspiracy and racketeering, and Miss Robinson could face up to 12½ years on an accessory charge.

Three different defendants are on trial in Goshen, N.Y., on state charges of robbery and murder involving solely the Brink's robbery and shootout in Rockland County.

Criteria For Racketeering Charge

Most of the state defendants were captured near the scene of the shootout with the police in Nyack on the day of the Rockland robbery. But the six Federal defendants were arrested later. Several others suspects are fugitives.

Judge Duffy, instructing the jury for five hours, said the main racketeering charge accused several defendants of being members of a group of robbers. To convict a defendant, he continued, the jury must find the defendant committed two or more crimes in "a pattern of racketeering activity."

The judge said the specific crimes in the charge were the robberies, the murders committed during the robberies and the kidnapping of two guards during the 1979 escape of Miss Chesimard from prison in Clinton, N.J. He said the case had "absolutely nothing to do with politics."

The four men on trial were also named in separate charges of armed bank robbery and killing people during the robberies.

In the trial, the prosecution presented more than 100 witnesses, including informers who descibed a robbery group called "the Family." The defense tried to discredit the informers and said the defendants were being prosecuted for their radical politics.

Judge Duffy **sequestered** the jury yesterday for the duration of the deliberations.

ON YOUR OWN: Jury Instructions in the News

Using newspapers and/or magazines, attempt to find other news articles involving jury instructions. For each news article you find, answer the three questions on page 150. Remember to bring your article and answers to class for discussion.

The Final Sentence

In states that have **capital crime** trials, jurors may serve for two trials. In the first trial, the jury must decide if the defendant is guilty of the capital crime. If the jury returns a verdict of guilty, then a second trial is held to fix the punishment. In most cases, the jury decides whether to recommend life imprisonment or the death penalty. If the jury decides on the death penalty, then the court sentences the defendant to be put to death. This final sentence is carried out in accordance with the state's death penalty laws.

YOUR TURN: Authorizing the Execution

Read the following death warrant and answer the questions that follow.

DEATH WARRANT
STATE OF FLORIDA

WHEREAS, DAVID LEROY WASHINGTON, did on the 20th day of September, 1976 murder Daniel Pridgen, and did on the 23rd day of September, 1976 murder Katrina Birk, and did on the 29th of September, 1976 murder Frank Meli, and

WHEREAS, DAVID LEROY WASHINGTON was found guilty of murder in the first degree in each case and was sentenced to death in each case on December 6, 1976; and

WHEREAS, the FLorida Supreme Court upheld each sentence of death imposed on DAVID LEROY WASHINGTON on September 7, 1978 and **certiorari** was denied by the United States Supreme Court April 30, 1979; and

WHEREAS, it has been determined that Executive Clemency, as authorized by Article IV, Section 8(a), Florida Constitution, is not appropriate; and

WHEREAS, attached hereto is a copy of the record pursuant to Section 922.0:9, Florida Statutes;

NOW, THEREFORE, I, BOB GRAHAM, as Governor of the State of Florida and pursuant to the authority and responsibility vested by the Constitution and Laws of Florida do hereby issue this warrant directing the Superintendent of the Florida State Prison to cause the sentence of death to be executed upon DAVID LEROY WASHINGTON on some day of the week beginning noon, Friday, the 6th day of July, 1984 and ending noon, Friday, the 13th day of July, 1984, in accord with the provision of the laws of the State of Florida.

IN TESTIMONY WHEREOF, I have hereunto set my hand and caused the Great Seal of the State of Florida to be affixed at Tallahassee, The Capitol, this 15th day of June, 1984.

Bob Graham
_____
GOVERNOR

1. Who was found guilty of murder in the first degree and sentenced to death on December 6, 1976?

2. Did the Florida Supreme Court uphold this death penalty? On what date did the court make this decision?

3. Who issued this death warrant?

4. Who was directed to cause the sentence of death to be executed?

5. When was the execution to occur? How many years were there between the death penalty sentence and the execution date?

ON YOUR OWN: A Real Trial

Visit a court to observe a real trial. After the trial, be prepared to answer the following questions:

1. Did the trial involve a civil case or a criminal case?
   A. Who were the parties (prosecution and defense or plaintiff and defendant)?
   B. What kind of relief was being sought from the court?

2. What was the case about?

3. Which steps in the trial did you observe?

ON YOUR OWN: Understanding Jury Instructions

Ask the following questions to three adults who have been on a jury. Discuss the results in class and send a summary of the responses obtained to the jury commission for your community.

1. How often have you been on a jury?

2. Did you understand the instructions given by the judge?

3. What was most difficult about the instructions?

4. What do you think could be done to make jurors better able to fulfill their duties?

Settlement Outside the Judicial Process: Mediation

Most legal problems are not solved by passing new laws or by judicial decisions. Many legal problems may be resolved outside the formal judicial process. Going to court should be the last resort after exhausting all other ways to solve the legal problem. One means of resolving problems is through mediation. Mediation is a form of negotiation. Mediation usually involves an independent third person who acts to help resolve a dispute. The mediator hears both sides of the problem. Then the mediator helps the sides reach a mutually agreed upon decision to resolve the problem. The mediator does not decide the solution, but helps the parties to examine alternatives to reach a satisfactory solution by themselves.

In settling disputes through mediation, the following guidelines are suggested:

1. Mediators should introduce themselves to the disputants and introduce the disputants to each other. Then the mediator should briefly describe how the mediator can help resolve the dispute.

2. Mediators should engage in active listening. The mediator should ask each disputant to state what he/she believes to be the dispute. To make sure all parties understand what is being said, the mediator may wish to paraphrase and repeat what each disputant has said, (that is, stating "I hear you saying . . .") As an added feature of fairness, the mediator may wish to select which disputant goes first by flipping a coin. The mediator must avoid making value judgments about what is being said. That is, the mediator should never say "that is foolish" or any other negative statement that may interfere with open communications.

3. After each disputant has described the problem, the mediator should attempt to formulate a definition of the problem that is mutually agreed to by each disputant. The mediator should remind the disputants that they have just reached a mutual agreement in defining the problem.

4. After defining the problem, the mediator should ask each disputant to recommend a solution of the commonly defined problem. The mediator should listen carefully and attempt to identify any common areas of agreement.

5. The mediator should begin to write an agreement to resolve the dispute based on the recommendation of each disputant. This is the working draft and should state all of the agreed upon recommendations.

6. After developing and writing the agreed upon resolution(s), all three participants (the disputants and the mediator) should sign the agreement and then shake hands.

YOUR TURN: Mediate a Solution to the Problem

Divide into groups of three or four students. Each group will be assigned one of the following disputes to resolve. Each person in the group will be assigned one of the following roles:

Disputant (Party) A — One party to the dispute.

Disputant (Party) B — The other party in the dispute.

Mediator (Party) M — The mediator who is responsible for listening to both sides and then helping them reach a satisfactory solution to their dispute.

Observer — The observer should take notes on the actual mediation process and then discuss his or her observations at the conclusion of the mediation (use the suggested steps above).

Each group should do the following:

1. Identify the major problem(s) in the dispute.

2. With the help of the mediator, list some possible solutions to the problem.

3. Party A and Party B, with the aid of the mediator, should agree on at least one solution to try to resolve the dispute. If no agreement can be reached, the parties may have to decide whether to seek settlement in court.

Dispute #1

Party A — A tenant in a four-unit apartment building. This tenant, a woman living alone, has a large dog in her apartment. She has the dog for companionship and protection. The dog has a very loud bark and barks anytime it hears someone in the hallway of the apartment building.

Party B — A neighbor of Party A. Party B is a single parent with two small children. Party B has just delivered a complaint to Party A. The complaint says that Party B and the two other tenants in the apartment building are tired of being disturbed by Party A's dog barking at all hours. Also, Party B is afraid that the dog might attack the small children if it ever gets loose in the hallway. Party B is considering filing a peace disturbance complaint against Party A with the police.

Mediator — The mediator must help A and B define the problem and then reach a satisfactory solution.

Dispute #2

Party A — Joe, the husband and father. Joe has agreed to a separation from his wife Joy. Joe and Joy have two children, a daughter sixteen years old and a son nine years old. Joe wants custody of the children except for weekends when Joy is available to take them. Joe has a steady job as a computer technician and feels he can take better care of the two children than Joy.

Party B — Joy, the wife and mother. Joy has agreed to the separation from Joe. According to Joy, she and Joe fight constantly. Staying together will only cause more problems. Joy has a full-time job as a salesperson for a sporting goods firm. Joy's sales job sometimes requires that she travel to other cities. She may be gone for a week at a time. She claims that her mother has agreed to take care of the children but says that she is willing to allow Joe to have the children three weekends every month.

Mediator — The mediator must help A and B define the problem and then reach a satisfactory solution.

Dispute #3

Party A — Carlos Castro, a month-to-month tenant in an apartment. Mr. Carlos does not speak English very well and he reads only in Spanish. When Mr. Castro first rented his apartment, his lease was written in both Spanish and English. Recently his daughter and grandson moved into his apartment. They had been living in Mexico. Mr. Castro received a letter from the new owner of his apartment building. The letter from this landlord was in English only. It listed new rules for tenants. One of the new rules stated, "No children, persons under eighteen, are permitted to reside in these apartment units." Mr. Castro has been a quiet, respectable tenant for almost ten years in this apartment building.

Party B — The new owner and landlord of the apartment building where Mr. Castro lives. Upon discovering that Mr. Castro's seven-year-old grandson was living in the apartment, the landlord sent Mr. Castro another letter. This letter, also in English, warned Mr. Castro to remove his grandson or face possible eviction. A week later, the landlord visited Mr. Castro's apartment. The landlord got the assistance of an interpreter. The landlord told Mr. Castro about the "no children" rule. The landlord informed Mr. Castro that his grandson would have to find another residence by the end of the month. The landlord says Mr. Castro can stay but the grandson must go. The landlord claims that he can obtain a court order evicting Mr. Castro and his family if he does not abide by the new rules.

Mediator — The mediator must help A and B define the problem and then reach a satisfactory solution.

Dispute #4

Party A — The owner of a three-year-old auto. Party A took his car to a local service station for a state auto inspection. Party A told the manager of the service station to inspect the car and to make any necessary repairs under $100. Party A told the manager to call him for approval if the repair will cost more than $100. When Party A arrived to pick up the inspected car, the manager explained what happened and gave Party A the bill for $146. Party A refuses to pay $146 claiming that he authorized only $100 in repairs.

Party B — The service station manager. After inspecting the car, the mechanic informed the manager that the car needed three repairs to bring the car up to inspection standards. The total for the three repairs was $146. No single repair was more than $100. The manager called Party A at his office. Party A was out of the office and would not be back until the end of the day. The manager knew this was the last day of the month for Party A to have the car inspected without a fine. The manager told the mechanic to go ahead and make the repairs. Party B insists that Party A pay the $146 bill. Party B threatens to sue Party A for payment in Small Claims Court.

Mediator — The mediator must help A and B define the problem and then reach a satisfactory solution.

9

THE VICTIM IN THE JUDICIAL SYSTEM

Third-Graders Try To Understand Death Of 9-Year-Old Classmate

By George E. Curry
Of the Post-Dispatch Staff

Third-graders at Captain School in Clayton are having difficulty in understanding that a classmate, 9-year-old Noah Kimbrough, is dead.

Sally Ann Nickens, Kimbrough's teacher, said some of the students were having a hard time adjusting to the loss of their classmate, who was shot to death Tuesday night after two robbers broke into his West End home while his parents were out shopping for Christmas presents.

"Some of the students have nightmares," she said, "They see pictures of him if they look at an open window — like he's still there. Many of the parents said their children have had sleepless nights. They have a great love for Noah. They don't realize that he is not here — they think he's coming back."

But Noah died Wednesday at St. Louis Children's Hospital.

Two intruders watched Lloyd and Marilyn Kimbrough, Noah's parents, leave the house at 5815 Pershing Avenue at 7 p.m. Tuesday. The intruders then ransacked it and took some valuables. They ordered Noah and his brother, Miles Rutlin, 17, into the basement and forced them to lie face down.

One of the robbers shot Noah in the back of the head. He aimed at Noah's brother, but the pistol misfired. Ruthin was able to wrestle the weapon away, and the assailants fled.

On Thursday two suspects were charged with capital murder, first degree assault and first-degree robbery in connection with the case. They are Sammy D. Taylor Jr., 17 of the 6100 block of Shillington Drive in Berkeley, and Brock Seals, 18, of the 5800 block of Nina Place.

St. Louis Post-Dispatch

Woman Bilked by Pigeon Drop

Flora Harrell, 65, of the 5800 block of Matfitt Avenue, was bilked out of $500 Wednesday by a man posing as a policeman. Mrs. Harrell got a call from a man, who said he was trying to catch a thief who wanted to steal money from Mrs. Harrell's bank account. Mrs. Harrell cooperated in the ''scheme'' to catch the thief by withdrawing $500 from her bank and giving it to the man posing as the officer. The man later returned an envelope to Mrs. Harrell, but when she looked inside it contained only strips of paper.

St. Louis Post-Dispatch

Woman Robbed at Knifepoint

Katherine Hardman, 30, was robbed about 10:30 p.m. Wednesday in the 3800 block of McDonald Avenue. Ms. Hardman said two young men had demanded money and one had pressed a knife against her throat. She gave the robbers $20, and one youth struck her in the face, knocked her down and kicked her in the ribs. She was admitted for observation at Barnes Hospital.

St. Louis Post-Dispatch

Who do you think is affected by the **crime** in these articles? What are the consequences for these persons? How would you feel if you were any of these persons?

In one out of every three households, someone was the victim of a crime during the past year. To many of these victims and their families, the effects of the crime were life-shattering. For the victim, a crime is not over when the offender leaves the scene—the lives of victims are often never the same after the crime. But the public forgets the victim and focuses on the drama of the crime and the criminal. Victims have begun to speak out on the many harmful effects of crime on the victim:

"My name is Mel Patterson. A man mugged me and grabbed my wallet after I cashed my paycheck. My rent money was in the wallet and I was evicted from my apartment. I had no money to pay a deposit on a new apartment or to buy food for me and my three children. I had nowhere to go."

"My name is Armand Rodriquez. My daughter was hit by a drunk driver. Since the accident five years ago, she has been totally paralyzed. My wife quit work because my daughter requires a full-time attendant. The medical bills are so high I doubt that we will ever pay them off. All our money goes to those bills. My daughter will be a vegetable the rest of her life."

"My name is Brenda Tipton. I am a 45-year-old waitress at the West Side Cafe. One night as we were closing the cafe, the manager pulled me into the stockroom and raped me. He held a knife at my throat. I was shocked. I never expected that to happen to me. I felt humiliated by the medical examination and later by the questions in court. My husband looked at me like I was dirty. He couldn't get over it and left me. I hate men now."

"My name is Sharman Sayers. My father was shot in a robbery last year. He was in the hospital for six days before he died. We were left with no support. My mother had not worked before my father died. She didn't know what to do. I am so sad because I can't be with my father anymore and my mother is so nervous."

"My name is Joe Redcloud. My wife, children and I became seriously ill and we lost six of our prize horses after we worked in the stable yard. A dirt hauler had illegally dumped toxic wastes in our stable. The horses were our main source of income. We are suffering severe hardships without them. Also, our children suffer partial blindness."

"My name is Lester Hogan. Six months ago my house was burglarized. The burglars made a mess of the house. They stole things worth about $1000. Since then my happy 10-year-old son has been moody. He is afraid to leave the house alone. In the house he follows us from room to room. His grades in school have fallen. Although we cannot afford it, we are taking him to a counselor. We may just have to move out of our house and our neighborhood to help him forget the experience."

These victims and members of their families have related some of the consequences of crime for victims. Some other consequences can be:

— Loss of a home and personal possessions resulting from arson;
— Fear of revenge for testifying against an offender;
— Loss of personal treasures and sentimental things;
— Loss of a job because of time taken off to testify;
— Loss of a job because of physical injuries and emotional effects;
— Inconvenience and cost of replacing keys, credit cards, or driver's license;
— Cost of replacing a car, a television, or other stolen item;
— Cost of repairing a home, a car, a window, or other damaged item;
— Loss of means of transportation;
— Physical pain.

YOUR TURN: Victims Tell Their Stories

A Task Force on Victims of Crime is holding hearings to allow victims to tell their stories. By listening to victims, the task force may better understand the needs of victims when it makes recommend- ations on new laws and policies to help crime victims.

Your class has been chosen as a location for a hearing of the local Crime Victims Task Force. The entire class will be the task force. Several students can be appointed as reporters to take notes on the testimony, or the teacher can be the reporter. Each student will play the role of a victim. When you tell your story to the task force, base it on personal experience, experiences of persons you know, or stories you have read in the newspaper. After all students have testified, the task force should be prepared to discuss the kinds of problems faced by victims. The following questions may be used to guide the discussion:

1. How did you feel as a victim? What did you learn about victims from playing the role of one?

2. What do you think can be done to help these victims?

3. What do you think can be done to help victims?

ON YOUR OWN: How Has Crime Affected People You Know?

Do a survey of your family and neighbors to find out how they may have been affected by crime. Ask three people these questions. Mark an X by the appropriate answer. Keep in mind that people may still be upset about crimes against them even though the crimes oc- curred some time ago. You should be sensitive and considerate of people and their privacy.

Respondents

	#1	#2	#3	
Yes	____	____	____	1. Have you or a close friend, neighbor, or relative ever been a victim of a crime?
No	____	____	____	
Yes	____	____	____	2. Have you or a close friend, neighbor, or relative been a victim of crime during the past twelve months?
No	____	____	____	

Respondents

#1   #2   #3

Yes	_____	_____	_____
No	_____	_____	_____

3. Have you ever had property taken from you in a crime?
   a. What was the property worth?

	_____	_____	_____
	_____	_____	_____
	_____	_____	_____
	_____	_____	_____
	_____	_____	_____
	_____	_____	_____

     Less than $10
     $10 to $100
     $101 to $1,000
     $1,001 to $5,000
     Over $5,000
     Priceless, sentimental value

Yes	_____	_____	_____
No	_____	_____	_____

   b. Did you ever get the property back?

Yes	_____	_____	_____
No	_____	_____	_____
Yes	_____	_____	_____
No	_____	_____	_____
Yes	_____	_____	_____
No	_____	_____	_____
Yes	_____	_____	_____
No	_____	_____	_____

4. Have your ever been injured physically as a result of a crime?
   a. Did you have to pay a doctor or hospital for treatment?
   b. Did you miss any work or school because of your injuries?
   c. Did you have any permanent injuries?

	_____	_____	_____
	_____	_____	_____
	_____	_____	_____
	_____	_____	_____

5. Where did the crime occur?
   At home
   On the street
   At work or school
   Other _____

	_____	_____	_____
	_____	_____	_____
	_____	_____	_____
	_____	_____	_____
	_____	_____	_____

6. How old were you at the time of the crime?
   Under 18
   18 – 29
   30 – 45
   46 – 60
   Over 60

Yes	_____	_____	_____
No	_____	_____	_____

7. Did you report this crime to the police?

8. In what ways did the crime change your life?

#1 _____

#2 _____

#3 _____

Respondents

	#1	#2	#3	
Yes	_____	_____	_____	9. Do you feel afraid to be alone in your
No	_____	_____	_____	home?
Yes	_____	_____	_____	10. Do you feel afraid to be alone on the
No	_____	_____	_____	street at night?

11. What do you think should be done to aid victims of crime?

#1_____

#2_____

#3_____

Helping the Victim

Reread the newspaper articles at the beginning of this chapter. Using the list on page 161, identify the financial costs to the crime victims and their families. Who do you think will pay these financial costs?

Usually crime victims and their families pay most or all of these costs. The people who are most likely to be victims—the lower in-comed, the young, the elderly—often have no insurance. And, even when a victim has insurance, it may not cover all the losses from a crime.

To most people, it seems unfair that victims have to pay the costs of putting their lives back together after a crime. In our legal system, the person who causes injuries or damage may be held legally responsible for the costs resulting from his or her conduct. Yet, even though in most cases victims are not at all responsible for the crime, they are the ones to pay.

> Who do you think should pay the costs of crime?
> Who is responsible for the occurrence of the crime and for its effects on the victim?

The person responsible for the crime and its effects is the offender. In some cases, state laws authorize the judge sentencing a person convicted of a crime to order **restitution.** Restitution means that the offender must pay back the victim. Usually this is done by paying back the victim's money or paying for the victim's property as part of the sentence. Judges who do not order restitution believe that it may discourage offenders and make it harder for them to earn a living legally. Even when judges do order restitution, most victims do not get relief. Can you think of any reasons why?

Another way a victim might obtain money from the offender is by a **civil** lawsuit. For example, a victim of a criminal **assault and battery** could sue the offender for money damages for the **tort** called assault. Similarly, a victim of a theft could sue the thief to return the property or pay the value of it. The local prosecutor would be the lawyer in the criminal case; the victim's lawyer would handle the civil suit. For every crime committed against a victim, there is a civil lawsuit that the victim could file against the offender.

Most often, however, a civil lawsuit will not help. A victim can only sue a person whose identity is known. Many victims never find out who committed the crime against them. Also, most offenders have little or no money to pay to victims. One recent study showed the average income of offenders was less than $5,000 per year. The money the offender does have is likely to be used for lawyers in the criminal case. And, an offender sentenced to prison will not earn much money while in prison. For most victims, civil lawsuits are expensive, time-consuming dead ends.

To help victims of crime, most states have passed victim compensation laws. Victims can now apply to a state agency or a court for compensation covering their "out-of-pocket" medical expenses and income lost due to injuries. The benefits are paid from a special victim compensation fund. In some states, contributions to the fund come from special fines each person convicted of a crime must pay. In most states, however, victims cannot get compensation for property damages, for pain, or for emotional shock.

Who qualifies as a victim differs from state to state. In some states, only victims of violent crimes may get compensation; other states limit compensation to victims of certain crimes; still other states allow compensation to all injured crime victims, regardless of the type of crime. People injured while committing a crime or in connection with a crime they have committed do not qualify. Also, individuals who contribute to their own injuries, like someone injured in a family quarrel, generally cannot get compensation or get only reduced compensation. In some states, only people with low incomes can get compensation.

Many victims do not know they can apply for victim compensation.

To make sure that victims do know about the benefits, some state laws require police to inform victims of their right to compensation.
The following is from the New York victim statement law:

MANDATORY INFORMATION FOR INNOCENT VICTIMS OF CRIME

1. Injured innocent victims of crime or their dependents may recover cost of medical treatment and reimbursement for loss of wages.

2. If death results from a criminal act, the victim's funeral expense may be paid by the State.

Every Police Station, precinct House or other appropriate Law Enforcement location in New York State where a crime may be reported has information, brochures and application forms.

It is estimated that nearly one third of all crime goes unreported. But no one can get victim compensation benefits unless he or she reports the crime to the police and cooperates with the authorities in the arrest and prosecution. Victim compensation laws, therefore, can help victims and lead to more arrests and prosecution of offenders.

YOUR TURN: Analyzing and Applying a Victim Compensation Law

1. Analyze the excerpts below from a sample victim compensation law and answer the following questions:
   a. Who qualifies as a "victim" entitled to compensation?
   b. Who does not qualify?
   c. What do you think are the reasons for the qualifications?

2. Examine the statements of the victims on pages 160-161. For each victim, decide whether the individual qualifies for compensation under this law. If not, what would you recommend that the victim do? Do the benefits available under the victim compensation law cover all the costs?

Victim Compensation Law
595.010. Definitions
(10) "Injured victim" shall mean any person:
  (a) Killed or receiving a personal injury in this state as a result of another person's commission of or attempt to commit any crime;
  (b) Killed or receiving a personal injury in this state while in a good faith attempt to assist a person against whom a crime is being perpetrated or attempted;
  (c) Killed or receiving a personal injury in this state while assisting a law enforcement officer in the apprehension of a person who the officer has reason to believe has perpetrated or attempted a crime;
(11) "Offender," a person who commits a crime;
(12) "Personal injury," actual bodily harm;
(15) "Victim," a person who suffers personal injury or death as a direct result of a crime, as defined in subdivision (1) of this section;
595.020. Eligibility for compensation
1. Except as hereinafter provided, the following persons shall be eligible for compensation pursuant to sections 595.010 to 595.070:
  (1) a victim of a crime; and
  (2) In the case of the death of the victim as a direct result of the crime, a dependent of the victim.
2. An offender or an accomplice of an offender, a member of the family of the offender, a person living with the offender or a person maintaining sexual relations with the offender shall in no case be eligible to receive compensation with respect to a crime committed by the offender.
595.030. Compensation
1. No compensation shall be paid unless the division of worker's compensation finds that a crime was committed, that such crime directly resulted in personal physical injury to, or the death of, the victim, and that police record show that such crime was promptly reported to the proper authorities.
2. Any compensation paid . . . for death or personal injury shall be in an amount not exceeding out-of-pocket loss, together with loss of earnings or support resulting from such injury or death.
4. Any compensation for loss of earnings or support

shall be in an amount equal to the actual loss sustained; provided, however, that no award . . . shall exceed ten thousand dollars ($10,000).

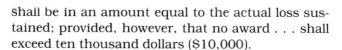

In many communities, victims of crime and other concerned citizens have formed organizations to help crime victims. The organizations provide services to victims and try to get other people to help victims. Following are some of the things organizations for crime victims do:

. . . Give counseling

. . . Help victim find temporary housing

. . . Arrange transportation to the doctor, police, work

. . . Help victim get financial help

. . . Talk to victim's employer to prevent loss of job or wages for time missed

. . . Go to court with victim

. . . Make minor home repairs

. . . Provide crime prevention information

. . . Talk with prosecutors to make sure victim is consulted on decisions

. . . Assist victim in filling out forms

. . . Explain criminal justice system to victims

. . . Monitor the trial

. . . Arrange for a translator for victim

. . . Educate the public about the problems of victims

. . . Meet with victims for support

. . . Lobby for change in the law

ON YOUR OWN: Help for Victims in Your Community

1. Find out whether your state or local community has a victim compensation law or any other laws that may help victims. Ask

your teacher to invite a lawyer or a member of the victim compensation agency to discuss how the law works and whether victims are really helped. Find out how victims learn about victim compensation benefits in your community. How is the victim compensation program listed in the telephone directory?

2. Find out what organizations and agencies in your community help crime victims. Complete the following form with the results of your research.

  A. The following organization(s) in our community gives financial aid to crime victims: _____

  _____

  _____

  B. The following organization(s) in our community gives information and counseling to crime victims: _____

  _____

  _____

  C. The following organization(s) in our community lobbies for the passage of new laws to help crime victims: _____

  _____

  _____

  D. The following organization(s) in our community provides food, clothing, and house repairs to crime victims: _____

  _____

  _____

  E. The major problems for crime victims in our community are:_____

  _____

  _____

If your community has no victim aid organization, ask your teacher to invite someone from the office of the local prosecuting attorney to discuss the problems. Find out what your class can do to help victims know about resources available to help them.

★★★★★★★★★★★

Rights of Victims

Many people say that victims of crime are the forgotten people in our criminal justice system. Criminal suspects have well-defined rights under the Constitution and other laws. Law enforcement authorities have definite rights in the criminal justice process. But what rights do victims have?

The chart below illustrates the extremes between the treatment of the victim and the accused. Look at the chart. What rights do persons accused or convicted of crimes have that victims do not have? What do you think are the reasons for the differences?

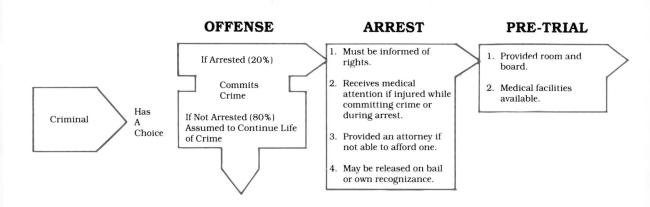

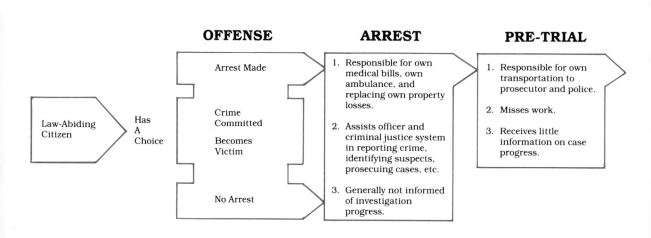

170

Victims traditionally have had few rights in our legal system. By definition, a crime is a violation of law; not an injury to an individual. The government—the police, the prosecutor, and the courts—prosecutes the suspect for breaking the law, not for injuring the victim. Because the victim is not involved in that dispute, the criminal justice system has long overlooked the needs, concerns and convenience of the victim.

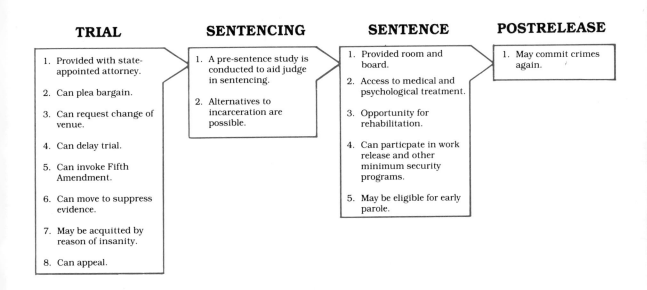

TRIAL

1. Provided with state-appointed attorney.
2. Can plea bargain.
3. Can request change of venue.
4. Can delay trial.
5. Can invoke Fifth Amendment.
6. Can move to suppress evidence.
7. May be acquitted by reason of insanity.
8. Can appeal.

SENTENCING

1. A pre-sentence study is conducted to aid judge in sentencing.
2. Alternatives to incarceration are possible.

SENTENCE

1. Provided room and board.
2. Access to medical and psychological treatment.
3. Opportunity for rehabilitation.
4. Can participate in work release and other minimum security programs.
5. May be eligible for early parole.

POSTRELEASE

1. May commit crimes again.

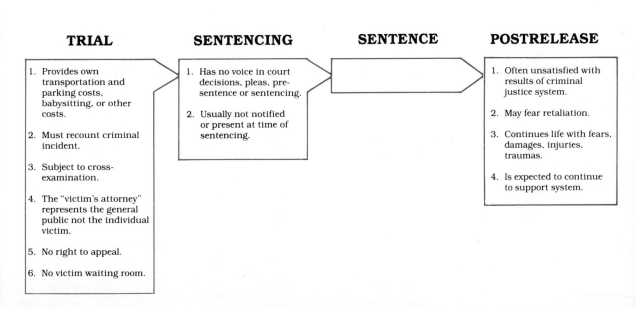

TRIAL

1. Provides own transportation and parking costs, babysitting, or other costs.
2. Must recount criminal incident.
3. Subject to cross-examination.
4. The "victim's attorney" represents the general public not the individual victim.
5. No right to appeal.
6. No victim waiting room.

SENTENCING

1. Has no voice in court decisions, pleas, pre-sentence or sentencing.
2. Usually not notified or present at time of sentencing.

SENTENCE

POSTRELEASE

1. Often unsatisfied with results of criminal justice system.
2. May fear retaliation.
3. Continues life with fears, damages, injuries, traumas.
4. Is expected to continue to support system.

In a criminal case, the suspect faces the power of government on the other side. The suspect therefore has certain rights guaranteed to make the fight more balanced: the right to remain silent, the right to counsel, the right to confront witnesses, the right to protection from cruel and unusual punishment, and other rights in the Constitution. But the victim has the government fighting for him or her. As a result, it has usually been thought that the victim does not need legal protections like those available to suspects. Recently, people have begun to question this thinking.

Besides becoming more sensitive to victims and their problems, people have begun to recognize the importance of victims to law enforcement. Without the cooperation of victims, few lawbreakers would be convicted. By giving victims more rights, more people may be encouraged to help the police and the courts.

Looking After the Victim

Victim organizations and some elected officials are working to see that laws are passed to help and to protect crime victims. Some of the proposed laws seek to protect citizens from crime. Others seek to give help to victims and give them a greater voice in the legal system. Here are some examples:

— Provide more judges and courts

— Give longer prison terms for repeat offenders

— Encourage use of burglar alarms

— Deny bail for suspects who are threats to society

— Treat victims with dignity

— Require restitution

— Protect victims from being fired for missing work when appearing in court

— Return victim's stolen property

— Right to information about procedures and status of case

— Right to notice of rescheduled or cancelled hearings

— Right to notice of suspect's release on **bail** or release from prison

— Right to participation in all hearings

— Right to **counsel**

Why do you think victims in many communities do not have these rights now?

YOUR TURN: Proposals for Helping Victims

After reading the proposals above, brainstorm a list of other proposals to add to the list. Using this list of proposals, conduct a debate on the pros and cons of each proposal. You should be prepared to respond to the arguments on the other side. Think about the following questions as you prepare your arguments.

1. What would be the advantages and disadvantages of the proposal? How would it help victims?

2. What problems might occur if this proposal were enacted?

3. Would the proposal be expensive for the government to put into effect? Is it more important than spending money on roads? On schools? On courts for civil cases?

4. Would the proposal help all victims or would it favor certain victims? Is the law fair?

5. Would the proposal violate any constitutional rights of suspects? Would the proposal create a possibility that an innocent person might be convicted?

Which are the best proposals? You may wish to rank the proposals from most important to least important. What have you learned from the debates?

ON YOUR OWN: Expressing Your Views
on Proposals to Help Victims

Contact a legislator to find out what laws dealing with victims are being proposed at the national, state, or local level. Based on what you learned in the debates and discussions, write a letter to a legislator in support of or against a proposal that will affect victims.

10

INFLUENCING GOVERNMENT: LOBBYING

The Meaning of Lobbying

Reprinted by permission of Mrs. Walt Kelly

People are a source of many problems, but they can also be a part of the solution. The two major ways of changing government policy in our republic are by voting and by **lobbying.** Both are rights protected by the U.S. Constitution. The term "lobbying" is not used in the Constitution, but the First Amendment clearly protects the right to influence government decision making:

> Congress shall make no law . . . abridging the freedom of speech or of the press; or of the right of the people peaceably to assemble and to petition the Government for redress of grievances.

Free speech, free press, peaceful assembly, and petition are powerful means to influence government decisions. And people exercise these powers in a variety of ways.

The following letter was sent to the members of a state organization to protect animals:

> Dear Member:
>
> We need your help to pass a new law regulating kennels. As you know, some kennel operators in this state treat animals cruelly and inhumanely. Animals are often crowded into small cages with no room to move around or exercise. The cages are rarely cleaned so the animals have to lie in their own filth. Some kennel operators feed the animals so poorly that a number of dogs have died of starvation!
>
> We think a state law regulating kennels will help prevent this cruel treatment of animals. We are very close to having that state law! The state legislature passed the bill we proposed. But, in order for the bill to become law, the governor must sign it. The governor has received many phone calls from a small group asking the governor to veto this important law. We must respond! Call Jane Roddy, the governor's assistant legislative counsel, at 999-9999 to tell her that you want the governor to sign this bill immediately.
>
> If we animal lovers do not make our voices heard, the governor may bow to pressure and veto the bill.
>
> Remember, we are 25,000 members STRONG. We live in 100 counties and our concerns *do* make a difference. Tell Ms. Roddy. Call her as soon as possible!!
>
> Sincerely,
>
> Pat Clifford
> Director

In writing the letter, the director of the organization was asking members of the organization to be lobbyists. A lobbyist is a person who tries to influence the decisions of elected officials on public policies. The term "lobbyist" comes from seventeenth century England where interested persons would corner legislators in the outer waiting room of the legislature—the lobby.

Anyone can be a lobbyist. Citizen lobbyists are private citizens who lobby public officials for or against changes in the law. Private citizens can lobby government as part of a group or organization or they can lobby as a single individual. People lobby when they care strongly about a particular issue. But not everyone who lobbies does so because of personal feelings about an issue. Some persons lobby because that is their job.

Professional lobbyists are persons hired by businesses, unions, or organizations to influence legislators on issues important to their clients. For example, a lobbyist for an American car manufacturer might be hired to lobby Congress to limit the import of Japanese and other foreign cars. The first paid lobbyists appeared in legislatures in the early nineteenth century. Professional lobbyists work in Washington, D.C., and all fifty state capitals. In 1980 more than fifteen thousand professional lobbyists were in Washington, D.C. These lobbyists spend more than $2 billion annually to influence legislation. In addition, many government bodies (government agencies, city and county legislatures, mayors, and supervisors) have their own lobbyists.

Many people have a negative image of lobbyists. This is because some professional lobbyists use money and favors to influence decision making by public officials. Some legislators vote the way the lobbyists tell them to vote rather than considering the needs of the people. Some lobbyists even help write legislation. Consider the editorial cartoon on the right:

'Why Don't We Just Vote For The Lobbyists?
They Write The Laws More Than The Legislators Do'

© 1982 Engelhardt in the St. Louis Post-Dispatch
— reprinted with permission

To prevent misconduct by lobbyists, state and federal laws regulate lobbying activities. Massachusetts enacted the first law regulating lobbyists in 1890. Other states followed its example. In many states, all lobbyists—both individual citizens and paid professionals—must register with the state before speaking at any **public hearing.** Congress enacted the Federal Regulation of Lobbying Act in 1946. Current federal law requires all persons paid to lobby in Congress to submit reports with the following information:

— The amount of money received and spent for lobbying;

— The names of all persons who received the money;

— The purposes for which the money was spent;

— The names of all magazines or newspapers in which the lobbyist has had articles or editorials published;

— The proposed laws the lobbyist is employed to support or oppose.

YOUR TURN: Legislating Honesty in Lobbying

Review the above information on the federal law on lobbying and answer the following questions:

1. What do you think is the purpose of laws regulating lobbyists?

2. How do you think that requiring lobbyists to provide the information above will affect the lobbying process?

3. What other ways can you think of to control lobbying? Briefly explain your answer.

ON YOUR OWN: Your State Lobbying Law

Find out how lobbyists are regulated in your state. Who is covered by the law — all lobbyists or only professionals? What does the law require lobbyists to do? What are some groups that employ professional lobbyists in your state?

Lobbying Laws and Free Speech

Much of the money used in lobbying is to "buy speech" — that is, to pay for lobbyists' salaries, to print literature, to advertise to get the message to government decision makers, and to build public opinion for a particular policy. Some lobbyists have argued that any attempt to regulate speech violates the First Amendment's protection of freedom of expression. But in a challenge to the 1946 federal law regulating lobbyists, the U.S. Supreme Court upheld the constitutionality of this law. The Supreme Court ruled that Congress was not attempting to prohibit lobbying. The Court said that Congress "wants only to know who is being hired, who is putting up the money, and how much."

Making campaign contributions to candidates for public office is another form of lobbying. In 1971, in response to charges of influence buying, Congress passed the Federal Election Campaign Act to regulate elections for federal offices. The federal law requires:

— Public disclosure of the names of all individual political contributions above $100;

— Public disclosure by political committees and candidates of their receipts and expenditures;

— Limits on the amounts of money that candidates might spend for the purchase of radio and television time;

— Limits on the total amount any candidate for federal office can spend.

Some people strongly opposed the new federal regulations. Like those opposed to the 1946 law, these people believed that any effort to regulate lobbying violated the First Amendment.

YOUR TURN: Case Study on the Federal Election Campaign Act

Read the following case, summarizing *Buckley v. Valeo*, 424 U.S. 1 (1976), and answer the questions that follow.

United States Senator James Buckley, presidential candidate Eugene McCarthy, and the New York Civil Liberties Union filed a lawsuit against the federal government in federal court to challenge the Federal Election Campaign Act. They argued that the strict disclosure laws would have a "chilling effect" on some contributors who did not want their contributions to become publicly known. They also argued that the limits on the amount of money that could be spent for radio and television time and the limits on total spending restricted free speech. The limits were therefore unconstitutional.

In defending the Federal Election Campaign Act, attorneys for the federal government argued that the government has an interest in preventing the buying of elections by big money. They argued that the limits on spending and contributions were fair and equitable. They said the limits helped to equalize the ability of individuals and groups to influence the outcome of elections. According to them, the public interest in keeping the election process fair outweighed the First Amendment free speech argument.

YOU BE THE JUDGE — Answer the following questions:

1. What are the important facts in this case? Who are the parties in the case? What is the problem?

2. What laws and constitutional issues are involved in this case?

3. What are the major arguments for both sides in this case?

4. If you were the judge in this case, what would you decide and why?

5. What are some other ways of resolving this problem?

★★★★★★★★★★★★

Getting the Lobbying Job Done

Lobbyists use many different techniques to promote the interests of the groups for which they work. Following are some of those techniques:

1. Place political advertisements in the news media;

2. Initiate letter-writing campaigns to get hundreds or thousands of letters on an issue written by individuals and sent to their legislators;

3. Get influential persons to send letters and telegrams to legislators;

4. Attend committee hearings to keep informed about the progress of the bill;

5. Testify at public hearings;

6. Provide information for legislative staff members who actually write the bill;

7. Develop pamphlets to be sent to legislators and/or their **constituents;**

8. Work with legislators and their staff members to negotiate changes or **amendments** in proposed laws.

   To be effective, a lobbyist must understand the legislative process. Lobbyists need to know the chairperson and members of the legislative committees to which the bills are assigned. Committee members, particularly the chairperson, are all important for passage of a bill. If a committee chairperson opposes a bill, the bill is unlikely to be reported out of committee. This means the whole legislature will not have a chance to consider it. In some cases a bill could be assigned to one of several committees. Then lobbyists try to get a bill assigned to the committee that is most likely to view the bill the same way they do.

   An effective lobbyist knows everything about an issue. For most issues, that means doing a lot of research. Research can include gathering statistics on the problem, conducting public opinion polls, collecting information on laws in other states or countries, and even performing tests of products. By presenting well-documented research to legislators, lobbyists provide a service to legislators and help their decision making.

THE SKILL OF PERSUASION

   The key to effective lobbying is persuading others to adopt a particular position on an issue. Following are some tips on how to be persuasive in discussing an issue with a legislator.

1. *Do your homework.* Know the facts about the issue. Know the costs and benefits of the proposed law. If possible, find out the legislator's views in advance. Be aware of pressures on the legislator from constituents, other legislators, and other lobbyists.

2. *Plan your opener.* The most important part of any interview is getting off to a good start. Say something friendly instead of jumping right into a long speech on the reason for your call or visit.

3. *Be direct.* Be accurate and honest about the importance of your issue and your opponent's position. Explain your opinion in a strong, direct way, without rambling. Present your position clearly with good supporting information.

4. *Listen as well as talk.* Communication is a two-way street. It is just as important to listen and learn from the legislator as it is to say what you think.

5. *Ask good questions.* Find out where the legislator stands. Prepare your questions in advance: identify the information you want to find out and develop questions that will help you get it. If you want more than a "yes" or "no" response, prepare your questions to get more information. Try to get specific answers. If an answer is vague or incomplete, be ready to probe: "That's interesting. Could you explain that a little more?" or "Let's see, you said. . . . Exactly how do you mean that?"

6. *Look for an opening to come back.* If a question arises that you cannot answer on the spot, do not be afraid to say so. Find the answer if you can and use that as an opener for a return call or visit.

7. *Try to identify your opposition.* The legislator will probably be willing to tell you who else is lobbying on your issue and what the views are. The legislator might be able to suggest other legislators whom you should lobby.

8. *Know your opponent's arguments.* Be prepared to argue effectively against each of your opponent's arguments.

Can you think of any other tips for making a persuasive presentation to a legislator? What are they?

YOUR TURN: Persuading a Legislator

Six students will be selected as legislators. Divide the rest of the class into six groups. Each group will be assigned a proposed law.

Using the tips above, three groups should prepare to lobby *for* their proposed law and three groups should prepare to lobby *against* their proposed law. Each group will present its interview to two legislators.

Legislator	Proposed Law
1. Local legislator	Ban billboards on public streets
2. State representative	Make school year one month longer
3. U.S. Senator	Prohibit sale of handguns

After all the interviews have been completed, the legislators will discuss the following questions:

> What was especially persuasive in the interview?
> What in the interview was not so persuasive?
> Did the students conducting the interview follow the tips for persuasive lobbying?
> Was it clear what information was being sought from the legislator?
> How did the questions help get the information desired?

★★★★★★★★★★★

Individual Citizens Can Make a Difference

One advantage that professional lobbyists often have over citizen lobbyists is their ongoing relationship with legislators and their staffs. But citizen lobbyists can be very effective. The following is a case in point.

A Tennessee doctor became upset over the number of children killed in car accidents because they were not in safety seats. He proposed a law requiring children riding in cars to be in safety seats, and he worked with state legislators to pass the bill. He also worked to educate the public about the law and to push for its enforcement by the state highway patrol. In the first five years after passage of the law, only one child strapped in a safety seat died; that was in a head-on collision with a tractor-trailer.

The doctor and other citizens did a number of things to get the law passed. These included (1) researching statistics of child deaths in car accidents; (2) persuading a legislator to sponsor the bill and to testify at hearings; (3) writing letters to legislators; (4) making phone calls to legislators and support groups; (5) attending legislative hearings; (6) testifying at legislative hearings; (7) writing letters to local newspapers; (8) writing pamphlets to educate the legislators and public about the need for the law; and (9) persuading local, state, and national safety councils, and the American Association of Pediatricians to support the bill. The Tennessee law on car safety seats is a success story. It shows what one determined person can accomplish.

YOUR TURN: The Arguments on Mandatory Child Safety Seats

Read the material below. Then identify each point as either *FOR* or *AGAINST* mandatory safety seat legislation. Using the information in the material, write two letters to a state legislator, one *for* a mandatory safety seat law and one *against* such a law. In writing the letters, be sure to follow these guidelines: (a) state your position clearly in the beginning; (b) clearly explain the points in your favor; (c) explain why the legislator should support your position; and (d) think of other information that would be helpful for you to include in your letter. For example, what has been the result of child restraint laws in states that have enacted them? What has been the cost?

1. A recent study by the Institute for Highway Safety found that the highest death rate among children traveling in cars is among children one year old or younger.

2. In an accident, a child sitting in a parent's lap can be crushed between the car's interior and the parent. Even if the parent is wearing a seat belt, in a 30-MPH collision a ten-pound child exerts a three hundred-pound force against the parent's grip. Even a strong adult would be unable to hold a child in such a situation.

3. A mandatory child restraint law would create a hardship for low income parents who have several children.

4. A mandatory child restraint law would interfere with parental responsibility. Parents have a right under the Constitution to protect the privacy of their home and property.

5. The U.S. Consumer Product Safety Commission requires all child safety seats manufactured since January 1, 1981, to pass federal safety tests that measure the movements of a child in a 35-MPH crash.

6. The American Association of Pediatricians estimates that 90 percent of deaths of young children and 80 percent of the injuries to them could have been avoided if the victims had been secured in properly designed and tested safety seats.

7. Because of their lower height on vehicle seats, infants and small children in crashes are more likely than adult occupants to have head and face contact with lower areas of the instrument panel and front seat backs.

8. In many states, mandatory child restraint laws have been enacted or are pending.

9. A mandatory car restraint law would be a problem for relatives who travel with young children such as aunts, uncles, and grandparents.

10. Many children hate car seats and cry when they are in these restraints. The crying might disturb parents and result in car accidents.

Grassroots Lobbying

In order to pass the mandatory child restraint bill in Tennessee, the doctor who originated the idea needed help. He had to mobilize supporters and then had to influence legislators and other public officials. An outpouring of citizen opinion can influence public officials. For citizen lobbyists, demonstrations of grassroots support by large numbers of constituents may be the most effective lobbying technique.

Whether a person acts alone or as a member of a pressure group, the most important first step is to place the issue in front of the public, Whatever the issue — the appointment of a judge, the placement of a hazardous waste dump near a city, or the appointment of a federal official — public attention is the first priority. Citizen lobbyists also need to get support from any existing organizations or groups.

One way to bring attention to an issue is to get good media coverage. To make sure the story is covered, a press release is generally the best way to begin. The press release should be on the stationery of the group. The following is a good form for a press release:

Name of Contact Person:_____   In the right hand corner
                                           put IMMEDIATE
Address:_____   RELEASE (or release at
                                           such-and-such date)
Phone Number:_____

Begin with a lead sentence that grabs the reader's attention. Then give information on who, what, where, when, and how.

Brief highlights, keeping them short and concise, could be added. One page is generally the preferable length. The news media receive a lot of press releases. Therefore, the press release should include information that attracts the attention of the media.

Sample Press Release

Disabled Veterans for Life

For further information contact: IMMEDIATE RELEASE
Bob Allen
P.O. Box 113047
Wichita, Kansas 67206
758-2097

   Disabled Veterans for Life are holding a wheelchair rally in favor of House Bill 97 at the Governor's Mansion on Friday, February 9. This rally is to demonstrate the importance of the bill to disabled Americans. Veterans in wheelchairs will begin the rally at the Disabled Veterans headquarters. The veterans will roll their wheelchairs down Main Street to the Governor's Mansion.

The public can influence the actions and policies of government officials in a variety of ways. Many television and radio stations offer individuals and pressure groups the opportunity to voice opinions to large audiences. Another way to influence public officials is to put a stamped message on each piece of mail that a group sends to legislators, such as "20 million disabled Americans VOTE!!!"

YOUR TURN: Effectiveness of Lobbying Techniques

1. Read the following newspaper items. Each article highlights one way concerned people have chosen to publicize their issues. Analyze each example and then answer these questions:

   A. What was the group or person trying to accomplish by this method?
   B. How might this method be an advantage or disadvantage to the cause?

2. Name other techniques these groups and individuals could use to publicize their concerns.

   Some lobbyists plan face to face meetings with lawmakers.

AP/Wide World Photos

Lobbyists gather in a corridor of the California State Capital building in Sacramento. A display of photographs helps lobbyists identity the lawmakers they wish to meet with to discuss legislation and other matters of public policy.

Some lobbyists make use of newspaper or magazine columns:

Dear Abby
Why children should be strapped into safety seats

By ABIGAIL VAN BUREN

Dear Abby: Here in New York, the state legislature recently passed a law requiring all car passengers 4 years old and under to be strapped into approved safety seats.

There is a $25 fine for parents who have not equipped their cars as yet, and that $25 goes toward the purchase of a seat. I can't believe all the grumbling and complaining about this law.

We moved here four years ago, leaving behind in Ohio a deep, dark secret we never mention here. Six years ago I was driving with my 6-month-old daughter, unbelted, sitting in her carrier beside me. Five blocks from home, I was broadsided by a mail truck. My car was flipped over twice, and my precious baby girl was tossed around inside like a pingpong ball. She died 72 hours later of massve head injuries. I was told it was a blessing — that she would ave been a vegetable had she lived.

Going home to an empty nursery drove me crazy with guilt. I had always been so careful. I had padded her crib, made sure she had only the safest toys, guarded her with my life and loved her with all my heart. If I had only known what I know now, she would have ridden home from the hospital as a newborn baby in a safety seat instead of in my arms.

We buried the truth with Tina and moved here to escape the memories. No one here knows we ever had a child. My husband finds it too hard to talk about. Since I can't tell the story, I beg you to do it for me, Abby. If it saves only one child's life, Tina's death will not have been in vain.

Learned Too Late

Some lobbyists write letters to the editor:

Joint Custody

Testifying before a House Ways and Means subcommittee, Margaret Heckler, Secretary of Health and Human Services, quoted a Census Bureau estimate that children are due $4 billion a year in child-support payments by delinquent parents. Secretary Heckler spoke for a bill to require states to dock wages as well as federal and state tax refunds of these delinquent parents. Certainly parents who have been ordered to make child support payments must do so.

The same Census Bureau referred to by Ms. Heckler also reported that in more than "95 percent of all single parent homes in the U.S., the mother has custody of the children." Hence, the delinquent parents are fathers. The divorce process is for most people the worst experience they will ever have. The process wherein the mother is awarded custody and left to raise her children by herself is supported and encouraged by society. But we see how difficult it often is for her to cope with the situation. So then we have to create numerous, costly social and psychological services to help her survive. A simpler, more cost-effective solution would be to award custody to both parents.

Recent studies state that children have fewer mental and emotional problems when they have a close personal relationship with their fathers. Other studies show that those fathers with joint custody arrangements that allow free and easy access to their children continue their child support payments.

The current system under which most divorces are granted is not fair to anyone, and the real victim is the child, I urge everyone — men, women, and children, especially children — to write to Dan Rostenkowski, Chairman, House Ways and Means Committee, Suite 1102, Longworth Office Bldg., Washington, D.C. 20515, expressing your views and ideas about divorce. In addition I urge all men who have ever had a problem with visitation or custody arrangements to send their child-support payments for the week of Aug. 15 to Mr. Rostenkowski. Be sure to include the case or cause number as well as the name and address of the proper court so that Mr. Rostenkowski can forward said payment.

James E. Phillips, St. Francis, Wis.

St. Louis Post-Dispatch

Some lobbyists pay newspapers or magazines to publish advertisements:

Can You be Indifferent?

In January of 1970 the President of the United States promised the people "peace with nature." Yet, in the summer of 1970, men were sent forth to murder 60,000 sentient animals: 9,000 for Japan, 9,000 for Canada — and 42,000 ostensibly for the people of the United States.

As president of Friends of Animals, I, Alice Herrington, spent ten days on the Pribilof Islands, our Federal public territory, to observe and report on this massacre of seals. Hour after hour I watched helpless animals being driven inland a mile or more, until their lungs were bursting; watched the clubs being raised over and over as the seals were battered into insensibility. As my eyes watched, my mind recalled the litany of the bureaucrats, remembered their statements that this is mercy killing, done to save the seals from starvation and disease. And then I moved closer to the seals as they grouped together in terror. The men were killing only the healthy seals whose coats would gleam on fashion row. The seal with fish net imbedded in its fur was ignored after only one bash of the club — a bash which removed an eye. And I remembered these same bureaucrats' statement that only 15 out of every 100 seals born survives the first three years. And there they were, the 15 three-year-old seals nature wanted to survive, being crushed at that very moment by employees of the United States Government.

That individual man often engages his lust to kill is apparent. That our society, our government, condones murder for profit is abominable. And then the profit is only for the Fouke Fur Company which holds a monopoly contract with the government; the whole barbaric "program" is subsidized by the tax dollar of the American people.

If you are one who feels, one who recognizes that all life is bound together on this earth, won't you join and ask Congress to pass this law:

A. To permit the Aleut native on the Pribilofs to kill, for their own commercial profit, 18,000 seals per year: the sealskins — not the American dollars — to be delivered to Japan and Canada . . . until the current agreement to kill for those countries runs out.

B. To ban the import into the United States of all products, raw or finished, from marine mammals (seals, whales, walrus, polar bear, otters, etc.).

C. To direct the administration to initiate a truly international agreement to protect marine mammals.

As the prime consumer of the world's resources, we owe it to the world and the coming generations of all species not to abuse the world. Please join and write your representatives in the Congress today, asking them to sponsor this measure.

Committee for Humane Legislation, Inc.
11 West 60th Street
New York, New York 10023

I cannot be indifferent. I enclose my donation of $_____(payable to CHL) to aid the passage of animal protective legislation. Please add my name to your mailing list.

Name

Address

City, State, Zip Code   CHL-I

Reprinted with permission of the Committee for Humane Legislation, Inc.

YOUR TURN: Planning a Lobbying Campaign

Select one of the following issues or develop one of your own. As a group, develop strategies for mobilizing public opinion about your issue. Develop a lobbying plan setting out specific lobbying strategies. Number the strategies in the order you would perform them. Write a press release about any event in your lobbying plan. Present your plan to the class.

ISSUE A:

Your group opposes the appointment of a new director for the State Office of Mental Health Services. You are opposed to her appointment because you feel that she believes in putting patients in mental hospitals. Your group believes in letting people with mental problems live in community settings with proper support services.

ISSUE B

Your group wants a new prison to relieve serious overcrowding of prisons in your state. The legislature has passed a bill to **appropriate** money for a new prison. The governor has the bill and is considering vetoing the bill.

ISSUE C

Your group wants the state legislature to appropriate money for driver's education courses.

ISSUE D:

Your group favors passage of a local ordinance requiring helmets for motorcycle riders. You are trying to influence your city legislators.

ISSUE E:

Your issue.

QUESTION FOR DISCUSSION:

How are the strategies your group used particularly suited to your issue?

ON YOUR OWN: Effective Lobbying Techniques

Write to groups that lobby to ask them to identify their most successful lobbying techniques. At the same time, write to legislators and other government officials to ask them to identify the lobbying techniques that are most effective in influencing decision making. Compare the answers from both groups.

11

INFLUENCING GOVERNMENT: VOTING

Empowering the Powerless: The Right to Vote

> Our government and other institutions have grown so large and complicated that most people feel powerless. They complain of being "planned upon." They are seldom consulted or asked for ideas about their own future.
>
> Alvin Toffler, *Future Shock*

Almost daily, citizens echo Alvin Toffler's description of feeling powerless: "I'm tired of all these taxes—sales tax, income tax, property tax, and on and on—they take my money and I have nothing to say about it" or "People running the country don't really care what happens to me." How can people make sure government cares about their opinions? How can people influence government decisions about taxation and other matters?

In some countries people feel they can only influence their government by overthrowing it. In the United States, however, people can affect government without resorting to violence. Two of the major means of influencing government are the right to lobby and the right to vote. These rights are protected by the Constitution.

Every citizen can lobby and vote. People lobby by writing letters to government officials, by talking and persuading others to write letters to lawmakers, and by attending and testifying before legislative committees. Lobbyists communicate with government officials in an attempt to influence public policy. By voting, citizens attempt to elect officials to represent their points of view on public issues. People also vote to express opinions on issues. In many states, voters can vote directly on public issues by **initiative** and/or **referendum**.

Voting is a means of participating in the decision making process. Voters share in shaping history. History is full of examples of votes shaping events. For example, votes cast for Abraham Lincoln in 1860 helped to lead the nation on a far different course than that offered by Lincoln's opponents: Stephen Douglas, John Breckenridge, and

© 1972 United Feature Syndicate, Inc.

John Bell. Lincoln was the only candidate to firmly oppose the expansion of slavery. Lincoln said, "There is a judgment and a feeling against slavery in this nation, which has cast at least a million and a half of votes."

People exercise the right to vote in a number of ways before they ever enter a formal voting booth. Young people vote for team captains, elect student council representatives, and sometimes even vote on school or classroom rules. Make a mental list of the times that you have voted?

Read the cartoon on the previous page. What is Marcy saying about the power of voting?

Who Can Vote?

Specific voting laws are the responsibility of state governments. The United States Constitution protects and extends the right to vote to millions of citizens. Pages 13 through 16 of this book detail the history of the right to vote in this country.

The following are the constitutional cornerstones of the right to vote:

Fifteenth Amendment
(ratified, 1870)

Extends the right to vote to black males.

Nineteenth Amendment
(ratified, 1920)

Extends the right to vote to women.

Twenty-Third Amendment
(ratified, 1961)

Extends the right to vote to qualified persons living in the District of Columbia.

Twenty-Fourth Amendment
(ratified, 1964)

Protects the right to vote of persons who cannot afford to pay a poll tax.

Twenty-Sixth Amendment
(ratified, 1971)

Extends the right to vote to persons eighteen or older.

State constitutions, federal statutes, and state laws have extended the right to vote as well. As a result, almost all states have the following general qualifications for voting. A person must be:

1. A citizen of the United States;

2. At least eighteen years of age; and

3. A resident of the community in which he or she wants to vote.

In other words, fourteen year olds cannot vote. Persons living in Iowa cannot vote in Illinois. Noncitizens cannot vote. Why not?

The citizenship requirement for voting is very basic and broad. What is a citizen? The Fourteenth Amendment states, "All persons born or naturalized in the United States . . . are citizens of the United States and of the State wherein they reside." Anyone born in the United States or with parents who are United States citizens is automatically a citizen. Persons born in other countries who live in the United States can become citizens through **naturalization.**

To become a naturalized citizen, a person must meet the following qualifications set by Congress: must be eighteen years of age; must have resided in the U.S. for five years; must be able to read and write; must pass a citizenship test requiring knowledge of the history and principles of American government; must take an oath of allegiance to the United States; and must renounce allegiance to his or her former country.

U.S. citizens and those eligible for citizenship have an interest in the affairs and decisions of the U.S. government and their local communities. Some might say that people from other nations also have an interest in the decisions of the U.S. government, and therefore, they should be able to vote in U.S. elections. But voting is a privilege of citizenship. A citizen of another country who lives in the United States may vote in the other country but not in the United States. Citizenship and residency are related requirements. An analogy with school student council elections illustrates these requirements. Should students from another school be able to vote in student council elections in your school? It is reasonable to restrict voting in student council elections to students in the school electing the student council. Similarly, restricting voting in Iowa, for example, to citizens residing in Iowa is also reasonable.

The age requirement is also considered reasonable. It is impossible to test everyone in the country to see if he or she is competent to vote. Therefore, the law arbitrarily assumes that when people reach a certain age, they are competent to vote. Until the ratification of the Twenty-Sixth Amendment, many states, restricted voting to citizens twenty-one or older. Many lawmakers thought that twenty-one-year-olds were likely to be more mature and better informed than those under twenty-one.

Other lawmakers believed that twenty-one was too high an age limit. They believed that persons eighteen to twenty years old could be just as mature and well informed as a twenty-one-year old. On March 8, 1971, Congress passed and sent to the states for ratification the Twenty-Sixth Amendment. The Twenty-Sixth Amendment states, "The right of citizens of the United States, who are eighteen years of age or older, to vote shall not be denied or abridged by the United States or by any state on account of age." By July 5, 1971, thirty-nine of the fifty state legislatures had ratified the Twenty-Sixth Amendment. Do you think the Twenty-Sixth Amendment prohibits states from lowering the voting age below eighteen?

YOUR TURN: Are They Eligible to Vote and Why?

Read each of the situations below. Then answer the following questions.

1. Identify each person who *is* eligible to vote. Give at least one reason why this person is eligible to vote.

2. Identify each person in the situation who *is not* eligible to vote. State why the person is not eligible.

3. In your opinion, should the laws be changed in order to give the ineligible person the right to vote? Briefly explain your answer. If you believe the law should be changed, explain how the law should be changed.

Situation 1

John, age nineteen, and Josie, age seventeen, are both enrolled in Ms. Bright's American Government class. Ms. Bright always urges students to learn about government and recognize the impact of government on their daily lives. Ms. Bright also encourages students to take an active role in community affairs by lobbying and, when possible, voting. Josie is a well-informed student. She writes editorials for the school newspaper on contemporary issues such as the military draft, the equal rights amendment, and nuclear power. Ms. Bright has even said, "Josie is better informed than most voters I know."

John, however, thinks American Government is boring; he rarely listens to the news and almost never reads a newspaper. He told Ms. Bright, "I registered to vote because you gave us extra credit, but I've never voted and I don't plan to. My vote is not going to make any difference anyway."

Situation 2

Josea, Angel, and Carlos are all twenty-five-years-old. They came to the United States from Mexico. Carlos entered the United States legally. Angel and Jose are illegal aliens. This means they entered the United States illegally. All three work in a small textile factory in New Mexico. They have worked in this factory for seven years. They have a small home and they pay their taxes.

After five years, Carlos applied for naturalization to become a citizen of the United States. Carlos is now a citizen. Carlos enjoys the rights and privileges of citizenship. Angel and Josea would like to have some say about government decisions.

Situation 3

Eddie, age sixty-six, and Eve Long, age seventy, have been retired for the last six years. The Longs own a home in Detroit, Michigan, where they were born and raised, but they spend most of the winter in their condominium in Florida. Their official residence is in Michigan but they pay property taxes in both Michigan and Florida. When the Longs make their winter move to Florida in mid-October, they discover that a proposal to increase local property taxes in their Florida community will be on the November ballot.

Matt and Marge Manners are in their late fifties and live near the Long's winter home. The Manners are life-long residents of Florida. The Manners have family in other states but their home is in Florida.

Voter Registration

In most states, persons who are qualified to vote must first register to vote before they can actually vote in an election. Voting is at least a two-step process. First, a person registers (signs up) within a set time prior to an election. Then at the next election the person may vote.

Laws governing voter registration vary from state to state. All states provide some central locations for registering, such as city hall, county courthouses, and election boards. Some states permit registration by mail.

YOUR TURN: Register to Vote

Examine the voter registration form on the following page. After reading the registration form, answer the following questions:

1. What are three requirements that must be met before a person can register to vote in Montgomery County, Maryland?

2. Who is the applicant?

3. What is his political party?

4. Why must applicants list a political party on their voter registration form?

5. Can the applicant vote as soon as this form is filled out? Explain.

6. How can persons who have been convicted of a crime find out if they are eligible to vote?

7. Where can a person get a voter registration form in your community?

ON YOUR OWN: Voting Requirements in Your State

Contact your local library, the Board of Election Commissioners, the League of Women Voters, or a state legislator to assist you in answering the following questions:

1. What are the basic qualifications for voting in your state?

2. Are the qualifications established by the state constitution or by state statute?

3. Can persons convicted of a crime vote in your state? Briefly explain the answer.

4. Where can persons register to vote? Are any special provisions made for persons unable to register due to illness, disability, or other situations that keep a person from normal means of registration? What are they?

5. How may persons vote by absentee ballot in your state?

Excel in Civics

Sample Voter Registration Form:

BOARD OF SUPERVISORS OF ELECTIONS for Montgomery County, Maryland	Box 333, Rockville, MD 20850 Telephone: 279-1507

INSTRUCTIONS

DO NOT USE THIS FORM if you are already registered to vote in Montgomery County, Maryland. If you are unsure of your registration status, call the elections office, 279-1507.
USE THIS FORM to register to vote in Montgomery County if you are

- A citizen of the United States.
- At least 17 years old and will be 18 years old on or before the next General Election.
- A resident of Montgomery County.
- Not convicted of a disqualifying crime.
- Not under guardianship for mental disability.

GIVING FALSE INFORMATION TO PROCURE VOTER REGISTRATION IS **PERJURY** AND IS PUNISHABLE BY IMPRISONMENT FOR NOT LESS THAN TEN YEARS.

This application must be received by the elections office no later than 9 P.M. on the fifth Monday prior to an election in order for you to be registered to vote in that election.

If your application is received on time and if it is complete, it will be processed and a Voter Notification form mailed to you. YOU ARE NOT A REGISTERED VOTER UNTIL YOU RECEIVE THAT NOTIFICATION.

The Board of Supervisors of Elections is not responsible if application is late or registration information is incomplete or inaccurate.

PLEASE COMPLETE 1 THROUGH 14:

1. Daytime Telephone number (in the event we need clarifying information)_____ *none*

2. NAME (PRINT)

LAST	FIRST	MIDDLE
HOLLOMAN	*CURTIS*	*ROY*

3. RESIDENCE (PRINT)

STREET NO.	STREET	APT. NO.
717	*GREENLEAF AVENUE*	

4. CITY OR TOWN	5. ZIP	6. SEX (M or F)	9. PARTY AFFILIATION CHOICE (CHECK ONE)
Rockville, MD	*20850*	*M*	DEMOCRAT _____ REPUBLICAN _____
7. DATE OF BIRTH (MONTH-DAY-YEAR) *9/27/51*	8. PLACE OF BIRTH (STATE OR FOREIGN COUNTRY) *NORTH CAROLINA*		OTHER (SPECIFY) *Independent* DECLINES TO AFFILIATE_____

DO NOT WRITE IN SPACE BELOW
DATE OF REGISTRATION

DIST.	PREC.

ID NUMBER

I AM A CITIZEN OF THE UNITED STATES AND A RESIDENT OF MONTGOMERY COUNTY, MARYLAND. I HAVE NOT BEEN CONVICTED OF A DISQUALIFYING CRIME. I AM NOT UNDER GUARDIANSHIP FOR MENTAL DISABILITY.
UNDER PENALTIES OF PERJURY, I DO SOLEMNLY SWEAR (OR AFFIRM) THAT THE INFORMATION SET FORTH HEREON ABOUT MY PLACE OF RESIDENCE, NAME, PLACE OF BIRTH, CRIMINAL OFFENSES, QUALIFICATIONS AS A VOTER, AND MY RIGHT TO REGISTER AND VOTE UNDER THE LAWS OF THIS STATE IS TRUE.

10. _____ *Curtis Ray Holloman* _____
(SIGNATURE OF APPLICANT)

11. PRIOR REGISTRATION. Have you ever registered to vote here or anywhere in the United States before?
Yes _____ No *✓*

12. If yes, complete the following:
Name on last registration_____

Address on last registration_____

(CITY OR TOWN)	(COUNTY)	(STATE)

Party affiliation on last registration_____

13. Date of birth_____ *9/27/61*

14. Signature_____ *Curtis Roy Holloman*

RESIDENCE. Registering to vote in this county is declaration of residence in this county and state, and authorization to cancel any prior registration in another Maryland locality or another state.
PARTY AFFILIATION. Only voters affiliated with the Democratic or Republican Party vote in the primary election of their party. All registered voters vote in a general election and in nonpartisan Board of Education elections.
DISQUALIFYING CRIME. Contact Montgomery County Board of Supervisors of Elections, 279-1507 if you have been convicted of a crime.

The Vanishing Voter

More people appear to take an interest in one afternoon of football at the Super Bowl than in examining the candidates and issues and casting votes that may affect lives for generations. Ask someone to describe the strengths and weaknesses of Super Bowl teams and ask whom they favor to win. Then ask this person to describe the strength and weaknesses of the candidates for president, or Congress, or state or local offices. Ask whom they favor to win and why. What can be done to generate as much enthusiasm for voting as for sporting events?

Since 1960, voter participation by persons eligible to vote has steadily declined throughout the United States. The following illustrates this steady decline:

1960 — 65 percent of the voting-age population (VAP) voted in the Kennedy-Nixon presidential election

1964 — 63 percent of the VAP voted in the Johnson-Goldwater presidential election

1968 — 60 percent of the VAP voted in the Nixon-Humphrey presidential election

1972 — 55 percent of the VAP voted in the Nixon-McGovern presidential election

1976 — 54 percent of the VAP voted in the Carter-Ford presidential election

1980 — 53 percent of the VAP voted in the Reagan-Carter presidential election

1984 — 53 percent of the VAP voted in the Reagan-Mondale presidential election

In each of these elections, a *minority* of the voting-age population actually elected a president. For example, in 1980 Ronald Reagan was elected by 26 percent of the voting-age population.

Even fewer people vote in off-year congressional elections (that is, elections for the U.S. Senate and House of Representatives in non-presidential election years). Still fewer voters participate in local or special elections. Between 1960 and 1978, participation in off-year congressional elections fell from 47 percent of the voting-age population to 37 percent. This means that in many congressional elections only 20 percent of the voting age population elects members of the U.S. House of Representative and Senate. In local and special elections, less than 10 per cent of the voting age population may elect a member of the local city council or determines the fate of a school bond issue. A few votes can make a great difference in determining the decisions of governments. Yet, in almost every state, more needs to be done to encourage voter registration and participation.

YOUR TURN: Examining Voter Registration and Participation

Examine the chart on the following page and answer the following questions:

1. a. How many people were registered to vote in your state in 1980?

   b. What was the voting-age population (VAP) in your state in 1980?

   c. How many people actually voted in the 1980 election in your state?

2. How would you rank your state's voter participation in the 1980 election?

   High = more than 65 percent of voting-age population voted
   Average = 50-60 percent of voting-age population voted
   Low = Less than 50 percent of voting-age population voted

3. a. In your opinion, why are more people not registered to vote?

   b. In your opinion, why do registered voters not bother to vote?

ON YOUR OWN: Analyzing Recent Voter Trends

Using the library and/or the League of Women Voters, or the local or state Board of Election Commissioners, find the answers to the following questions. Compare your answers to the information found in your answer to question #1 above.

1. How many people were registered to vote in your state for the most recent off-year Congressional election (for example, 1986)?

REGISTRATION AND TURNOUT IN THE 1980 ELECTION BY STATE

State	Voting-Age Population (VAP)*	Number Registered	% of VAP Registered	Number Voted	% of Registered voters Voting	% of VAP Voting
Alabama	2,702,000	2,277,789	84%	1,341,929	58.9%	49.7%
Alaska	257,000	258,742**	100%	158,445	61.2%	61.7%
Arizona	1,779,000	1,121,169	63%	873,945	77.9%	49.1%
Arkansas	1,562,000	1,185,902	76%	837,582	70.6%	53.6%
California	16,956,000	11,361,020	67%	8,587,063	75.6%	50.6%
Colorado	2,050,000	1,434,257	55%	1,184,415	82.6%	57.8%
Connecticut	2,321,000	1,719,108	74%	1,406,285	81.8%	60.6%
Delaware	420,000	300,600	72%	235,900	78.5%	56.2%
Florida	6,876,000	4,809,721	70%	3,686,930	76.7%	53.6%
Georgia	3,629,000	2,466,786	68%	1,596,917	64.7%	44.0%
Hawaii	657,000	402,795	61%	303,287	75.3%	46.2%
Idaho	634,000	581,006	92%	437,431	75.3%	69.0%
Illinois	8,046,000	6,230,332	74%	4,749,721	76.2%	59.0%
Indiana	3,849,000	2,944,311	64%	2,242,033	76.1%	58.2%
Iowa	2,093,000	1,746,725	83%	1,317,661	75.4%	63.0%
Kansas	1,756,000	1,290,539	73%	979,795	75.9%	55.8%
Kentucky	2,532,000	1,824,469	72%	1,294,627	71.0%	51.1%
Louisiana	2,780,000	2,015,402	72%	1,548,591	76.8%	55.7%
Maine	790,000	759,978	96%	523,011	68.8%	66.2%
Maryland	3,039,000	2,064,883	68%	1,540,496	74.6%	50.7%
Massachusetts	4,298,000	3,142,908	73%	2,524,298	80.3%	58.7%
Michigan	6,557,000	5,725,713	87%	3,909,725	68.3%	59.6%
Minnesota	2,957,000	2,787,277	94%	2,051,980	73.6%	69.4%
Mississippi	1,650,000	1,484,140	90%	892,620	60.1%	54.1%
Missouri	3,569,000	2,845,023	80%	2,099,824	73.8%	58.8%
Montana	560,000	496,402	89%	363,952	73.3%	65.6%
Nebraska	1,138,000	856,182	75%	640,854	74.9%	56.3%
Nevada	533,000	297,318	56%	247,885	83.4%	46.5%
New Hampshire	657,000	553,236	84%	383,990	69.4%	58.4%
New Jersey	5,398,000	3,761,428	70%	2,975,684	79.1%	55.1%
New Mexico	869,000	652,687	75%	456,971	70.0%	52.6%
New York	12,900,000	7,869,587	61%	6,201,959	78.8%	48.1%
North Carolina	4,055,000	2,774,844	68%	1,855,833	66.9%	45.8%
North Dakota	469,000	***	—	301,545	—	64.3%
Ohio	7,701,000	5,887,488	76%	4,283,603	72.8%	55.6%
Oklahoma	2,131,000	1,469,320	69%	1,149,708	78.2%	54.0%
Oregon	1,909,000	1,569,222	82%	1,181,516	75.3%	61.9%
Pennsylvania	8,652,000	5,754,287	67%	4,561,501	79.3%	52.7%
Rhode Island	687,000	547,472	80%	416,072	76.0%	60.6%
South Carolina	2,069,000	1,235,521	60%	894,071	72.4%	43.2%
South Dakota	485,000	447,508	92%	327,703	73.2%	67.6%
Tennessee	3,205,000	2,359,002	74%	1,617,616	68.6%	50.5%
Texas	9,648,000	6,639,661	69%	4,541,636	68.4%	47.1%
Utah	901,000	781,711	87%	604,222	77.3%	67.1%
Vermont	359,000	311,919	87%	213,299	68.4%	59.4%
Virginia	3,817,000	2,302,405	60%	1,866,032	81.0%	48.9%
Washington	2,978,000	2,236,603	75%	1,742,394	77.9%	58.5%
West Virginia	1,357,000	1,034,546	76%	737,715	71.3%	54.4%
Wisconsin	3,446,000	***	—	2,273,221	—	66.0%
Wyoming	335,000	219,423	65%	176,713	80.5%	52.8%
District of Columbia	475,000	288,837	61%	175,237	60.6%	36.8%
National	160,491,000	—	—	86,515,443	—	53.9%

*U.S. Bureau of the Census Current Population Reports, Series P-25, #879, Projections of the Population of Voting Age for States: November 1980, (includes military and insitutionalized persons).

**See text page 2.　***No statewide registration.

Information complied by the Election Research Center, Washington, D.C. and reprinted with permission.

2. How many people actually voted in your state's most recent off-year Congressional elections?

3. How does this turnout compare to the 1980 registration and turnout in your state?

4. How many people were registered and how many actually voted in your state in the 1984 presidential election?

5. How does this turnout compare to the 1980 registration and turnout in your state?

6. What are some reasons for the differences in turnout in your state in the 1980 and 1984 presidential elections?

7. How many people are registered in your local community? How many actually voted in the most recent local or special election?

Young Voter Participation: A Right and Responsibility

> No right is more precious in a free country than that of having a voice in the election of those who make the laws under which, as good citizens, we must live. Other rights, even the most basic, are illusory if the right to vote is undermined.
>> Majority opinion written by U.S. Supreme Court Justice Hugo Black, *Wesberry v. Sanders*, 376 U.S. 1 (1964)

Voting is not only a right, it is a responsibility. Voting has been called the "great equalizer." That is because the vote of the poorest citizen is equal to the vote of the richest citizen. Yet many eligible voters fail to exercise this fundamental right. In 1980 more than 160 million people were eligible to vote, but only half, or 85 million people, voted.

There are millions of eligible voters between eighteen and twenty-one. Yet, since the passage of the Twenty-Sixth Amendment, only about one out of three eligible young people bother to vote. The eligible voters between eighteen and twenty-one have the lowest record of voter registration and voting compared to other age groups.

Do you know anyone between eighteen and twenty-one who is not registered to vote? Why do not more young people exercise their right to vote?

YOUR TURN: Too Young to Vote?

Read each of the statements below. Then choose the letter that best expresses *your* opinion about the statement. Use the following code:

SA = Strongly   A = Agree   U = Undecided
      Agree

          D = Disagree   SD = Strongly
                                      Disagree

Briefly explain your answer after each statement. Survey other students in school and compare their opinions with yours.

1. Most eighteen to twenty-one-year-olds are too immature to vote.

2. The voting age should be raised to twenty-one because persons twenty-one and older are more responsible and better informed than those under twenty-one.

3. Most young people do not vote because they have not had much practice or experience voting.

4. Most young people believe voting is a waste of time because their one vote is not going to make much difference.

5. The voting age should be lowered to sixteen or seventeen because many sixteen and seventeen-year-olds know as much about candidates and issues as persons eighteen or older.

6. Every student should be required to take and pass a course on the importance of voting.

★★★★★★★★★★★

Improving Voter Participation

Your vote can make a difference. A number of critical elections would have turned out differently if just one more person in each precinct had voted the other way. For example, it is claimed that if only one more voter per precinct had voted for Richard Nixon in 1960, Nixon would have been elected president at that time. And in 1968, if only one more voter per precinct had voted for Hubert Humphrey, Humphrey would have been elected president. United States senators have been elected by fewer than fifty votes in some states. In 1982 thirteen congressional elections were decided by fewer than fifteen hundred votes. In 1982 some candidates actually received more votes at the polls than their opponents, but they lost the elections because their opponents received more **absentee votes.**

Your vote *can* make a difference. Your vote can help decide who is elected and therefore help determine government policy. Your vote can mean more aid for education or more money for the military. Yet, many people still refuse to vote.

One reason people do not vote is that they have to register first. In 1963 the Presidential Commission on Registration and Voting concluded that the major reason for non-voting was restrictive voter registration laws. The commission made the following recommendations to improve voter participation:

— Each state should set up a commission on registration and voting participation, or . . . survey in detail its election law and practices.

— Local residency requirement should not exceed 30 days.

— New state residents should be allowed to vote for President.

— Voter registration should extend as close to election day as possible, and should not end more than 3 or 4 weeks before election day.

— **Literacy tests** should be abolished.

— Voting by 18 year olds should be considered by the states.

— The right to vote should be extended to those living on federal reservations (that is, native Americans, living on reservations).

— The **poll tax** as a qualification for voting should be eliminated.

As a result of the Voting Rights Act of 1964, federal court decisions, the Twenty-Fourth and Twenty-Sixth Amendments, and various state laws, all of these recommendations have been implemented. Yet, voter participation has continued to decline.

The Committee for the Study of the American Electorate has recently analyzed nonvoting in the United States. The committee is a bipartisan group of civic, educational, labor, business, and political leaders.

Their analysis indicates that many eligible voters do not register and vote for the following reasons:

— They are not interested in voting;

— They do not believe their vote makes a difference;

— They believe there is very little difference in the candidates and therefore the results will not make much difference in the direction of government.

These same studies confirm that more people vote when they believe their vote will make a difference.

For example, in the 1983 election for mayor of Chicago, nearly 89 percent of the registered voters voted. Many people say such a high turnout occurred because of a clear difference in the candidates' views on major issues and a belief among voters that the election was important and would be close. Harold Washington, the Democratic candidate, ran on a platform promising major changes and reform of city government. Bernard Epton, the Republican candidate, promised not to make major changes and urged voters to elect him "before it's too late." On April 12, 1983, a record number of voters ventured to the polls—1,291,858. Washington received 668,176 votes, or 51.7 percent of the votes cast. It was estimated that more than 100,000 of the votes were cast by newly registered voters. As one political observer noted, "The Washington campaign created a sense of excitement and optimism about the possibilities of power in people who had given up on the political system." Clearly, those voters thought their vote would make a difference.

YOUR TURN: Increasing Voter Participation

Divide the class into groups. Each group should be assigned one of the following proposals (bills) for increasing voter participation.

Each group should read and study the assigned proposal. Then answer the following questions:

1. Would this bill be likely to increase voter registration and voting? Briefly explain your answer.

2. Which, if any, of the commission recommendations on page 206 does the bill adopt?

3. What is at least one negative aspect of the bill?

4. What is at least one positive aspect of the bill?

5. If you were voting on this bill, how would you vote, and why?

Example:

Bill #X   A law requiring automatic registration of all persons of voting-age in the population. The state government will record all births and birth dates, and compile them in a voter data bank. Whenever a citizen becomes eighteen, the data bank indicates to all election officials that this person meets the state age qualifications for voting. This person may vote in all elections as long as he or she has some proof of residency (for example, a driver's license). All polling places will have computer terminals with access to the state voting data bank. All citizens eighteen or older would automatically be eligible. The election judges in the polling place will only need to verify the residency requirement.

Possible answers to questions:

1. Yes, this bill would result in almost 100 percent voter registration and, therefore, may increase the likelihood of voting since eligible voters would not have to register first.

2. It does not adopt any specific recommendation but it meets the general purpose of eliminating restrictive voter registration laws.

3. Adoption of this proposal would increase the role of "big government" and might lead to abuse of the data bank information by other government departments (for example, the Selective Service System might use the information to identify those who failed to register for the military draft when they became eighteen).

4. This proposal makes voting an easy one-step process. The formal registration process would be eliminated and the eligible voter would only have to be concerned about actually voting.

5. You decide!

Bills to be studied by small groups:

Bill #1 A law permitting same-day registration for voting. All persons wishing to vote may register and vote on election day by demonstrating proof of age and residency and by swearing that they are citizens of the United States. Upon meeting these requirements, persons will be permitted to vote in the election.

Bill #2 A law making all state and federal elections official holidays. Any eligible voter failing to vote will be subject to a fine.

Bill #3 A law establishing weekends, Saturday and Sunday, as official election days. All elections would be held over a two-day weekend and the polls would be open from 7 A.M. to 7 P.M. on both Saturday and Sunday.

Bill #4 A law to extend the hours that polls will be open. The polls would open at 5 A.M. and close at midnight, permitting eligible voters to vote at anytime during those hours.

Bill #5 A law authorizing the Election Commission to hire and deputize election commissioners to go door-to-door to verify the accuracy of the voter registration lists by checking each address with the name(s) on the registration list. The commissioners would be authorized to register all unregistered voters right at the door. Registration postcards will be distributed where no one answers. Eligible but unregistered voters will have an opportunity to complete the registration cards and mail to the Election Commission. The returned postcard will serve as the voter's registration.

Bill #6 A law requiring the following words to appear below the list of candidates for an office: 'None of the Above is Acceptable.' Any eligible voter may vote against all candidates for the same office by placing an X or punching the appropriate square before the words 'None of the Above.' If 'None of the Above' receives a plurality of the votes cast, a new election will be scheduled and additional candidates will have an opportunity to file and campaign for this office.

ON YOUR OWN: A Survey on Voting

Interview at least five people aged eighteen or older and ask them to answer the following questions:

1. VOTER REGISTRATION AND PARTICIPATION — Which of the following reasons helps to explain why all eligible voters are not registered and why they do not vote?

   a. Apathy — Most people who are not registered do not care about voting. They are not interested in politics.

   b. Alienation — Most people who are not registered and do not vote do not believe their votes make a difference. They believe that voters have little choice in elections so they do not bother to register or to vote.

   c. Registration and voting process is too difficult — Many people do not know how to register. They believe it is probably too difficult and time-consuming. Other registered voters confused by new voting machines and procedures. To avoid confusion they do not bother to vote.

   d. Other reasons.

2. INCREASING VOTER REGISTRATION — Which of the following suggestions would you recommend to increase the number of registered voters? (You may choose more than one.)

   a. Same-day registration — Voters may register the same day as they vote.

   b. Postcard registration — Election officials send postcards to each household; to register, voters would just tear off and return the card with their signature.

   c. Automatic registration — Using date of birth information from county records or Social Security, everyone becomes automatically registered at age eighteen.

   d. Keep the current process for registration.

   e. Other suggestions.

3. INCREASING VOTER PARTICIPATION — What can be done to increase the number of voters? (You may choose more than one.)

   a. Make national election days official holidays and fine anyone who fails to vote.

b. Have elections over a two-day weekend (for example, polls would be open from 7 A.M. to 7 P.M. on Saturday and Sunday).

c. Extend the number of hours the polls will be open.

d. Increase awareness among citizens of the importance of voting by media efforts (for example, television and radio commercials) and by education campaigns (for example, every high school student participates in a mock election using actual voting machines and procedures).

e. Give voters more choice on the ballots (for example, make it easier for third and fourth parties to get on the ballot).

f. Keep things as they are — those that care enough will vote.

g. Other suggestions.

4. What should be done to better inform citizens of the importance of voting?

After sharing your survey results, write an article for the school or local newspaper reporting the findings.

Technology May Change the Future of Voting

Maybe more people would vote if it were as simple as making a phone call. Many experts believe that today's technology provides an opportunity for more direct participation in government decision making. The telephone, two-way television sets, and home computers are examples of the technology that could be used to increase voter participation. For example, the telephone could be used to record a vote for a candidate, or *for* or *against* an issue. To protect this process from abuse, the voter would be given a code word and would make a voice imprint of that word prior to the election. On election day the voter would dial a special number. A recording would provide the caller with all the necessary information and the voter would then identify his or her voice by giving the code word. After the voice imprint is verified, the voter would vote on the candidates or issues by stating clearly his or her candidate or issue preference.

211

Television is another form of technology that may be used for voting in the future. The two-way cube now used by some cable television subscribers provides voters with the opportunity to vote for candidates or speak out on proposed legislation. For example, a voter could view a debate on a bill before the U.S. House of Representatives. After the debate, the home viewer could register his or her views on the bills by teletype. These views would go directly to a computer in the office of their congressional representative. The representative could then review the **constituent's** views immediately prior to voting on the bill. The voter would be given a confidential code in order to protect the system from abuse (that is, the voter would first punch in his or her code number and then be given clearance to vote by cube).

These changes are possible. Because of the enormous costs of conducting elections today, many believe that such changes may be economically, socially, and politically acceptable.

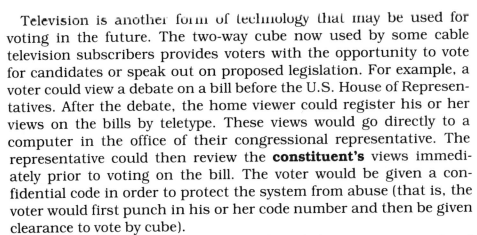

YOUR TURN: Should Voting Laws Change as Technology Changes?

Read the following bill called Televote. The bill would change the voting law to make use of new technology.

TELEVOTE BILL

A law to provide all eligible voters with the means of voting by telephone in all elections conducted by the state. This will not immediately replace normal voting procedures at designated polls but will serve as an alternative means of voting. To guard against voter fraud or abuse, voters wishing to vote by telephone would make a voice imprint for the Election Commission and each voter would be given a code name and number for use in actual voting. The voice imprint and the code are entered into the statewide voter databank. Every polling place will be equipped with computer terminals with access to the statewide voter databank. When a voter casts a vote by telephone or at the local polls, it is automatically recorded in the statewide databank.

The teacher will select six students who will testify on the Televote proposal—three students as witnesses *for* Televote and three students as witnesses *against* Televote before the state legislature's

Election Committee. The remainder of the class will represent members of the state legislature's Election Committee.

Follow these steps in preparing for this hearing:

1. Each student chosen to be a witness should read the given witness statement. This testimony is provided as an informational resource. Students should testify in their own words *for* or *against* the Televote bill.

2. While witnesses prepare to testify, the remaining students should meet in small groups. Each small group should be assigned one witness whom they will be responsible for questioning as members of the legislature's Elections Committee. Each small group should then read the witness's testimony and develop a list of at least five questions to ask its respective witnesses based on the given testimony.

3. The teacher should then arrange for the formal hearing. The teacher should write the proposed bill on the chalkboard. The following steps are recommended:
   a. Call the three witnesses for the Televote bill.
   b. Each witness should identify who he or she is (name and occupation). Each witness may give an opening statement to the class (the members of the Elections Committee).
   c. The members of the small group assigned to question a particular witness should ask its witness the questions they have listed. Members of the group may need to adjust their questions as needed as the witness gives his or her opening statement and answers questions.
   d. After the three witnesses for the bill have testified, call the three witnesses against the bill. Follow the same procedures as those outlined in steps a, b, and c.

4. After all witnesses have testified, the teacher should ask for other questions or comments that anyone wishes to make on the proposed legislation. Allow approximately 10–15 minutes for this closing discussion and/or debate.

5. The teacher should ask the committee members (the class other than the witnesses) to vote *for* or *against* the proposed Televote legislation. The teacher should record the votes as they are cast on the chalkboard near the stated bill.

213

WITNESSES *FOR* THE TELEVOTE LEGISLATION.

Witness #1 — Professor of Political Science

"I have conducted numerous studies and have published a number of articles and books analyzing voting behavior in the United States. My studies and others document the fact that eligible citizens in our nation vote far less than voters in other industrialized democracies (like Canada, Great Britain, France, and Italy). This poor participation is also documented in the steady decline in voting of the voting age population in presidential and off-year congressional elections since 1960. I have also concluded that every change made to increase registration and actual voting results in an increase of 3–5 percent participation among the voting age population. Many of those representing this increase are new and first-time voters. Evidence indicates that the change led to their registration and actual voting.

"I would predict that the enactment of this Televote legislation will immediately increase voter turnout by 3–5 percent, and with continued voter education drives, this can double to a 10 percent increase by the end of the decade. I suggest that the legislature make use of the technology and enact Televote as soon as possible."

Witness #2 — Director of Voter Power

"I am the Director of Voter Power. Voter Power is a national organization established to increase citizens' awareness and exercise of their right to vote. Voter Power concentrates on strategies to register voters. We provide follow-up voter education to ensure actual voting and increased participation.

"Our experience with voter registration shows that the easier and more convenient the registration procedures, the greater the number of persons registering to vote. For example, in areas with mail registration or deputized volunteer registrars that go into the community to register voters, the number of registered voters increases. Of course, registration is only one step in the voting process. Registration only has meaning if the registered voter actually votes.

"Passage of the Televote legislation could promote registration and actual voting by providing the simple alternative of voting by telephone. Televote could simplify voter registration by developing a simple process of registering by telephone. And, regardless of the registration process, Televote will increase the likelihood of registered voters voting. One of the most common follow-up methods of getting out the vote is the telephone call "reminder to vote." Using this method would remind registered voters of the ease of immediately casting their telephone votes. Televote could revolutionize voter participation."

Witness #3 — Professor of Communications and Technology.

"Televote is technologically possible. As professor of communications and technology, I have specialized in improving two-way communications technology. My consulting work with telecommunications has led to explorations of video telephones, two-way television communication machines, and other technological innovations designed to enhance communication. Telephones can give access to computer systems as well. Therefore, the process is possible.

"The process and technology can be implemented in a way that guards against voter fraud and abuse. The short-term costs of installing a statewide voter databank with local and portable terminals may be high, but in the long run money will be saved. The process with the centralized computer will produce faster, more accurate election results than the present procedures. In addition, money will be saved because fewer persons will need to be hired for election day service (for example, as election judges and counters). I predict that one day all voting will be done by telephone."

WITNESSES *AGAINST* THE TELEVOTE LEGISLATION

Witness #1 — Professor of American History and Distinguished Lecturer of Social Sciences

"I have researched and published a number of articles and books on the effects of registration laws and election procedures on actual voter turnout. I have concluded that laws designed to make registration and voting easier have only a minimal effect on voter turnout. Even in states with same-day registration, the voter turnout averages only 1–3 percent higher than in states with more complicated procedures.

"More recently, I have conducted an analysis of the research studies on the impact of computers and video technology on interpersonal relations. On the whole, these studies have found that as use of computers and video games increases, the quantity and quality of interpersonal relations decreases. In other words, when people spend more and more time with computers and in front of video screens, they decrease their actual face-to-face contact with others.

Also their communication skills become less effective.

"In my judgment, enactment of the Televote legislation will add to this problem. Televote provides an antisocial situation. The voter loses contact with the interpersonal qualities of the election process. The voter would likely lose contact with the election judges from the local community, and with candidates and campaign workers outside polling places. I believe more energy and effort should be spent in encouraging every eligible voter to become more personally involved in the political process. Such efforts will result in a richer democracy."

Witness #2 — Director, State Board of Election Commissioners

"I am here to testify against passage of the Televote legislation. As Director of the State Board of Election Commissioners, I know the human and economic costs of this legislation.

"First and foremost, the costs of installation and implementation of Televote, including the centralized voter databank and network terminals throughout the state, will be astronomical. If the state legislature wishes to appropriate more money to improve voter registration and turnout, then the money would be more wisely spent on voter education programs and not on technological gimmickry.

"I grew up and practiced politics by meeting the people, talking with them, and encouraging them to vote. The political and electoral process should keep people communicating with one another. We should not allow the process to degenerate into pushing or dialing numbers on the telephone. Also, I am greatly concerned about the loss of jobs for all of our temporary election employees. These employees are a vital part of our political tradition. Each employee is honored to perform his or her civic responsibility for the state. They are proud to be a part of the election process. Losing these jobs would be a blow to them and to the state. A telephone and computer will never replace the smile and service of an election judge at the polls.

"I urge the committee to vote against this proposed legislation."

Witness #3 — President of P.I.T., Privacy In Technology, a private security firm

"I am here to urge you to vote against the proposed Televote legislation because of its potential for increased fraud and abuse. I have worked as a security specialist for a number of computer firms and corporations using large databanks. While much can be done to

216

reduce computer fraud and databank break-ins, there are no sure ways of guaranteeing the system against possible abuse. As security tightens, the costs of security increases.

"Televote creates the possibility that a person's secret vote may be accessible to someone able to break into the master statewide voter databank. Thus protection of a voter's confidentiality could not be guaranteed. I realize that all voting procedures have a history and potential of fraud and abuse, but as an expert in high-tech security, I wanted you to be aware of the potential for fraud and abuse with Televote."

★ ★ ★ ★ ★ ★ ★ ★ ★ ★

Appendix

The Constitution of the United States

Preamble. We, the people of the United States, in order to form a more perfect Union, establish justice, insure domestic tranquility, provide for the common defense, promote the general welfare, and secure the blessings of liberty to ourselves and our posterity, do ordain and establish this Constitution for the United States of America.

Article I.

Section 1. All legislative powers herein granted, shall be vested in a Congress of the United States, which shall consist of a Senate and House of Representatives.

Section 2. The House of Representatives shall be composed of members chosen every second year by the people of the several States; and the electors in each State shall have the qualifications requisite for electors of the most numerous branch of the State Legislature.

No person shall be a Representative who shall not have attained the age of twenty-five years, and been seven years a citizen of the United States, and who shall not, when elected, be an inhabitant of that State in which he shall be chosen.

Representatives ~~and direct taxes~~[1] shall be apportioned among the several States which may be included within this Union, according to their respective numbers, ~~which shall be determined by adding to the whole number of free persons, including those bound to service for a term of years, and excluding Indians not taxed, three fifths of all other persons~~. The actual enumeration shall be made within three years after the first meeting of the Congress of the United States, and within every subsequent term of ten years, in such manner as they shall by law direct. The number of Representatives shall not exceed one for every thirty thousand, but each State shall have at least one Representative, ~~and until such enumeration shall be made, the State of New Hampshire shall be entitled to choose three, Massachusetts eight, Rhode Island and Providence Plantations one, Connecticut five, New York six, New Jersey four, Pennsylvania eight, Delaware one, Maryland six, Virginia ten, North Carolina five, South Carolina five, and Georgia three~~.

When vacancies happen in the representation from any State, the Executive authority thereof shall issue writs of election to fill such vacancies.

The House of Representatives shall choose their Speaker and other officers; and shall have the sole power of impeachment.

Section 3. The Senate of the United States shall be composed of two Senators from each State, chosen ~~by the legislature thereof~~, for six years; and each Senator shall have one vote.

~~Immediately after they shall be assembled, in consequence of the first election, they shall be divided equally as may be into three classes. The seats of the Senators of the first class shall be vacated at the expiration of the second year, of the second class at the expiration of the fourth year, and of the third class at the expiration of the sixth year~~, so that one third may be chosen every second year; ~~and if vacancies happen by resignation, or otherwise, during the recess of the legislature of any State, the Executive thereof may make temporary appointments until the next meeting of the legislature, which shall then fill such vacancies~~.

No person shall be a Senator who shall not have attained the age of thirty years, and been nine years a citizen of the United States, and who shall not, when elected, be an inhabitant of that State for which he shall be chosen.

The Vice-President of the United States shall be President of the Senate, but shall have no vote, unless they be equally divided.

The Senate shall choose their other officers, and also a President *Pro Tempore,* in the absence of the Vice-President, or when he shall exercise the office of President of the United States.

The Senate shall have the sole power to try all impeachments. When sitting for that purpose, they shall be on oath or affirmation. When the President of the United States is tried, the Chief Justice

---

[1]Those parts of the U.S. Constitution that are no longer applicable or which have been changed by amendments are marked through with colored lines.

shall preside; and no person shall be convicted without the concurrence of two thirds of the members present.

Judgment in cases of impeachment shall not extend further than to removal from office, and disqualification to hold and enjoy any office of honour, trust or profit, under the United States; but the party convicted shall nevertheless be liable and subject to indictment, trial, judgment, and punishment according to law.

Section 4. The times, places and manner of holding elections for Senators and Representatives, shall be prescribed in each State by the legislature thereof; but the Congress may at any time by law make or alter such regulations, except as to the places of choosing Senators.

The Congress shall assemble at least once in every year, ~~and such meeting shall be on the first Monday in December~~, unless they shall by law appoint a different day.

Section 5. Each House shall be the judge of the elections, returns, and qualifications of its own members, and a majority of each shall constitute a quorum to do business; but a smaller number may adjourn from day to day, and may be authorized to compel the attendance of absent members, in such manner, and under such penalties, as each House may provide.

Each House may determine the rules of its proceedings, punish its members for disorderly behaviour, and, with the concurrence of two thirds, expel a member.

Each House shall keep a journal of its proceedings, and from time to time publish the same, excepting such parts as may, in their judgment, require secrecy; and the yeas and nays of the members of either House on any question, shall, at the desire of one fifth of those present, be entered on the journal.

Neither House, during the session of Congress, shall, without the consent of the other, adjourn for more than three days, nor to any other place than that in which the two Houses shall be sitting.

Section 6. The Senators and Representatives shall receive a compensation for their services, to be ascertained by law, and paid out of the Treasury of the United States. They shall, in all cases, except treason, felony, and breach of the peace, be privileged from arrest during their attendance at the session of their respective Houses, and in going to, and returning from, the same; and for any speech or debate in either House, they shall not be questioned in any other place.

No Senator or Representative shall, during the time for which he was elected, be appointed to any civil office under the authority of the United States, which shall have been created, or the emoluments whereof shall have been increased during such time; and no person holding any office under the United States, shall be a member of either House during his continuance in office.

Section 7. All bills for raising revenue shall originate in the House of Representatives; but the Senate may propose or concur with amendments as on other bills.

Every bill which shall have passed the House of Representatives and the Senate, shall, before it becomes a law, be presented to the President of the United States; if he approves he shall sign it, but if not he shall return it, with his objections, to that House in which it shall have originated, who shall enter the objections at large on their journal, and proceed to reconsider it. If after such reconsideration two thirds of that House agree to pass the bill, it shall be sent, together with the objections, to the other House, by which it shall likewise be reconsidered, and if approved by two thirds of that House, it shall become a law. But in all cases the votes of both Houses shall be determined by yeas and nays, and the names of the persons voting for and against the bill shall be entered on the journal of each House respectively. If any bill shall not be returned by the President within ten days (Sundays excepted) after it shall have been presented to him, the same shall be a law in like manner as if he had signed it, unless the Congress by their adjournment prevent its return, in which case it shall not be a law.

Every order, resolution, or vote, to which the concurrence of the Senate and House of Representatives may be necessary (except on a question of adjournment), shall be presented to the President of the United States; and before the same shall take effect, shall be approved by him, or being disapproved by him, shall be re-passed by two thirds of the Senate and House of Representatives, according to the rules and limitations prescribed in the case of a bill.

Section 8. The Congress shall have power

To lay and collect taxes, duties, imposts and excises, to pay the debts, and provide for the common defense and general welfare of United States; but all duties, imposts, and excises shall be uniform throughout the United States;

To borrow money on the credit of the United States;

To regulate commerce with foreign nations, and among the several States, and with the Indian tribes;

To establish an uniform rule of naturalization, and uniform laws on the subject of bankruptcies throughout the United States;

To coin money, regulate the value thereof, and of foreign coin, and fix the standard of weights and measures;

To provide for the punishment of counterfeiting the securities and current coin of the United States;

To establish post-offices and post-roads;

To promote the progress of science and useful arts, by securing, for limited times, to authors and inventors, the exclusive right to their respective writings and discoveries;

To constitute tribunals inferior to the Supreme Court;

To define and punish piracies and felonies committed on the high seas, and offences against the law of nations;

To declare war, grant letters of marque and reprisal, and make rules concerning captures on land and water;

To raise and support armies, but no appropriation of money to that use shall be for a longer term than two years;

To provide and maintain a navy;

To make rules for the government and regulation of the land and naval forces;

To provide for calling forth the

militia to execute the laws of the Union, suppress insurrections and repel invasions;

To provide for organizing, arming, and disciplining the militia, and for governing such part of them as may be employed in the service of the United States, reserving to the States respectively, the appointment of the officers, and the authority of training the militia according to the discipline prescribed by Congress;

To exercise exclusive legislation, in all cases whatsoever, over such district (not exceeding ten miles square) as may, by cession of particular States, and the acceptance of Congress, become the seat of the government of the United States, and to exercise like authority over all places purchased by the consent of the legislature of the State in which the same shall be, for the erection of forts, magazines, arsenals, dock-yards, and other needful buildings; And,

To make all laws which shall be necessary and proper for carrying into execution the foregoing powers, and all other powers vested by this Constitution in the government of the United States, or in any department or officer thereof.

Section 9. ~~The migration or importation of such persons as any of the States now existing shall think proper to admit, shall not be prohibited by the Congress prior to the year one thousand eight hundred and eight; but a tax or duty may be imposed on such importation, not exceeding ten dollars for each person.~~

The privilege of the writ of *habeas corpus* shall not be suspended, unless when in cases of rebellion or in-vasion the public safety may require it.

No bill of attainder or *ex post facto* law shall be passed.

~~No capitation, or other direct tax, shall be laid, unless in proportion to the census or enumeration herein before directed to be taken.~~

No tax or duty shall be laid on articles exported from any State.

No preference shall be given by any regulation of commerce or revenue to the ports of one State over those of another; nor shall vessels bound to, or from, one State be obliged to enter, clear, or pay duties in another.

No money shall be drawn from the treasury, but in consequence of appropriations made by law; and a regular statement and account of the receipts and expenditures of all public money shall be published from time to time.

No title of nobility shall be granted by the United States; and no person holding any office of profit or trust under them, shall, without the consent of the Congress, accept of any present, emolument, office, or title of any kind whatever, from any king, prince, or foreign state.

Section 10. No State shall enter into any treaty, alliance, or confederation; grant letters of marque and reprisal; coin money; emit bills of credit; make any thing but gold and silver coin a tender of payment of debts; pass any bill of attainder, *ex post facto* law, or law impairing the obligation of contracts, or grant any title of nobility.

No State shall, without the consent of the Congress, lay any imposts or duties on imports or exports, except what may be absolutely necessary for executing its inspection laws; and the net produce of all duties and imposts, laid by any State on imports or exports, shall be for the use of the treasury of the United States; and all such laws shall be subject to the revision and control of the Congress. No State shall, without the consent of Congress, lay any duty of tonnage, keep troops, or ships of war, in time of peace, enter into any agreement or compact with another State, or with a foreign power, or engage in war, unless actually invaded, or in such imminent danger as will not admit of delay.

Article II.

Section 1. The executive power shall be vested in a President of the United States of America. He shall hold his office during the term of four years, and together with the Vice-President, chosen for the same term, be elected as follows:

Each State shall appoint, in such manner as the legislature thereof may direct, a number of electors equal to the whole number of Senators and Representatives to which the State may be entitled in the Congress; but no Senator or Representative, or person holding an office of trust or profit under the United States, shall be appointed an elector.

~~The electors shall meet in their respective States, and vote by a ballot for two persons, of whom one at least shall not be an inhabitant of the same State with themselves. And they shall make a list of all the persons voted for, and of the number of votes for each; which list they shall sign and certify, and transmit sealed to the seat of the government of the United States, directed to the Presi-~~

~~dent of the Senate. The President of the Senate shall, in the presence of the Senate and House of Representatives, open all the certificates and the votes shall then be counted. The person having the greatest number of votes shall be the President, if such number be a majority of the whole number of electors appointed; and if there be more than one who have such majority, and have an equal number of votes, then the House of Representatives shall immediately choose by ballot one of them for President. But in choosing the President, the votes shall be taken by States, the representation from each State having one vote; a quorum for this purpose shall consist of a member or members from two thirds of the States, and a majority of all the States shall be necessary to a choice. In every case, after the choice of the President, the person having the greatest number of votes of the electors shall be the Vice-President. But if there should remain two to more who have equal votes, the Senate shall choose from them by ballot the Vice-President.~~

The Congress may determine the time of choosing the electors, and the day on which they shall give their votes; which day shall be the same throughout the United States.

No person except a natural born citizen, ~~or a citizen of the United States, at the time of the adoption of this Constitution,~~ shall be eligible to the office of President; neither shall any person be eligible to that office who shall not have attained the age of thirty-five years, and been fourteen years a resident within the United States.

In case of the removal of the President from office, or of his death, resignation, or inability to discharge the powers and duties of the said office, the same shall devolve on the Vice-President, and the Congress may by law provide for the case of removal, death, resignation, or inability, both of the President and Vice-President, declaring what officer shall than act as President, and such officer shall act accordingly until the disability be removed, or a President shall be elected.

The President shall at stated times, receive for his services, a compensation, which shall neither be increased nor diminished during the period for which he shall have been elected, and he shall not receive within that period any other emolument from the United States or any of them.

Before he enter on the execution of his office, he shall take the following oath or affirmation:

"I do solemnly swear (or affirm) that I will faithfully execute the office of President of the United States, and will, to the best of my ability, preserve, protect, and defend the Constitution of the United States."

Section 2. The President shall be Commander-in-Chief of the Army and Navy of the United States, and of the militia of the several States, when called into the actual service of the United States; he may require the opinion, in writing, of the principal officer in each of the executive departments, upon any subject relating to the duties of their respective offices, and he shall have power to grant reprieves and pardons for offences against the United States, except in cases of impeachment.

He shall have power, by and with the advice and consent of the Senate, to make treaties, provided two thirds of the Senate present concur; and he shall nominate, and by and with the advice and consent of the Senate, shall appoint ambassadors, other public ministers and consuls, judges of the Supreme Court, and all other officers of the United States, whose appointments are not herein otherwise provided for, and which shall be established by law. But the Congress may by law vest the appointment of such inferior officers, as they think proper, in the President alone, in the courts of law, or in the heads of departments.

The President shall have power to fill up all vacancies that may happen during the recess of the Senate, by granting commissions which shall expire at the end of their session.

Section 3. He shall, from time to time, give to the Congress information of the state of the Union, and recommend to their consideration such measures as he shall judge necessary and expedient. He may on extraordinary occasions, convene both Houses, or either of them; and in case of disagreement between them with respect to the time of adjournment, he may adjourn them to such time as he shall think proper. He shall receive ambassadors and other public ministers. He shall take care that the laws be faithfully executed; and shall commission all the officers of the United States.

Section 4. The President, Vice-President, and all civil officers of the United States, shall be removed from office on impeachment for, and conviction of, treason, bribery, or other high crimes and misdemeanors.

Article III.

Section 1. The judicial power of the United States shall be vested in one Supreme Court, and in such inferior courts as the Congress may, from time to time, ordain and establish. The judges, both of the Supreme and inferior courts, shall hold their offices during good behavior; and shall, at stated times, receive for their services, a compensation, which shall not be diminished during their continuance in office.

Section 2. The judicial power shall extend to all cases, in law and equity, arising under this Constitution, and laws of the United States, and treaties made, or which shall be made, under their authority; to all cases affecting ambassadors, other public ministers, and consuls; to all cases of admiralty and maritime jurisdiction; to controversies to which the United States shall be a party; to controversies between two or more States, ~~between a State and citizens of another State,~~ between citizens of different States, between citizens of the same States claiming lands under grants of different States, and between a State, or the citizens thereof, and foreign states, citizens or subjects.

In all cases affecting ambassadors, other public ministers and consuls, and those in which a State shall be party, the Supreme Court shall have original jurisdiction. In all the other cases before mentioned, the Supreme Court shall have appellate jurisdiction, both as to law and fact, with such exceptions, and under such regulations, as the Congress shall make.

The trial of all crimes, except in cases of impeachment, shall be by jury; and such trial shall be held in the State where the said crimes shall have been committed; and when not committed within any State, the trial shall be at such place or places as the Congress may by law have directed.

Section 3. Treason against the United States shall consist only in levying war against them, or in adhering to their enemies, giving them aid and comfort. No person shall be convicted of treason unless on the testimony of two witnesses to the same overt act, or on confession in open court.

The Congress shall have power to declare the punishment of treason, but no attainder of treason shall work corruption of blood, or forfeiture, except during the life of the person attained.

Article IV.

Section 1. Full faith and credit shall be given in each State to the public acts, records and judicial proceedings of every other State. And the Congress may by general laws prescribe the manner in which such acts, records, and proceedings shall be proved, and the effect thereof.

Section 2. The citizens of each State shall be entitled to all privileges and immunitites of citizens in the several States.

A person charged in any State with treason, felony, or other crime, who shall flee from justice, and be found in another State, shall, on demand of the executive authority of the State from which he fled, be delivered up to be removed to the State having jurisdiction of the crime.

~~No person held to service or labor in one State, under the laws thereof, escaping into another, shall, in consequence of any laws or regulation therein, be discharged from such service or labor, but shall be delivered up on claim of the party to whom such service or labor may be due.~~

Section 3. New States may be admitted by the Congress into this Union; but no new State shall be formed or erected within the jurisdiction of any other State; nor any State be formed by the junction of two or more States, or parts of States, without the consent of the legislatures of the States concerned, as well as of the Congress.

The Congress shall have power to dispose of and make all needful rules and regulations respecting the territory or other property belonging to the United States; and nothing in this Constitution shall be so construed as to prejudice any claims of the United States, or of any particular State.

Section 4. The United States shall guarantee to every State in this Union a republican form of government, and shall protect each of them against invasion; and on application of the legislature, or of the executive (when the legislature cannot be convened), against domestic violence.

Article V. The Congress, whenever two thirds of both Houses shall deem it necessary, shall propose amendments to this Constitution, or on the application of the legislatures of two thirds of the several States, shall call a convention for proposing amendments, which, in either case, shall be valid to all intents and purposes, as part of this Constitution, when ratified by the legislatures of three fourths of the several States, or by conventions in three fourths thereof, as the one or the other mode of ratification may be proposed by the Congress; provided ~~that no amendment, which may be made prior to the year one thousand eight hundred and eight, shall in any manner affect the first and fourth clauses in the ninth section of the first article; and~~ that no State, without its consent, shall be deprived of its equal suffrage in the Senate.

Article VI. All debts contracted, and engagements entered into, before the adoption of this Constitution, shall be as valid against the United States, under this Constitution, as under the confederation.

This Constitution and the laws of the United States which shall be made in pursuance thereof, and all treaties made, or which shall be made, under the authority of the United States, shall be the supreme law of the land; and the judges, in every State, shall be bound thereby, any thing in the constitution or laws of any State to the contrary notwithstanding.

The Senators and Representatives before mentioned, and the members of the several State legislatures, and all executive and judicial officers, both of the United States and the several States, shall be bound, by oath or affirmation, to support this Constitution; but no religious test shall ever be required as qualification to any office or public trust under the United States.

Article VII. ~~The ratification of the conventions of nine States, shall be sufficient for the establishment of this Constitution between the States so ratifying the same.~~

TEN ORIGINAL AMENDMENTS: THE BILL OF RIGHTS

(These first 10 amendments were adopted in 1791.)

Amendment I. Congress shall make no law respecting an establishment of religion, or prohibiting the free exercise thereof; or abridging the freedom of speech, or of the press; or the right of the people peaceably to assemble, and to petition the government for a redress of grievances.

Amendment II. A well regulated militia being necessary to the security of a free State, the right of the people to keep and bear arms shall not be infringed.

Amendment III. No soldier shall, in time of peace, be quartered in any house without the consent of the owner; nor in time of war, but in a manner to be prescribed by law.

Amendment IV. The right of the people to be secure in their persons, houses, papers, and effects, against unreasonable searches and seizures, shall not be violated; and no warrants shall issue, but upon probable cause, supported by oath or affirmation, and particularly describing the place to be searched, and the persons or things to be seized.

Amendment V. No person shall be held to answer for a capital or otherwise infamous crime, unless on a presentment or indictment of a grand jury, except in cases arising in the land or naval forces, or in the militia, when in actual service, in time of war or public danger; nor shall any person be subject for the same offence to be twice put in jeopardy of life or limb; nor shall be compelled, in any criminal case, to be witness against himself; nor be deprived of life, liberty, or property, without due process of law; nor shall private property be taken for public use without just compensation.

Amendment VI. In all criminal prosecutions the accused shall enjoy the right to a speedy and public trial, by an impartial jury of the State and district wherein the crime shall have been committed, which district shall have been previously ascertained by law, and to be informed of the nature and cause of the accusation; to be confronted with the witnesses against him; to have compulsory process for obtaining witnesses in his favour; and to have the assistance of counsel for his defence.

Amendment VII. In suits at common law, where the value of controversy shall exceed twenty dollars, the right of trial by jury shall be preserved; and no fact tried by a jury shall be otherwise re-examined in any court of the United States than according to the rules of common law.

Amendment VIII. Excessive bail shall not be required, nor excessive fines imposed, nor cruel and unusual punishments inflicted.

Amendment IX. The enumeration in the Constitution of certain rights, shall not be construed to deny or disparage others retained by the people.

Amendment X. The powers not delegated to the United States by the Constitution, nor prohibited by it to the States, are reserved to the States respectively or to the people.

AMENDMENTS SINCE THE BILL OF RIGHTS

Amendment XI (1795). The Judicial power of the United States shall not be construed to extend to any suit in law or equity, commenced or prosecuted against one of the United States by citizens or subjects of any Foreign State.

Amendment XII (1804). The electors shall meet in their respective States, and vote by ballot for President and Vice-President, one of whom, at least shall not be an inhabitant of the same State with themselves; they shall name in their ballots the person voted for as President, and in distinct ballots the person voted for as Vice-President; and they shall make distinct lists of all persons voted for as President, and of all persons voted for as Vice-President, and of the number of votes for each, which list they shall sign and certify, and transmit sealed to the seat of the government of the United States, directed to the President of the Senate; the President of the Senate shall, in the presence of the Senate and House of Representatives, open all the certificates, and the votes shall then be counted; the person having the greatest number of votes for President shall be the President, if such number be a majority of the whole number of electors appointed; and if no person have such majority, then from the persons having the highest numbers, not exceeding three, on the list of those voted for a President, the House of Representatives shall choose immediately, by ballot, the President. But in choosing the President, the vote shall be taken by States, the representation from each State having one vote; a quorum for this purpose shall consist of a member or members from two thirds of the States, and a majority of all the States shall be necessary to a choice. ~~And if the House of Representatives shall not choose a President whenever the right of choice shall develop upon them, before the fourth day of March next following, then the Vice-President shall act as President, as in the case of the death or other constitutional disability of the President.~~

The person having the greatest number of votes as Vice-President shall be the Vice-President, if such number be a majority of the whole number of electors appointed; and if no person have a majority, then from the two highest numbers on the list the Senate shall choose the Vice-President; a quorum for that purpose shall consist of two thirds of the whole number shall be necessary to a choice.

But no person constitutionally ineligible to the office of President shall be eligible to that of Vice-President of the United States.

Amendment XIII (1865).
Section 1. Neither slavery nor in-

229

voluntary servitude except as a punishment for crime whereof the party shall have been duly convicted, shall exist within the United States, or any place subject to their jurisdiction.

Section 2. Congress shall have power to enforce this article by appropriate legislation.

Amendment XIV (1868).

Section 1. All persons born or naturalized in the United States, and subject to the jurisdiction thereof, are citizens of the United States and of the State wherein they reside. No State shall make or enforce any law which shall abridge the privileges or immunities of citizens of the United States; nor shall any State deprive any person of life, liberty, or property, without due process of law, nor deny to any person within its jurisdiction the equal protection of the laws.

Section 2. Representatives shall be apportioned among the several States according to their respective numbers, counting the whole number of persons in each State, excluding Indians not taxed. But when the right to vote at any election for the choice of electors for President and Vice-President of the United States, or the members of the legislature thereof, is denied to any of the ~~male~~ inhabitants of such State, being ~~twenty-one years of age, and~~ citizens of the United States, or in any way abridged, except for participation in rebellion or other crime, the basis of representation therein shall be reduced in the proportion which the number of such ~~male~~ citizens shall bear to the whole number of ~~male~~

citizens ~~twenty-one years of age~~ in such State.

Section 3. No person shall be a Senator or Representative in Congress, or elector of President and Vice-President, or hold any office, civil or military, under the United States, or under any State, who having previously taken an oath, as a member of Congress, or as an officer of the United States, or as a member of any State legislature, or as an executive or judicial officer of any State, to support the Constitution of the United States, shall have engaged in insurrection or rebellion against the same, or given aid or comfort to the enemies thereof. But Congress may by a vote of two thirds of each house remove such disability.

Section 4. The validity of the public debt of the United States, authorized by law, including debts incurred for payment of pensions and bounties for services in suppressing insurrection or rebellion, shall not be questioned. But neither the United States nor any State shall assume or pay any debt or obligation incurred in aid of insurrection or rebellion against the United States, or any claim for loss or emancipation of any slave; but all such debts, obligations, and claims shall be held illegal and void.

Section 5. The Congress shall have power to enforce, by appropriate legislation, the provisions of this article.

Amendment XV (1870).

Section 1. The right of citizens of the United States to vote shall not be denied or abridged by the United States or by any State on account of race, color, or previous condition of servitude.

Section 2. The Congress shall have power to enforce this article by appropriate legislation.

Amendment XVI (1913). The Congress shall have power to lay and collect taxes on incomes, from whatever source derived, without apportionment among the several States, and without regard to any census or enumeration.

Amendment XVII (1913). The Senate of the United States shall be composed of two Senators from each State, elected by the people thereof, for six years; and each Senator shall have one vote. The electors in each State shall have the qualifications requisite for electors of the most numerous branch of the State legislatures.

When vacancies happen in the representation of any State in the Senate, the executive authority of such State shall issue writs of election to fill such vacancies: *Provided,* That the legislature of any State may empower the executive thereof to make temporary appointments until the people fill the vacancies by election as the legislature may direct.

This amendment shall not be so construed as to affect the election or term of any Senator chosen before it becomes valid as part of the Constitution.

Amendment XVIII (1919).

Section 1. After one year from the ratification of this article the manufacture, sale, or transportation of intoxicating liquors within, the importion thereof into, or the exportation thereof from the United States and all territory subject to the jurisdiction thereof for beverage purposes is hereby prohibited.

Section 2. The Congress and the several States shall have concurrent power to enforce this article by appropriate legislation.

Section 3. This article shall be inoperative unless it shall have been ratified as an amendment to the Constitution by the legislatures of the several States, as provided in the Constitution, within seven years from the date of the submission hereof to the States by the Congress.

Amendment XIX (1920). The right of citizens of the United States to vote shall not be denied or abridged by the United States or by any State on account of sex.

Congress shall have power to enforce this article by appropriate legislation.

Amendment XX (1933).

Section 1. The terms of the President and Vice-President shall end at noon on the 20th day of January, and the terms of Senators and Representatives at noon on the 3rd day of January, of the years in which such terms would have ended if this article had not been ratified; and the terms of their successors shall then begin.

Section 2. The Congress shall assemble at least once in every year, and such meeting shall begin at noon on the 3rd day of January, unless they shall by law appoint a different day.

Section 3. If, at the time fixed for the beginning of the term of the President, the President elect shall have died, the Vice-President elect shall become President. If a President shall not have been chosen before the time fixed for the beginning of his term, or if the President elect shall have failed to qualify, then the Vice-President elect shall act as President until a President shall have qualified; and the Congress may by law provide for the case wherein neither a President elect nor a Vice-President elect shall have qualified, declaring who shall then act as President, or the manner in which one who is to act shall be selected, and such person shall act accordingly until a President or Vice-President shall have qualified.

Section 4. The Congress may by law provide for the case of the death of any of the persons from whom the House of Representatives may choose a President whenever the right choice shall have developed upon them, and for the case of the death of any of the persons from whom the Senate may choose a Vice-President whenever the right of choice shall have devolved upon them.

~~**Section 5.** Sections 1 and 2 shall take effect on the 15th day of October following the ratification of this article.~~

~~**Section 6.** This article shall be inoperative unless it shall have been ratified as an amendment to the Constitution by the legislatures of three-fourths of the several States within seven years from the date of its submission.~~

Amendment XXI (1933).

Section 1. The eighteenth article of amendment to the Constitution of the United States is hereby repealed.

Section 2. The transportation or importation into any State, Territory, or possession of the United States for delivery or use therein of intoxicating liquors, in violation of the laws thereof, is hereby prohibited.

~~**Section 3.** This article shall be inoperative unless it shall have been ratified as an amendment to the Constitution by conventions in the several States, as provided in the Constitution, within seven years from the date of the submission hereof to the States by the Congress.~~

Amendment XXII (1951).

Section 1. No person shall be elected to the office of the President more than twice, and no person who has held the office of President, or acted as President, for more than two years of a term to which some other person was elected President shall be elected to the office of the President more than once. ~~But this Article shall not apply to any person holding the office of President when this Article was proposed by the Congress, and shall not prevent any person who may be holding the office of President, or acting as President, during the term within which this Article becomes operative from holding the office of President or acting as President during the remainder of such term.~~

Amendment XXIII (1961).

Section 1. The District constituting the seat of Government of the United States shall appoint in such manner as the Congress may direct: A number of electors of President and Vice-President equal to the whole number of Senators and Representatives in Congress to which the District would be entitled if it were a State, but in no event more than the least populous State; they shall be in addition to those appointed by the States, but they shall be considered, for the purposes of the election of President and Vice-President, to be electors appointed by a State; and they shall meet in the District and perform such duties as provided by the twelfth article of amendment.

Section 2. The Congress shall have the power to enforce this article by appropriate legislation.

Amendment XXIV (1964).

Section 1. The right of citizens of the United States to vote in any primary or other election for President or Vice-President, for electors for President or Vice-President, or for Senator or Representatives in Congress, shall not be denied or abridged by the United States or any State by reason of failure to pay any poll tax or other tax.

Section 2. The Congress shall have the power to enforce this article by appropriate legislation.

Amendment XXV (1967).

Section 1. In case of the removal of the President from office or his death or resignation, the Vice-President shall become President.

Section 2. Whenever there is a vacancy in the office of the Vice-President, the President shall nominate a Vice-President who shall take office upon confirmation by a majority vote of both houses of Congress.

Section 3. Whenever the Presi-dent transmits to the President *Pro Tempore* of the Senate and the Speaker of the House of Representatives his written declaration that he is unable to discharge the powers and duties of his office, and until he transmits to them a written declaration to the contrary, such powers and duties shall be discharged by the Vice-President as Acting President.

Section 4. Whenever the Vice-President and a majority of either the principal officers of the executive departments or of such other body as Congress may by law provide, transmit to the President *Pro Tempore* of the Senate and the Speaker of the House of Representatives their written declaration that the President is unable to discharge the powers and duties of his office the Vice-President shall immediately assume the powers and duties of the office as Acting President.

Thereafter, when the President transmits to the President *Pro Tempore* of the Senate and the Speaker of the House of Representatives his written declaration that no inability exists, he shall resume the powers and duties of his office unless the Vice-President and a majority of either the principal officers of the executive departments or of such other body as Congress may by law provide, transmit within four days to the President *Pro Tempore* of the Senate and the Speaker of the House of Representatives their written declaration that the President is unable to discharge the power and duties of his office. Thereupon Congress shall decide the issue, assembling within 48 hours for the purpose if not in session. If the Congress, within 21 days after receipt of the latter written declaration, or, if Congress is not in session, within 21 days after Congress is required to assemble, determines by two-thirds vote of both houses that the President is unable to discharge the powers and duties of his office, the Vice-President shall continue to discharge the same as Acting President; otherwise, the President shall resume the powers and duties of his office.

Amendment XXVI (1971).

Section 1. The right of citizens of the United States, who are eighteen years of age or older, to vote shall not be denied or abridged by the United States or any State on account of age.

Section 2. The Congress shall have the power to enforce this article by appropriate legislation.

Appendix

Case Citations

Chapter 1: THE LAW IS . . .

Cherokee Nation v. Southern Kansas Railway Company. 33 F. 900 (D.D.C. 1888), pg. 3

Baldinger v. Banks, 26 Misc. 2d 1086, 201 N.Y.S. 2d 629 (Sup. Ct. N.Y. 1960), pg. 10
Also p. 11 — Regulation 99.11, U.S. Department of Education.

Chapter 3: STATE AND LOCAL LAWMAKING

Wisconsin v. Yoder, 406 U.S. 205, 92 S. Ct. 1526, 32 L. Ed. 2d 15 (1972), pg. 39

Gong Lum v. Rice, 275 U.S. 78, 48 S. Ct. 91, 72 L. Ed. 172 (1927), pg. 39

Cooper v. Aaron, 358 U.S. 1, 78 S. Ct. 1401, 3 L. Ed. 2d 5 (1958), pg. 39

**Chapter 4 CONFLICTS OF POWER: FEDERAL, STATE, AND LOCAL
            LAWMAKING**

Rosenfeld v. Southern Pacific Company, 444 F. 2d 1219 (9th Cir. 1971), pg. 61

Glossary

Absentee vote. Voting by mail or other means if the voter has an approved reason to miss going to the polls on election day.

Acquittal. A finding that a person is not guilty of a crime.

Amendment. (1) A change or addition in a law; (2) A change in a bill during its passage through a legislature.

Appeal. To request that a higher court review the actions of a lower court in order to correct mistakes.

Appeals Court. A court that reviews decisions of other courts. An appeals court does not hear evidence, but only looks at what was done in the lower court.

Appropriate. To designate a fund for a distinct use, or for the payment of a particular purpose.

Arrest. The taking of a person into custody by law enforcement officers to answer criminal charges.

Articles of Confederation. The document that provided the legal foundation of the thirteen original colonies before the adoption of the U.S. Constitution.

Assault. Assault is a tort and a crime. In criminal law, assault is an unlawful act creating a reasonable fear of receiving physical injury with the intent to create either the fear or the injury. In both, the actual infliction of injury need not be shown. As a tort, assault is an intentional threat to commit a battery against someone with apparent ability to carry out the threat.

Bail. Money, property, or bond put up to allow the release of a person in jail until time of trial. The purpose of bail is to assure that the released defendant appears in court for trial.

Battery. Battery is a tort and a crime. In criminal law, battery is the unlawful application of force to the person of another; it is any intentional unprovoked, harmful physical contact of one person by another person. As a tort, battery is any wrongful or offensive, physical contact inflicted without a person's consent.

Beyond a reasonable doubt. The level of proof required to convict a defendant of a crime. If a judge or juror has any justifiable doubt that the defendant committed the crime, the defendant must be found not guilty.

Bill. A proposal for a law considered by a legislative body such as Congress, a state legislature, or a local lawmaking body.

Bond or bail bond. A sum of money, in the amount designated in an order fixing bail, posted by a defendant to secure release from jail while awaiting trial. The money

is forfeited if the defendant fails to appear in court.

Bureaucracy. A governmental body of nonelected officials and administrators, sometimes considered to follow procedures rigidly without thinking.

Burglary. Unlawfully entering the building or inhabitable structure of another person with the intention of committing a felony, or with intent to steal property of value.

Cabinet. The body of persons appointed by the president to head the major departments of the executive branch and to act as his or her advisers.

Certified to stand trial. In juvenile proceedings, a determination by the court that a juvenile should be tried as an adult, based on the following factors: minor's age; seriousness of crime; previous history of delinquency; degree of criminal sophistication; and chance for the minor to be rehabilitated in the juvenile justice system.

Certiorari. A writ of common law origin issued by a superior to an inferior court requiring the latter to produce a certified record of a particular case tried therein. The writ is issued in order that the court issuing the writ may inspect the proceedings and determine whether there have been any irregularities. It is most commonly used to refer to the Supreme Court of the United States, which uses the writ of certiorari as a discretionary device to choose the cases it wishes to hear. The trend in state practice has been to abolish such writ.

Charter. The basic starting document granted by a state government giving a local government the right to exist, similar to a constitution.

Chief Justice. The presiding judge of the highest court of a state or of the U.S. Supreme Court. Judges of the highest court are called *justices.*

Civil. Having to do with any part of the law other than crimes. In a civil case, one person sues another person for damages or other relief with respect to an injury or wrong.

Common law. Law developed from court decisions (sometimes called judge-made law), as distinguished from statutes and regulations.

COMPLAINANT. *See* PLAINTIFF.

Constituent. A voter in a district represented by an elected official.

Constitution. The fundamental law of a nation or state, setting forth basic principles, and establishing the framework of its government.

Contempt of court. Failure of a person to do what a court has ordered him or her to do. A person found to be in contempt of court can be fined or jailed.

Contract. A legally enforceable agreement between two or more persons.

Conviction. A finding that a person is guilty of a crime.

Counsel. A lawyer.

Crime. An illegal act or failure to act.

Cross examination. The questioning of an opposing witness during a trial or hearing.

Damages. (1) The injuries or losses suffered by one person because of the fault of another. (2) Money asked for or ordered by court to be paid for the injuries or losses suffered.

Deceptive business practices. Activities of businesses that cheat or unreasonably confuse consumers; for example, false promises in advertising.

Defendant. The person against whom a legal action is brought. In a civil case, the defendant is the person being sued. In a criminal case, the defendant is the person accused of committing a crime.

Desegregate. To eliminate unlawful racial separation.

Direct examination. The questioning of a witness in a trial or a hearing by the side that called the witness.

Due process of law. A constitutional protection that entitles every person involved in a legal dispute the right to proper notice and a fair hearing or trial. The specific requirements of due process may vary from situation to situation, but in general, due process requires that no law or government procedure be arbitrary or unfair. Due process is fair treatment. *See the Fifth and Fourteenth Amendment.*

Equal protection of laws. A constitutional requirement prohibiting government from subjecting people, in similar situations, to unequal treatment without a legitimate reason to do so. *See the Fourteenth Amendment.*

Executive order. A law issued by the president or a governor that does not need to be passed by the legislature.

Executive privilege. The right of the president and subordinates to keep some information (primarily documents) from public disclosure.

Federal Bureau of Investigation (FBI). The branch of the Justice Department that investigates violations of federal law not specifically handled by other agencies.

Federal system. A type of government in which the power to govern is divided among a national government and state governments.

Felony. A serious crime punishable by a prison sentence of one year or more or by death.

Hearing. (1) A trial in a court or administrative agency at which witnesses give evidence or lawyers make arguments, and the court or agency makes an order with respect to a dispute. (2) A meeting of a commission or legislative committee to gather information. A *public hearing* is a meeting at which the public may comment on proposed action by a legislative body or administrative agency.

Initiative. The power of the people to enact laws by voting directly on the proposals, without the need for passage by the legislature.

Injunction. A court order to do or not to do a particular thing. By an injunction, a court enjoins a person to do (or from doing) something.

Jurisdiction. (1) The geographical area within which a court, agency, or public official has the power to act. (2) The persons and/or the subject matters about which a court, agency, or official has the power to make decisions.

Jury. A group of persons selected by law and sworn to examine facts presented at a trial and to determine which party should win the trial.

Justice Department. The U.S. Cabinet department that is responsible for federal law enforcement and crime prevention.

Kitchen cabinets. A term used to refer to the informed network of close friends and family who confer with presidents about matters of public policy.

Larceny. Stealing of any kind.

Liable. To be legally responsible for civil injuries.

Lobbying. Attempting to persuade a lawmaker to take a particular position on an issue.

Misdemeanor. A criminal offense less serious than a felony that is usually punishable by a fine or less than a year in jail.

Naturalization. The process of becoming a citizen of a country.

Negotiation. Communications among parties with a view to reaching a settlement or agreement.

Nolo contendere. A defendant's plea of *no contest* in a criminal case, meaning that he or she does not directly admit guilt, but submits to sentencing or other punishment. It is a Latin expression, translating "I will not contest it."

Ordinance. A municipal statute, or local law.

Overrule. A judge's decision to reject an objection or motion by a lawyer.

Pardon. (1) A president's or governor's power to release a person from punishment for a crime. (2) The official act releasing a person from punishment for a crime granted by the governing authority (president or governor).

Party. A person who brings a lawsuit or the person against whom a lawsuit is brought.

Perjury. Making false statements (lying) under oath. Perjury is a criminal offense.

Petition. The first document in a civil lawsuit, stating the wrong done to the plaintiff and requesting the court to take a particular action; also called *complaint.*

PETITIONER. *See* **PLAINTIFF.**

Petty larceny. Stealing a small amount in monetary value.

Plaintiff. A person who files a civil lawsuit against another person; also called *petitioner or complainant.*

Precedent. A rule of law established for the first time by a court for a particular type of case and thereafter referred to in deciding similar cases.

Preponderance of the evidence. The level of proof required in civil cases. The judge or jury must find in favor of the party that presents the greater weight of evidence, not as to quantity (in number of witnesses or facts) but as to quality (evidence that is more believable and convincing to the mind).

Probable cause. Sufficient facts to believe that a crime has been committed by the person to be arrested or that the objects sought will be found in the place to be searched. The constitution requires probable cause before a search warrant or an arrest warrant may be issued.

Prosecutor. A public official who presents the government's case against a person accused of a crime and who asks the court to convict the person.

Public hearing. *See* **HEARINGS.**

Rebuttal. Evidence that is offered by a party after he or she has rested his/her case and after the opponent has rested, in order to contradict the opponent's evidence.

Referendum. Putting an important law or constitutional amendment to a direct vote of the people rather than passing it through the legislature.

Regulation. A rule or order having force of law issued by a government, administrative agency.

Repeal. The cancellation of all or part of an existing law by a new law.

Reprieve. A postponement on enforcing a criminal sentence for a period of time after the sentence has been handed down.

Rule. An established standard or guide.

Segregate. To separate persons in housing, schooling, and other aspects of life on the basis of their race, color, sex, religion, age or nationality.

Sequester. To separate or isolate. For example, to sequester jurors is to isolate them from contact with the public during the course of a trial.

Small Claims Court. A court that handles civil cases under a certain amount of money (often about $1,000). These courts have simpler procedures, faster action, and often make it possible for persons to go to court without a lawyer.

Statute. An act of the legislature declaring, commanding, or prohibiting something; a law passed by the legislature.

Subpoena. A court order to appear at a certain time and place to give testimony or produce physical evidence upon a certain matter.

Suit. A lawsuit; a civil action in court.

Summons. A legal notice to respond to a lawsuit, or to appear in court at a certain time.

Sustain. A judge's decision to support an objection or motion made by a lawyer.

Testimony. Evidence given by a witness under oath.

Tort. A legal wrong causing harm or injury to another person. A tort is a civil wrong that is not based on an obligation under a contract. For an act to be a tort, there must be a legal duty owed by one person to another, a breaking of that duty, and harm done resulting from the action. Example of torts are negligence, battery, and libel.

Verdict. The jury's decision.

Voir dire. Translation means "to speak the truth." The process in which opposing lawyers question prospective jurors, and attempt to eliminate those who indicate an unfair bias or prejudice towards one side or the other. (For example, in a criminal trial involving a defendent charged with first degree robbery, the defense attorney might ask a prospective juror if he or she had ever been a victim of crime? If yes, what type of crime? Was the crime solved? Will the experience of being a victim of crime interfere with his or her ability to serve as a fair an impartial juror?). The process provides opposing lawyers an opportunity to select an acceptible jury.

Watergate. A political scandal involving illegal activities by President Nixon's reelection campaign in 1972 which resulted in President Nixon's resignation in 1974. (Watergate is the name of the building in Washington, D.C., that housed Democratic National Committee headquarters. The headquarters was broken into by men connected with President Nixon's reelection campaign.)

Index